Becoming a Minister

THOMAS C. ODEN

Classical Pastoral Care

VOLUME ONE
BECOMING A MINISTER

Baker Books

A Division of Baker Book House Co
Grand Rapids, Michigan 49516

For James and Sarah Hampson

© 1987 by Thomas C. Oden
Originally published 1987 by The Crossroad Publishing Company

Published by Baker Books
a division of Baker Book House Company
P.O. Box 6287, Grand Rapids, MI 49516-6287

Printed in the United States of America

ISBN: 0-8010-6763-4

Library of Congress Cataloging-in-Publication data on file in Washington, D.C.

Contents

Preface to the Baker Edition

EVANGELICALS STAND POISED to rediscover the classical pastoral tradition. This series seeks the revitalization of a discipline once familiar to evangelical Protestant scholarship, but now regrettably crippled and enervated.

It has been commonly observed that there is a deep hunger and profound readiness among evangelicals for neglected classical Christian roots as a resource for counsel, teaching, exegesis, and the work of ministry (see the writings of Robert Webber, Mark Noll, Ward Gasque, Donald Bloesch, James I. Packer, Michael Horton, Clark Pinnock, and Os Guinness).

It is well known that classic Protestant and evangelical teachers made frequent and informed references to the ancient Christian pastoral writers. Calvin was exceptionally well grounded in Augustine, but was also thoroughly familiar with the texts of Cyprian, Tertullian, John Chrysostom, Ambrose, Jerome, Leo, and Gregory the Great, and ecumenical council definitions such as those of Nicea, Constantinople I, and Chalcedon. Philipp Melancthon and Martin Chemnitz were especially gifted scholars of classical pastoral care. This tradition was carried forth and deepened by Reformed pastoral theologians (Gerhard, Quenstedt, Bucanus, Ursinus, Wollebius, and Cocceius), and survived healthily well into the eighteenth-century evangelical revival among leading teachers like J.A. Bengel, Philip Doddridge, Jonathan Edwards, John Wesley, and Johann Neander, all of whom read classic Christian writers handily in their original languages. Not until the late nineteenth century did the study of the ancient pastoral writers atrophy among Protestant pastors.

What is notably missing in today's picture is the classic pastoral texts themselves in accessible form, and a vital community of pastors and care-givers in living dialogue with these foundational prototypes.

1

A major long-range objective of this edition is the mentoring of young evangelical pastors and counselors toward greater competence in the classical pastoral tradition. Deliberately included in this collection are the voices of women from the classic Eastern and Western traditions of spiritual formation, exegesis, martyrology, catechesis, and piety. While the documentation of their poignant utterances is regrettably infrequent, they still are exceedingly powerful commentators on care-giving—I am thinking of such voices as Amma Theodora, Julian of Norwich, Hildegaard of Bingen, and Teresa of Avila.

Will benefits accrue to persons in teaching and helping professions who have no evangelical commitments or interests? The study of classical pastoral care is fitting not only for pastors and professionals, but for lay readers interested in their own inward spiritual formation. The arguments contained in this series tend to elicit ripple effects on diverse readers in such widely varied fields as psychology, Western cultural history, liturgies, homiletics, and education. Classical pastoral care is long overdue in contributing something distinctive of its own to the larger dialogue on care-giving, empathy, behavioral change, and therapeutic effectiveness.

By the early eighties it began to be evident that someone needed to pull together a substantial collection of essential sources of classic Christian writers on major themes of pastoral care. The series was first published by Crossroad/Continuum Publishing Company, a general academic publisher of religious books with strong ties to the erudite Herder tradition of Catholic scholarship. In the intervening years, no serious rival or alternative to this collection has appeared. There exists no other anthology of texts of classical pastoral care that presents the variety of textual material offered in this series. I am now deeply pleased to see it come out in an edition more accessible to Protestants. This is the first time the series has been made available in paperback.

The four books can be read either as a single, unified sequence or separately as stand-alone volumes. To this day some readers know of only one or two volumes, but are not aware that each volume is part of a cohesive series. Baker has made this unity clearer by offering the four volumes as a series.

I am deeply grateful for the interest that many working pastors, counselors, and lay persons have shown in this Classical Pastoral Care series. Even though these volumes were chosen as a Religious Book Club selection over several years, the circulation has been disseminated largely through academic audiences. I am pleased that it is now being offered by Baker for the first time to evangelical pastors and evangelically oriented pastoral and lay counselors and lay readers.

These texts are sometimes hard to locate if one is approaching them topically in crumbling, antiquated editions with poor indexes. This edition provides for the first time a well-devised index for the whole series that makes the anthology much more accessible to readers who wish to dip into it thematically.

These four volumes are designed to display the broad range of classical Christian reflections on all major questions of pastoral care. Many practical subjects are included, such as care of the dying, care of the poor, marriage and family counseling, pastoral visitation and care of the sick, counsel on addictive behaviors, vocational counsel, the timing of good counsel, the necessary and sufficient conditions of a helping relationship, body language in pastoral counsel, pastoral care through preaching, pastoral care through prayer, the pastor as educator of the soul, preparing for the Lord's table, clergy homosexuality and sexual ethics, equality of souls beyond sexual difference, the path to ordination, charismatic, healing ministries, and preparation for the care of souls.

The four volumes are:

I. *On Becoming a Minister* (first published 1987)
II. *Ministry through Word and Sacrament* (1989)
III. *Pastoral Counsel* (1989)
IV. *Crisis Ministries* (1986)

This edition for the first time identifies the order of volumes more clearly. Since in the first edition the fourth volume (*Crisis Ministries*, with its bio-bibliographical addendum) appeared first, the sequential order of the series has been confusing to some readers. Many have never seen the four volumes in a collection together, and do not yet realize that the whole sequence is constructed in a well-designed order to cover all major topics of pastoral theology.

There is reason to believe that this series is already being regarded as a standard necessary accession of theological seminary libraries, as well as of the libraries of most colleges and universities in which religious studies are taught, and in many general public libraries.

Meanwhile, out of rootless hunger the prefix "pastoral" has come to mean almost anything. There is no constraint on ascribing any subject matter to the category of pastoral care. In this game pastoral can mean my ultimate concern, transcendental meditation, or worse, my immediate feeling process or group hugging or my racial identity or crystal-gazing—you name it, anything. Then what is called pastoral is no longer related to the work of Christian ministry at all.

The preaching and counseling pastor needs to know that current pastoral care stands in a tradition of two millennia of reflection on the tasks of soul care. If deprived of these sources, the practice of pastoral care may become artificially constricted to modern psychotherapeutic procedures or pragmatic agendas. During the sixties and seventies, these reductionistic models prevailed among many old-line Protestant pastors, and to some degree as the eighties proceeded they also took root among evangelicals. This anthology shows the classic historic roots of contemporary approaches to psychological change, and provides to some degree a critique of those contemporary models.

Pastors today are rediscovering the distinctiveness of pastoral method as distinguished from other methods of inquiry (historical, philosophical, literary, psychological, etc.). Pastoral care is a unique enterprise that has its own distinctive subject-matter (care of souls); its own methodological premise (revelation); its own way of inquiring into its subject-matter (attentiveness to the revealed Word through Scripture and its consensual tradition of exegesis); its own criteria of scholarly authenticity (accountability to canonical text and tradition); its own way of knowing (listening to sacred Scripture with the historic church); its own mode of cultural analysis (with worldly powers bracketed and divine providence appreciated); and its own logic (internal consistency premised upon revealed truth).

The richness of the classic Christian pastoral tradition remains pertinent to ministry today. The laity have a right to competent, historically grounded pastoral care. The pastor has a right to the texts that teach how pastors have understood their work over the centuries. Modern chauvinism has falsely taught us a theory of moral inferiority: that new ideas are intrinsically superior, and old patterns inferior. This attitude has robbed the laity of the pastoral care they deserve, and the ministry of the texts that can best inform the recovery of pastoral identity.

Thomas C. Oden
June, 1994

Introduction

PASTORAL CARE is that branch of Christian theology that deals with care of persons by pastors. It is pastoral because it pertains to the offices, tasks, and duties of the pastor. It is care because it has charge of, and is deliberately attentive to the spiritual growth and destiny of persons. Pastoral care is analogous to a physician's care of the body. Since that particular sphere over which one exercises care is the psyche (soul, anima, the animating, enlivening, energizing, motivating spring of human existence without which a body is a corpse), pastoral care is also appropriately called the care of souls.

Classical pastoral care is pastoral care as understood, practiced and set forth by key writers of the Christian tradition. That is classical which is versed in the classics. Classics are the works of highest rank and quality in a field of study, whose worth has been recognized over a long period of time.

The Classical Pastoral Care series presents especially those rare texts that have a gem-like quality, that one often hopes to find easily but for which much reading is often necessary. The search has often required extensive digging in a given period or series before coming across just that text that best embodies the pastoral tradition, that brightly illuminates its subject, or profoundly grasps the point, or states it more subtly than before. This has been the joy and vexation of this editorial effort, similar to panning for gold in a deserted stream, only rarely coming across the bright nugget.

In presenting these kernels, what one winnows out is precisely the less pertinent material, while saving the golden grain. That is precisely the nature of an anthology, structurally limited as a series of texts to which there may be added comment or exposition. A different way of doing this would have been to select a dozen key texts, write a sturdy introduction for each, provide intensive biographical and historical background on the author, and present a new translation of the text in a scholarly, critical edition with a fully annotated set of interpretive notes and extensive commentary on the allusions of the texts. That would have been less useful to pastors, yet more desirable from the view-point of historical critical analysis. While we hope that approach will be taken in due time by others, we have tried to respond to a more urgently felt need in the practice of ministry: accessible texts that convey the heart of the classical pastoral tradition.

The advantages of ordering this material in a logical sequence of topics rather than chronologically may be so self-evident as not to require detailed apology. The central advantage is that it makes it possible to bring together the views of many different pastoral writers on the same topic, to compare and contrast their views, to learn pastoral care through its classic models, and to provide preliminary indications of how these ideas have developed through centuries of pastoral experience. The reader will find in the juxtaposition of various texts much food for thought on how they illuminate and penetrate each other. This organization of texts invites the reader to bring a creative associative memory to bear on how texts relate to each other and to the larger spectrum of Christian wisdom.

There is more here than a collection of quotable sentences or dusty maxims. There are stories of human crises, vignettes of significant encounters, case studies of pastoral dilemmas, recollections of exemplary persons who engaged in soul care with extraordinary effectiveness, as well as selections from pastoral letters, teaching materials, prayers, homilies, exegetical studies, and poetry.

The texts of the pastoral tradition are composed of sentences intended to be read by others as meaningful, and as containers of meaning not strictly or absolutely tied to a particular historical context. Much of the spirit of Augustine, Raymond Lull, or Teresa of Avila can come directly through their own powerful sentences without the need of commentator or historical interpreter. The editor's task has been largely that of trying to stay out of the way so as to invite the texts to speak for themselves. It is not our intent to load the demands of historicist perfectionism on the backs of pastoral readers. We have preferred texts that are to a larger degree understandable apart from details of their immediate environment, and which are written with the intent of being read and applied in social, cultural, historical settings other than their own.

Some Protestants have the deeply reinforced habit of jumping directly from the first century to the twentieth, overleaping, as with seven league boots, all nineteen centuries of pastoral wisdom in between. Others are more likely to leap from the early fourth century to the sixteenth or nineteenth century over more than a thousand years of "dark ages," more dark in our own memories than anywhere else. This study wishes to reach out to evangelical Protestants to show how much biblically grounded pastoral wisdom is found in the soul care of those ages, and to appeal to Roman Catholic and Orthodox traditions to reclaim their historic pastoral traditions. Some may feel that they can proceed very well in ministry without classical models. It indeed is possible to do so, but the question remains whether ministry can better be done with them. It is often out of ignorance of ancient wisdoms that we say we do not need them. In any event, we do not know what we are missing if we have never had an opportunity to examine them.

Pastoral care has often been practiced in our time with narrow unhistorical, or even anti-historical assumptions and prejudices. The primary values of much modern pastoral care have come directly and unapologetically from psychologists such as Sigmund Freud, Fritz Perls, Carl Rogers, Eric Berne, et al. These psychologists have at times tended to demean and undercut potential dialogue with classical sources, and foreclosed any recognition of any need for awareness of them. Strict Rogerians would tend to view these classical texts largely as "introjected values," Freudians as "super-ego intrusions," Berne as inordinate "over-parenting," and Skinner as heteronomous reinforcement. Although modern pastors do well to read these psychologists, their views are not normative for pastoral care. Even if one is unpersuaded that the classical tradition contains therapeutic wisdom, at least one has a right to examine it critically. After five decades of numerous waves of various psychological hegemonies in pastoral care, it is time to give classical views a new hearing.

The reader is invited to enter into the language of these texts with an open spirit, willing to listen. The intent is not to provide a definitive set of normative texts for pastoral practice but, rather, to provide an exemplary group of texts that represent recurrent themes and useful modes of therapeutic wisdom in the classical pastoral tradition.

The implication is not that this collection is a definitive compendium, or the only legitimate form of classical pastoral understanding. This study does not assume that all pastors ought to practice ministry directly or woodenly out of the classical tradition. It does assume that the classical tradition deserves a fair hearing.

Pastoral themes have been systematically neglected in the past century of historical theology. Readers who have deliberately sought to identify these texts in current editions are often baffled by the obstacles. This is most evident in the way pastoral themes have been ignored in indices. Go to the indices of the Nicene and Post-Nicene Fathers, for example, and you will find meager choices when you look under such fundamental topics as care of souls, call to ministry, shepherd, pastor, ordination, counsel, empathy, admonition, self-examination, deception, anxiety, habit, and care for the dying. Yet patristic writers were quite concerned with these very themes that often do not appear in the index. It appears that the ecclesiastical literature has been edited by those who largely have had a curious disinterest in pastoral care. The whole apparatus of commentary and scholarship has shown a bias in the direction of philosophical, exegetical, and doctrinal questions to the neglect of the practical care of souls to which much of this literature has been passionately devoted.

It is easier to acquire some knowledge of soul care and psychotherapeutic work after 1700. But textual resources on soul care prior to the eighteenth century are not readily available. Most standard histories of psychology begin with British empiricism; some begin with the naturalistic psychologists in Germany such as Wundt or Helmholtz; many begin with Freud, as if nothing much happened before, assuming that everything after Freud is normative for everything before. This is why the cut-off period for our collection is 1700. This enables us to include in our collection many important classical Protestant writers, like George Herbert, Richard Baxter, and Philipp Jacob Spener. Regrettably, it does not allow us to continue the story through important pastoral writers like Wesley, Schleiermacher, Kierkegaard, Sailer and many others. Though worthy of being done at some future date, the greater need is to establish textually the fact that there is a pre-modern classical pastoral therapeutic tradition. We are not suggesting, however, by setting the cut-off date for this collection at 1700, that subsequent writings are less valuable, but only more accessible.

While these texts point toward a centrist, ecumenical pastoral tradition, they do not imply that every pastoral writer would agree on every point of that consensus or that it is an absolutely defined consensus. Rather we point to a long tradition of pastoral practice that has remarkable dimensions of variety as well as continuity, of both consensus and dissent. This collection gives evidence that there has been a community of persons doing pastoral care who have been writing about it, sharing common ways of looking at the task, trying to understand it, and who constantly return to a series of questions that have recurrently emerged in the practice of pastoral care. These are the questions that are explored in these pages.

1 The Pastoral Calling

THE SELF-UNDERSTANDING of the pastor precedes and shapes all pastoral acts. The identity and inner strength of the provider of care is prior to any act of caring. One who engages in the practice of ministry must first learn and understand what a minister is.

Care-giving does not occur without a care-giver. The preparation and calling of the care-giver precedes and determines the giving of care. Care of souls cannot be understood without understanding the vocation of the care-giver.

The pastoral tradition has sought carefully to define its grounding, the human needs to which pastoral care is a response, the nature of the pastoral calling, and personal qualities desirable in the care-giver. The call to care is a crucial presupposition of care-giving in the classical pastoral tradition.

I. ❧ PERSONAL QUALITIES REQUISITE TO THE CARE OF SOULS

Care of souls begins by defining those qualities that enable a person to be sufficiently trusted to give care. The classic pastoral writers sought accurately to define those personal qualities that enable soul care. As contemporary psychotherapies have found that the interpersonal relationship between care-giver and recipient decisively affects the quality of care, so did the ancient pastoral tradition learn early to focus upon the definition and development of these interpersonal qualities.

Polycarp, the bishop of Smyrna, an early martyr for the faith, (c. 70–c. 155), was considered a model of the faithful pastor. Since he had, according to Irenaeus, direct and personal links with eyewitnesses to Jesus' ministry, his testimony concerning the qualities requisite for ministry had special importance for subsequent pastoral writers. Polycarp described the compassion needed for ministry in this letter to Christians at Smyrna:

As for the clergy, they should be persons of generous sympathies, with a wide compassion for humanity. It is their business to reclaim the wanderers, keep an eye on all who are infirm, and never neglect the widow, the orphan, or the needy. Their care at all times should be for what is honourable in the sight of God and men. Any show of ill-temper, partiality, or prejudice is to be scrupulously avoided; and eager-

11

ness for money should be a thing utterly alien to them. They must not be over ready to believe ill of anyone, nor too hasty with their censure; being well aware that we all of us owe the debt of sin. If we pray to the Lord to forgive us, we ourselves must be forgiving. (Polycarp, ECW, p. 146)

Although this picture of desired pastoral excellences may seem to some to be highly idealized, such pictures are often found in the pastoral literature. If it is the case that not all pastors meet these criteria, it still remains the case that such qualities are earnestly desired and sought out. Personal stability and inter-personal maturity are important components of this ideal.

John Climacus thought that one who has not worked through one's own anger should not become a pastor, anticipating the psychoanalytic dictum that an analyst must have undergone significant analysis:

It is not right for a lion to pasture sheep, and it is not safe for one still tyrannized by the passions to rule over passionate men.

A fox found in the company of hens is an unseemly sight, but nothing is more unseemly than an enraged shepherd. The former agitates and destroys the hens, while the latter agitates and destroys rational souls.

See that you are not an exacting investigator of trifling sins, thus showing yourself not to be an imitator of God. (John Climacus, *To the Shepherd*, sec. 47—49, Appendix to *Ladder of Divine Ascent*, p. 238)*

One who cares for souls must not be a slave to one's own unexamined passions. Otherwise the souls entrusted to one's care may be subjected to manipulation by the supposed carer, whose passions are projected on to the relationship. The church has a responsibility to protect the flock from lions and foxes that would exploit the flock under the guise of "care." Given these assumptions, what kinds of persons should be encouraged to consider undertaking the care of souls? Gregory provided a precise, careful, dialectically balanced answer:

One who is not led to covet the things of others, but gives freely of his own; who through the bowels of compassion is quickly moved to pardon, yet is never bent down from the fortress of rectitude by pardoning more than is meet; who perpetrates no unlawful deeds, yet deplores those perpetrated by others as though they were his own; who out of affection of heart sympathizes with another's infirmity, and so rejoices in the good of his neighbour as though it were his own advantage. (Gregory the Great, *BPR*, Part I, Ch. 10, NPNF 2, X, p. 7)

Empathy, compassion, non-defensiveness, firmness, and joy—these qualities we love and need in a pastor. Polycarp noted also that courtesy should be considered among the prime behavioral requisites of pastoral work:

Give way to one another in the Lord's own spirit of courtesy, treating no one as an inferior. When it is in your power to do a kindness, never put it off to another time, for charity is death's reprieve. (Polycarp, *Letter to Philippians*, sec. 10, ECW, p. 148)

Another early writing, the Didache, sets forth five positively desired qualities and three habits to be avoided:

School yourself to forbearance, compassion, guilelessness, calmness, and goodness; and never forget to respect the teaching you have had. Do not parade your own merits, or allow yourself to behave presumptuously, and do not make a point of associating with persons of eminence, but choose the companionship of honest and humble folk. (*Didache*, sec. 3, ECW, pp. 228–229)

Counsel can hardly be welcomed from one who does not follow his own counsel. Ambrose observed:

We note therefore that in seeking for counsel, uprightness of life, excellence in virtues, habits of benevolence, and the charm of good nature have very great weight. Who seeks for a spring in the mud? Who wants to drink from muddy water? . . . Who will think a man to be useful to another's cause whom he sees to be useless in his own life? . . . Am I to suppose that he is fit to give me advice who never takes it for himself, or am I to believe that he has time to give to me when he has none for himself? . . . How can a person have time for giving counsel when one has none for quiet? (Ambrose, *Duties of the Clergy*, Bk. II, Ch. XII, secs. 60, 62, NPNF 2, X, p. 53)

The hoped-for profile of interpersonal qualities expected of those entering ministry is no secret or hidden mystery. It is clear from these early descriptions, upon which later descriptions have built.

II. ᕗ Can Soul Care Be Studied?

Since personal destinies hinge upon its effectiveness, the care of persons deserves close study. Pastoral work does not proceed merely out of impulsive emotional hunches or simple intuition without intelligent effort. Pastoral care is, and has been for almost two millennia, a distinctive and well-defined discipline of study. It deserves the best reflective efforts of its practitioners.

It is dangerous to the health of the church to enter ministry without preparing for it:

Anyone who is about to enter upon this walk of life needs to explore it all thoroughly beforehand and only then to undertake this ministry. And why? Because if he studies the difficulties beforehand he will at any rate have the advantage of not being taken by surprise when they crop up. (John Chrysostom, *On the Priesthood*, Ch. III, sec. 16, p. 94)

As early as Tertullian (c. 160–c. 220) pastoral writers were appealing to the wisdom of historical experience in understanding soul care. He recognized that each historical layer of developing pastoral experience should be funded by previous layers:

Earlier works are more fitted for the instruction of the soul than later ones which, for their part, had to submit to instruction by the earlier ones. (Tertullian, *Testimony of the Soul*, Ch. 5, FC 10, p. 142)

Many ideas thought to be exclusively modern were treated by the ancient writers, and often in better balance than by modern pastoral writers. It is largely because of our ignorance of the earlier works that we have come to imagine modern psychological ideas (like repression, free association, dream analysis, positive reinforcement, congruence, empathy, etc.) are exclusively modern inventions. One motive of this study is to show how heavily dependent (however unawarely) modern psychologies and psychotherapies are upon various precedents in the Judeo-Christian wisdom of soul care.

A sixteenth century appeal to classical understandings of human behavior was offered by the independent-minded English physician and psychological analyst, Thomas Browne:

Live by old ethics and the classical rules of honesty. Put no new names or notions upon authentic virtues and vices. Think not that morality is ambulatory; that vices in one age are not vices in another, or that virtues, which are under the everlasting seal of right reason, may be stamped by opinion. And therefore, though vicious times invert the opinions of things, and set up new ethics against virtue, yet hold thou unto old morality; and rather than follow a multitude to do evil, stand like Pompey's pillar conspicuous by thyself, and single in integrity. And since the worst of times afford imitable examples of virtue, since no deluge of vice is like to be so general but more than eight will escape, eye well those heroes who have held their heads above water, who have touched pitch, and not been defiled, and in the common contagion have remained uncorrupted. (Thomas Browne, *Christian Morals*, Part I, sec. 12, p. 238; *Angl.*, p. 641)

One may "touch pitch," i.e., get one's hands dirty doing one's work in the world where it needs to be done, yet pray for purity of heart. Browne was convinced that the vices of one age do not differ much from another, and that even the worse of times may elicit the nobility of character.

III. * AWARENESS OF URGENT NEED

A decisive precondition of the calling of the pastor is the capacity to empathize with human hurt and alienation, to see that someone is hurting and help is needed—urgently. Often the pastoral writers viewed their whole societies (and not individuals only) as deeply troubled, risking failure and collapse. Their call to ministry was shaped by their sense of both social and personal pain. They often recognized that the care of persons cannot be abstracted from its actual context of political powers, social crises, economic needs, and cultural transformations.

Saint John Chrysostom, the leading doctor of the eastern church, (c. 347–407), used the stunning metaphor of a burning house to describe the context that prevailed in his own church and society, that intensified his own sense of calling:

> You have often been present at the burning of large houses. You have noticed how the smoke keeps rising to the sky. If no one comes near to put a stop to the mischief, but every one keeps looking to himself, the flame spreads freely on, and devours everything. It may happen that the whole city will stand around; they will stand around merely as spectators of the evil, not to aid nor assist. And there you may see them one and all standing round, and doing nothing, with various individuals stretching out their hands, and pointing out to some one who may have just arrived, either a flaming brand that moment flying through a window, or beams hurled down, or a whole exterior wall forced to fall outward, and tumbling violently to the ground.
>
> And there may be some around who are more daring and venturesome, who will have the boldness even to come close to the very buildings themselves while they are burning, not in order to lift a finger to help them or to put a stop to the mischief, but that they may the more fully enjoy the sight, being able from the nearer place to observe closely all that which often escapes those standing at a distance. If the house should happen to be large and magnificent, it appears to them a pitiable spectacle, and deserving of many tears. And truly there is a pitiable spectacle for us to behold—capitals of columns crumbling to dust, and many columns themselves shattering to pieces, some consumed by the fire, others thrown down often by the very hands that erected them, that they may not add fuel to the flame. Statues which stood with so much gracefulness with ceilings resting on them now stand exposed, with the roof torn off, standing hideously disfigured in the open air. And why should one go on to describe the wealth stored up in the house—the gold interlaid fabrics, the vessels of silver? What has now become of the storehouse of fabrics and perfumes, and the caskets of the costly jewels stored in a room the owners seldom visited? It has all become one blazing fire. Now coming in and out of the house are persons coming from their baths, cleaning persons, servants and many others. The whole house is one muddle of fire and water, mud and dust, and half-burnt beams!
>
> Now why have I drawn out so full a picture as this? Not simply be-

cause I wish to picture the conflagration of a house, for that is no essential concern of mine. Rather I wish to set before your eyes, as vividly as I can, the calamities of the Church. For like a conflagration indeed, as if from a thunderbolt hurled from on high, a fire is blazing in the roof of the Church. Yet no one seems roused up by it yet. Meanwhile our Father's house is burning, and we have remained asleep. . . .

Upon awakenening we stand gazing in amazement at the flames, but no longer able to quench the evil, or if we do quench it for a while, after a short time a spark is rekindled from a heap of ashes and begins consuming everything just as before. So it is now occurring with the Church, just what happens during a conflagration. It has already devoured the supports of the very pillars of the Church. Even the most faithful who had been supporting the roof, and who formerly held the whole building together it has enveloped in the flame. So the fire moved easily to the rest of the outer walls. Just as in the case of buildings, when the fire penetrates the timbers, it is better armed for its attack upon the stones, and when it has brought down the pillars and leveled them with the ground, little more is needed to consume everything else in flames. For when the props and supports of the upper parts fall down, the rest will speedily follow.

This is just where we are today in the life of the church: the fire has penetrated into every part. . . . We are no longer able to counsel those who are under our guidance, because we ourselves also are possessed with the same fever as they. We who are appointed by God to heal others, need the physician ourselves. What further hope of recovery is there left, when even the very physicians themselves need the healing hand of others? (John Chrysostom, *Homilies on Ephesians*, Hom. X, NPNF 1, XIII, pp. 100–101)*

The need is desperate: valuable structures are burning; bystanders are cynically enjoying the excitement of collapse; the physicians are sick with fever; the fire has penetrated every room! It is not unusual to find the pastoral writers interpreting their own period as an era of unprecedented crisis and misery. Edward Reynolds, a sixteenth century Anglican pastor poignantly wrote:

We live in failing times. We have found those of low degree vanity, and those of high degree a lie. We have leaned on our house, but it did not stand. We have leaned on our staff, and it has gone into our hand. We trusted too much in Parliaments, and they have been broken; in Princes, and they have given up the ghost. "*Nec vitia nec remedia ferre possumus,*" (we have been afflicted both with our diseases and with our remedies). Fear, and the pit, and the snare have been upon us. We have been changed from vessel to vessel, and we break every vessel we are put into. Our ships have been broken, our trade broken, our estates broken, our government broken, our hopes broken, our Church broken; nothing but our hearts and our sins, unbroken. . . . Well; it has been our sin and our folly to trust in broken reeds, in dying and perishing comforts. (Edward Reynolds, The Brand Plucked Out of the Fire, Works, V, pp. 189f; *Angl.*, p. 772)*

Even if these descriptions of urgent need tend toward exaggeration, the modern reader cannot help but feel the power of the moral vision that underlies the excess. Pastors are often deeply troubled and dissatisfied with the church and society, yet it has been just this sense of urgency and disquietude that has led them toward the call to ministry.

One of those rare moments in which Calvin talked autobiographically about his own personal sense of calling is found in his Preface to Psalms, where he candidly recounts his patterns of intense avoidance and resistance to the call to ministry, and the social and political crisis, war, and injustice, that framed his commitment:

Being of a disposition somewhat unpolished and bashful, which led me always to love the shade and retirement, I then began to seek some secluded corner where I might be withdrawn from the public view. But so far from being able to accomplish the object of my desire, all my retreats were like public schools. In short, while my one great object was to live in seclusion without being known, God so led me about through different turnings and changes, that he never permitted me to rest in any place, until, in spite of my natural disposition, he brought me forth to public notice. Leaving my native country, France, I in fact retired into Germany, expressly for the purpose of being able there to enjoy in some obscure corner the repose which I had always desired, and which had been so long denied me. But while I lay hidden at Basle and known only to a few people, many faithful and holy persons were burnt alive in France. The report of these burnings having reached everywhere, they excited the strongest disapprobation among a great part of the Germans, whose indignation was kindled against the authors of such tyranny. In order to allay this indignation, certain wicked and lying pamphlets were circulated, stating that none were treated with such cruelty but Anabaptists and seditious persons, who by their perverse ravings and false opinions were overthrowing not only religion but also all civil order. Observing that the object which these instruments of the court aimed at by their disguises was not only that the disgrace of shedding so much innocent blood might remain buried under the false charges and calumnies which they brought against the holy martyrs after their death, but also, that afterwards they might be able to proceed to the utmost extremity in murdering the poor saints without exciting compassion towards them in the breasts of any, it appeared to me, that unless I opposed them to the utmost of my ability, my silence could not be vindicated from the charge of cowardice and treachery. This was the consideration which induced me to publish my Institutes of the Christian Religion. My objects were, first, to prove that these reports were false and calumnious, and thus to vindicate my brethren, whose death was precious in the sight of the Lord. . . . William Farel detained me at Geneva, not so much by counsel and exhortation, as by a dreadful imprecation, which I felt to be as if God had from heaven laid his mighty hand upon me to arrest me. As the most direct road to Strasburg, to which I then intended to retire, was shut up by the wars, I had resolved to pass quickly by Geneva, without staying longer than a single night in that city. . . . After having learned that my heart was set upon devoting myself to private studies, for which I wished to keep myself free from other pursuits, and finding that he gained nothing by entreaties, Farel proceeded to utter an imprecation that God would curse my retirement and the tranquillity of the studies which I sought, if I should withdraw and refuse to give assistance, when the necessity was so urgent. By this imprecation I was so stricken with terror, that I desisted from the journey which I had undertaken. (Calvin, Preface to Psalms, *SW*, pp. 26–28)*

Calvin was strongly disinclined to respond to the call, but he could not in good conscience avoid it. A culture-shock experience in which one becomes a conscience-stricken outsider to one's own country may become an occasion for awakening or intensifying the call to pastoral caring. Tragic social and political events thus may become the matrix through which one's sense of calling comes into focus. So it occurred in the case of Calvin, detained, plagued and spurred on by William Farel, whom Calvin knew spoke rightly. It was nothing less than the persecution of innocent victims, widespread murder, the horrible sufferings of war, and the state cover-up of these misdeeds, that drove Calvin into the arena of pastoral care, along with the growing awareness that if he himself did not speak up, perhaps no one ever would or could. Calvin only wanted a quiet place to study. The Geneva that he entered, in which he expected to spend only one day, became the arena of a vast, complicated, unexpected ministry, to which he committed the remainder of his life, with astonishing effect.

IV. ❧ IDENTIFICATION WITH THE DISPOSSESSED

Personal identification with the hurt and poor is an assumption of the call to ministry. Affirmation of blackness symbolizing social alienation may seem to be a modern theme, but it was also found in the hellenistic Gentile Church. The experience of social oppression, rejection, and hatred from controlling groups caused third century Christians to identify with the experience of the black poor.

Early African Christian pastors such as Origen intentionally affirmed the social metaphor of blackness. Those who were thought to be outsiders and pariahs became the core of the early pastoral tradition: persons whom the Romans thought of as outlaws and fanatics, whom Jews rejected as non-Jews, and who to whites were considered blacks. Amid the persecutions of early third century Africa, in Alexandria, this view emerged, as expressed by Origen (c. 185–c. 254):

Those are, therefore, the daughters of this earthly Jerusalem who, seeing the Church of the Gentiles, despise and vilify her for her ignoble birth; for she is baseborn in their eyes, because she cannot count as hers the noble blood of Abraham and Isaac and Jacob, for all that she forgets her own people and her father's house and comes to Christ.

The Bride knows that the daughters of the former people impute this to her, and that because of it they call her black, as one who has not been enlightened by the patriarchs' teaching. She answers their objections thus: "I am indeed black, O daughters of Jerusalem, in that I cannot claim descent from famous men, neither have I received the enlightenment of Moses' Law. But I have my own beauty, all the same. For in me too there is that primal thing, the Image of God wherein I was created; and, coming now to the Word of God, I have received my beauty. Because of my dark colouring you may compare me to the tents of Cedar and the curtains of Solomon." (Origen, *The Song of Songs*, Bk. 2, ACW 26, p. 92)

The context is, in Origen's commentary on the Songs of Solomon, a extended allegorical interpretation of the church as bride of Christ, as anticipated in Old Testament wisdom. But an unusual bride indeed. This bride comes from among the outsiders, and does not belong to the established order. This bride is "baseborn" and rejected by everyone except God.

The third century church was not only called black, but joyfully affirmed her blackness, in a direct anticipation of the contemporary motif of black self-affirmation: Black is beautiful, and beautiful in its own distinctive way. This blackness, despised by the world, is made in the image of God. Origen continued the remarkable analogy:

Indeed I am surprised, O daughters of Jerusalem, that you should want to reproach me with the blackness of my hue. How have you come to forget what is written in your Law, as to what Mary suffered who spoke against Moses because he had taken a black Ethiopian to wife? How is it that you do not recognize the true fulfilment of that type in me? I am that Ethiopian. I am black indeed by reason of my lowly origin; but I am beautiful through penitence and faith. (Origen, *The Song of Songs*, Bk. 2, ACW 26, p. 93)

Christian pastoral care from its beginnings has thought of itself as identified with outsiders, with the poor and alienated, baseborn and rejected.

Richard Baxter sought to sensitize his fellow pastors to listen to the urgent needs of those who cry out for help, and the even more urgent needs of those who will not or cannot cry out for help. He enunciated this pathos-laden maxim: Those who most resist receiving help are those who most need it:

Can you hear them cry to you, as the man of Macedonia to Paul, in his vision, "Come and help us" (Acts 16:9); and yet refuse our help? Are you entrusted with the charge of a hospital, where one languishes in one corner, and another groans in another. . . ? Remember that such persons are less miserable than those who will not cry for help. It is the hardened offender who cares not for your help that most needs it. (Baxter, *RP*, pp. 197–98)*

V. ❧ Defining the Office of Pastor

Christian pastoral care is sharply distinguished from the services rendered by civil religion. It is not a service rendered to Caesar or political operatives or business interests. It is a spiritual office for the well-being of the church, entrusted with three primary areas of responsibility: word, sacrament, and pardon. Martin Chemnitz concisely stated what the office is, and is not:

What is the nature of the ministry of the church? It is not civil government, by which political affairs, or the matters of this world, are administered. Lk. 22:25–26; 2 Ti 2:4. Nor is it spiritual power lording it arbitrarily and, as it were, by naked power over the church of God in matters of faith. 2 Co. 1:24: 1 Ptr 5:3. Nor is it a business or a tricky way of indulging greed. 1 Ti 3:2–3, 8; 6:5: 1 Ptr 5:2. But it is a spiritual, or ecclesiastic, office, instituted and ordained by God Himself for discharging and performing necessary functions of the church, so that pastors, or preachers are and ought to be ministers of God and of the church in the kingdom of Christ, and stewards of the mysteries of God. 1 Co 4:1; Cl 1:25; 2 Co 4:5.

What, then, is the office of ministers of the church? This office, or ministry, has been committed and entrusted to them by God Himself through a legitimate call—

I. To feed the church of God with the true, pure, and salutary doctrine of the divine Word. Acts 20:28; Eph 4:11; 1 Ptr 5:2.

II. To administer and dispense the sacraments of Christ according to His institution. Mt. 28:19; 1 Co 11:23.

III. To administer rightly the use of the keys of the church, or of the kingdom of heaven, by either remitting or retaining sins (Mt 16:19; Jn 20:23), and to fulfill all these things and the whole ministry (as Paul says, 2 Ti 4:5) on the basis of the prescribed command, which the chief Shepherd Himself has given His ministers in His Word for instruction. Mt. 28:20. (Chemnitz, *MWS*, Introduction, secs. 1–2, p. 26)

Word, sacrament and pardon are the pivotal concerns of the pastoral office. The ministry of the Word includes preaching and teaching. The ministry of the sacraments seeks to enable Christ's living presence to be received in the world. The personal side of pastoral care focuses primarily on sin and grace, using rightly the keys (positive and negative reinforcement, discipline) of the church in eliciting penitence and behavioral change. Chemnitz delineated four principal issues of the ordinal examination that readies candidates for soul care:

> There are four chief parts:
> 1. The call. 2. The doctrine of the Word and of the Sacraments. 3. Ceremonies to be observed in church assemblies and in the administration of the sacraments. 4. The life and conduct of ministers of the church. (Chemnitz, *MWS*, Introduction, sec. 4, p. 27)

Readiness for ministry requires grounding in a pastoral calling, Christian teaching of Word and sacrament, rites and ceremonial practices of the church, and behavioral qualities requisite for pastoral care. The office of the pastor was concisely described by Calvin in three-fold terms as a ministry of word, sacrament and counseling.

> As to the pastors, whom Scripture also sometimes calls elders and ministers, their office is to proclaim the Word of God, to instruct, admonish, exhort and censure, both in public and private, to administer the sacraments, and to enjoin brotherly corrections along with the elders and colleagues. Now in order that nothing happen confusedly in the church, no one is to enter upon this office without a calling. (Calvin, *Draft Ecclesiastical Ordinances*, 1541, *SW*, p. 230)

Pastors are duly called and authorized to act representatively for the whole body in areas where it would not be fitting for all members to act representatively for all. Baptism alone does not qualify one to preach, teach, administer sacraments or absolve representatively for the whole community. Either to feel inwardly called without being sent by the whole church, or to be ecclesiastically approved and sent without experiencing God's inward call, is inadequate grounding, according to the Anglican Thirty-Nine Articles of Religion (1563):

> It is not lawful for any man to take upon him the office of public preaching, or ministering the Sacraments in the Congregation, before he be lawfully called, and sent to execute the same. And those we ought to judge lawfully called and sent, which be chosen and called to this work by men who have public authority given unto them in the Congregation, to call and send Ministers into the Lord's vineyard. (Anglican Thirty-nine Articles, sec. XXIII, *CC*, p. 274)

The classical ecumenical consensus affirmed by Catholics and Protestants alike is that duly authorized ministers are entrusted with the selection process that continues the apostolic tradition in each new generation. Although there are some traditions that would differ on this point, as a rule the gift of sacred ministry has not been given or legitimated by populist standards. Although democratic procedures, due processes and equity considerations are factored into ordination, its deeper purpose is to discern the will of God. The one objective above all to which ordained ministry is committed is the continuity and maintenance of the apostolic tradition.

John Chrysostom argued that even though the priestly office could like everything else be corrupted, the office itself is not in itself the cause of corruption of priests. Rather it is the abuses of the pastoral office that tend toward corruption:

> I do not venture to blame the priestly office for these evils. God forbid that I should be such a fool! Wise men do not blame the knife for murder, nor wine for drunkenness, nor strength for insolence, nor courage for recklessness. No; they blame the men who make wrong use of the gifts of God, and punish them for it. The priestly office might well accuse us of not handling it rightly. It is not itself the cause of the evils I have mentioned. (John Chrysostom, *On the Priesthood*, Ch. III, sec. 9, p. 78)

VI. ❧ DISTINGUISHING THE SPHERE OF SOUL CARE

Pastoral writers in various periods have sought accurately to define the proper sphere of pastoral care and the range of its jurisdiction. Among the sharpest of delineations is Luther's attempt to show that ministry has a particular task and sphere of operation vividly distinguishable from the secular sphere of law, coercion, governmental authority and unaided natural reasoning. Modern consciousness may brace at terms like spiritual "rule" (which today might more appropriately be called spiritual direction or guidance) and the "kingly" sphere (that which is most highly authoritative in the temporal sphere). These terms may sound overbearing and controlling. But it should be born in mind that Luther's intent is to *limit* the sphere of the pastoral office, which had previously suffered from overextension:

> There you have the spiritual rule *(Regiment)*, which one should be sure to separate as far from temporal rule as heaven and earth are apart. Now the men who have charge of this spiritual rule are real kings, real princes, real masters; and it is their duty to govern. Note here, however, and learn how this rule is limited and how far it extends. It extends (as the words clearly say) over the entire world; and yet it is to deal only with sins. . . . One should be careful not to mix and mingle these two jurisdictions, as the pope and his bishops have done. They have used the spiritual rule in such a way that they became worldly lords too; and emperors and kings had to bow before them. Christ did not command His disciples to do this; He did not send them

out to exercise worldly rule. But He entrusted to them the office of the ministry and the rule over sin, so that a definition of the office of the ministry is as follows: it is to preach the Gospel of Christ and to forgive sin to crushed and fearful consciences . . . . I, as a preacher and ambassador of Christ, should teach you nothing about housekeeping, farming, marrying, making a livelihood, and other things; for God has given you your reason for that. But if you cannot properly adapt yourself to many of these matters, you may use worldly-wise people who are able to advise you. My jurisdiction and rule, however, pertain only to sin, to teaching you that because of your sins you must have been lost forever had not Christ paid and rendered satisfaction for them. (Luther, "Sermon on John 20:19–31, 1533," WA 52, p. 268; WLS 2, pp. 950–951)

The pastor comes into close quarters with each person in his charge concerning the witness of their own conscience and the pertinent address of God's forgiving word. Pastoral counseling is not reducible to economic counseling or political advice, that depends upon prudential reasoning, and does not necessarily require the premises of sin and forgiveness. The specific realm of responsibility for ministry is the troubled conscience and the divine word of forgiveness. If ministry functions well in that arena, it will have all the more relevance for vocational and domestic issues, for political and economic justice.

Many pastoral writers have sought in various ways to define the proper range and responsibility of the minister. Anglican Bishop Gilbert Burnet writing in 1692 on the "dignity of sacred employment," provided this sharp definition of the pastoral task:

As much as the soul is better than the body, and as much as the purifying and perfecting the soul is preferable to all those mechanical employments that relate to the body, and as much as eternity is more valuable than this short and transitory life; so much does this employment excel all others.

The clergyman by his character and design of life, ought to be a man separated from the cares and concerns of this world, and dedicated to the study and meditation of divine matters. Whose conversation ought to be a pattern for others; a constant preaching to his people; who ought to offer up the prayers of the people in their name, and as their mouth to God; who ought to be praying and interceding for them in secret, as well as officiating among them in public; who ought to be distributing among them the bread of life, the word of God; and to be dispensing among them the sacred rites, which are the badges, the union, and the supports of Christians. He ought to admonish, to reprove, and to comfort them, not only by his general doctrine in his sermons, but from house to house, in order that he brings things more effectively home than can be done from the pulpit. He is to watch over their souls, to keep them from error, and to alarm them out of their sins, by giving them warning of the judgments of God; to visit the sick, and to prepare them for the judgment and life to come (Burnet, *Of the Pastoral Care*, Ch. I, pp. 41f.)*

Burnet then set forth the relation of the pastor's character to the pastoral office:

This is the function of a clergyman; who, that he may perform all these duties with more advantage, and better effect, ought to behave himself so well, that his own conversation may not only be without offence, but be so exemplary that his people may have reason to conclude, that he himself does firmly believe all those things which he purposes to them; that he thinks himself bound to follow all those rules that he sets them; and that they may see such a serious spirit of devotion in him that from thence they may be induced to believe, that his chief design among them, is to do them good and to save their souls; which may prepare them as to esteem and love him, that they may not be prejudiced against any thing that he does and says in public, by any thing that they observe in himself in secret. He must also be employing himself so well in his private studies, that from thence he may be furnished with such a variety of lively thoughts, divine meditations, and proper and noble expressions, as may enable him to discharge every part of his duty, in such a manner, as may raise not so much his own reputation, as the credit of his function, and of the great message of reconciliation that is committed to his charge. Above all studies, he ought to apply himself to understand the holy scriptures aright; to have his memory well furnished that way, that so upon all occasions he may be able to inforce what he says out of them, and so be an able minister of the New Testament. (Burnet, *Of the Pastoral Care*, Ch. I, pp. 42, 43)

That toward which ministry directs its care is the *psyche* (*anima*, soul), the animating, motivating, lively dimension of human existence. On behalf of the soul's proper growth, the minister enters into creative conversation, prays, leads worship, visits, admonishes and comforts. The personal behavior of the care giver is an important test of the authenticity of his public speech. The responsible behavior of the pastor is the strongest evidence his hearers have that he takes his own counsel seriously.

A single pastor is ill-advised to try to extend one's care over a great many persons, according to Richard Baxter. The pastor who attempts to take care of too many souls might as well be saying, "Let them suffer":

Flocks must ordinarily be no greater than we are capable of overseeing. . . . If the pastoral office consists in overseeing all the flock, then surely the number of souls under the care of each pastor must not be greater than he is able to take such heed to as is here required. . . . O, happy would it have been for the Church, and happy for the overseers themselves, if this measure here intimated by the apostle had still been observed: that the diocese had been no greater than the elders or bishops could oversee and rule, so that they might have taken heed to all the flock. Better would it have been if pastors had been multiplied as churches increased, and the number of overseers proportioned to the number of souls, that they might not have let the work be undone, while they assumed the empty titles, and undertook impossibilities! . . . . The general that will command an army alone may as well say, Let it be destroyed for lack of command. The schoolmaster that will oversee or govern all the schools in the county by himself may as well say, Let them all be ungoverned. The physician that will undertake the care of all the sick people in a whole nation, or county, when he is not able to visit one hundredth of them may as well say, Let them perish. (Baxter, *RP*, pp. 88–90)*

These works of personalized ministry are not easily replicable in secular surrogates (such as state care of the poor, or hospitalization for the terminally ill) in which the preconditioning assumptions of religiously-motivated personalization of care have been taken away, leaving bare humanistic motives of self-interest and equity. If the pastor does distinctly pastoral tasks well, the larger public good will be served, as Luther argued:

He informs and instructs the various estates on how they are to conduct themselves outwardly in their several offices and estates, so that they may do what is right in the sight of God. Every day he can comfort and advise those who are troubled, compose difficulties, relieve troubled consciences, help maintain peace and settle and remove differences, and countless other works of this kind. For a preacher confirms, strengthens, and helps to sustain authority of every kind, and temporal peace generally. He checks the rebellious; teaches obedience, morals, discipline, and honor; instructs fathers, mothers, children, and servants in their duties; in a word, he gives direction to all the temporal estates and offices. Of all the good things a pastor does these are, to be sure, the least. Yet they are so high and noble that the wisest of the heathen have never known or understood them, much less been able to do them. (Luther, "Sermon on Keeping Children in School, 1530," LW 46, p. 226)

What clergy do is of the highest order of importance, yet hidden from view. It involves a constant caring for persons where they are. From within naturalistic and hedonic assumptions, the observer can only remain astonished at the life the flows out of the grace of God.

VII. ❧ ON GIVING RESISTANCE TO THE CALL TO MINISTRY

Resistance to the pastoral calling is a perennial feature of seriousness about it. It should not be surprising that one might offer considerable resistance to a vocation that promised minimal financial security, little control of working hours, required constant personal availability, and assumed that one would be caring deeply about each person encountered. Such resistance appears often in the pastoral literature. Those who have most deeply heard the call to ministry have had to struggle inwardly with themselves and outwardly with other significant companions, in order to reach a decision to make such a commitment. The pastoral literature has reflected the depths of this struggle.

At one point in Martin Luther's career, we find the strength and complexity of his own inner resistance emerging in his conversations with his Augustinian spiritual advisor, Johann von Staupitz, who wisely allowed these resistances to be candidly expressed:

Under this pear tree I advanced more than fifteen arguments to Dr. Staupitz; with them I declined my call. But they did me no good. When I finally said: Dr. Staupitz, you are taking my life; I shall not live a quarter-year, he replied: In God's name! Our Lord God has many things to do; He is in need of wise people in heaven too. (Luther, *Table Talk*, WA-T 3, #3143b; WLS 3, p. 1131)

Moses, Isaiah, Jeremiah, Peter and Paul have perennially served as biblical prototypes of those who have resisted mightily the call of God, sometimes for a long period, yet in due time have given exceptional leadership to the people of God:

When Moses was called of the Lord to lead the people out, he declined right heartily. He excused himself and complained that he was of a slow tongue; he did not desire the assigned function. Yes, he resisted so long that the Lord was angry with him. Ex. 4:10–15.

Isaiah dreaded to preach he Word of the Lord, and complained that he was of unclean lips until the angel purged them. Jeremiah was called by God and prepared from birth to be a prophet; and yet he said, Ah, Lord God! I am not fit to preach, for I am but a child. Jer. 1:6. Peter was asked three times by the Lord whether he loved him, before He would give him charge of His sheep. John 21:15. Paul was called from heaven and drafted by the Lord Himself in the service of the Gospel. (Menno Simons, Foundation of Christian Doctrine, 1539, *CWMS*, p. 161)

Menno reported his own belabored resistance to the call to ministry under outwardly hazardous conditions and with bewildering inward confusion:

Trouble and fear were on every side. On the one hand I was sensible of my limited talents, my unlearnedness, my weak nature, the timidity of my spirit, the exceedingly great wickedness, perversity, and tyranny of the world, the great and powerful sects, the subtlety of many minds, and the woefully heavy cross that would weigh on me not a little should I comply. On the other hand I saw pitifully great hunger and need of these God-fearing, pious children, for I saw plainly that they erred as do harmless sheep which have no shepherd.

At last, after much prayer, before the Lord and His church I gave these conditions: that we should pray earnestly to the Lord for a season. Then if it should be pleasing to His holy will that I could or should labor to His praise, He would give me such a mind and heart as would say to me with Paul, Woe is me, if I preach not the gospel. And if not, that He might employ means so that nothing would come of it. For Christ says, If two or three shall agree on earth as touching anything that they shall ask, it shall be done for them of my Father which is in heaven. for where two or three are gathered together in my name, there am I in the midst of them. (Menno Simons, Reply to Gellius Faber, 1554, *CWMS*, p. 672)

The inward struggle was heightened by a keen sense of personal inadequacy coupled with a profound awareness of the seeming impossibility of the task (lacking grace), and the immensity of need, yet with earnest prayer, it could be sustained by divine providence. If the pastoral teacher knew in advance all of the troubles and difficulties of the work of ministry, would the call ever be accepted? Luther speculated on his own case:

Unless those who are in the office of preacher find joy in him who sent them, they will have much trouble. Our Lord God had to ask Moses as many as six times. He also led me into the office in the same way. Had I known about it before hand, he would have had to take more pains to get me in. Be that as it may, now that I have begun, I intend to perform the duties of the office with his help. On account of the exceedingly great and heavy cares and worries connected with it, I would not take the whole world to enter upon this work now. On the other hand, when I regard him who called me, I would not take the whole world not to have begun it. (Luther, *Table Talk*, LW 54, #113, pp. 12–13)

Luther urged caution in the counseling of one who has some gifts for ministry and yet has not truly felt with clarity called of God:

If you are learned and understand God's Word well and think that you would present it to others faithfully and profitably, then wait. If God wants it, He will have no trouble finding you. My friend, do not let your ability burst your belly. God has not forgotten you. If you are to preach His Word, He will no doubt call on you to do so at His own time. Do not determine the time limit or the place for Him. (Luther,

"Sermon on Matt. 4:18–22, Lenten Postil, 1525," WA 17 II, p. 255; WLS 2, p. 939)

The decision to enter sacred ministry cannot rightly be coerced, but must be a freely willed choice:

"Do it, not under compulsion, but of your own free will" (1 Pet. 5:21). It is true that no one should force himself into this office without being called. But when he is called and required, he must go willingly and do what his office demands. For those who must do this by constraint and have no desire and love for it will not carry it out well. (Luther, "Sermons on the First Epistle of St. Peter, 1523," LW 30, p. 136, NEB)*

Within the monastic context, many sincere individuals struggled with the call to preach over against the call to prayer. Frequently they perceived the call to preach as an exceptionally hard choice, as did St. Francis, remembered through the eyes of Bonaventure:

What do you think, brothers, what do you judge better? That I should spend my time in prayer or that I should go about preaching? I am a poor little man, simple and *unskilled in speech*; I have received a greater grace of prayer than of speaking. Also in prayer there seems to be a profit and the accumulation of graces, but in preaching the distribution of gifts already received from heaven. In prayer our interior affections are purified and we are united with the one, "true and highest good" as well as strengthened in virtue; in preaching, we get dust on our spiritual feet, distraction over many things and relaxation of discipline. Finally, in prayer we address God, listen to him and dwell among the angels as if we were living an angelic life; in preaching we must think, see, say and hear human things, adapting ourselves to them as if we were living on a human level, for men and among men. . . . When he had mulled over these words for many days with his friars, he could not perceive with certainty which of these he should choose as more acceptable to Christ. Although he understood extraordinary things through the spirit of prophecy, this question he could not resolve with certainty on his own. (Bonaventure, *The Life of St. Francis*, CWS, pp. 291–293)

Some have gone to radical and absurd lengths to disqualify themselves from the burdens of soul care, as Palladius (c. 365–425) reported of Ammonius (the story presupposes the Old Testament tradition that the body of the priest must be unblemished):

The people approached the blessed Timotheus, begging him to appoint Ammonius as their bishop. He said to them: "Bring him to me and I will ordain him."

Then they went with envoys and Ammonius saw that he was trapped. He pleaded with them and solemnly swore that he would not accept the election, that he would not leave the desert. They did not give in to him. Then while they were looking on he took a pair of shears and cut off his left ear, right back to the head, and he said: "And from now on be assured that it is impossible for me, as the law forbids a man with his ear cut off to be ordained priest." (Palladius, *The Lausiac History*, Ch. 11, sec. 1–2, ACW, 34, p. 47)

VIII. &ۥ THE LANGUAGE OF CURACY

Certain Hebrew, Greek, and Latin terms have strongly influenced the language of curacy (care of souls). A broad classical consensus has generally agreed on root meanings of these key terms, even though many particular issues remain under debate. To a surprising degree the older consensus still remains and has been confirmed by recent studies.

The single selection that follows, the longest in this collection, offers a centrist account of the various terms and offices of ministry that would find reasonably wide consensus among both Catholic and Protestant pastoral writers. It is written irenically in the style of the Anglican middle way between Rome and Geneva. It synthesizes much in short space that would otherwise be scattered over many authors who would make the same points less well. It is from Bishop Gilbert Burnet's once widely read classic: *Of the Pastoral Care*, of 1692. The meaning of key metaphors and descriptive terms for curacy are introduced: shepherd, servant, elder, overseer, steward, ambassador, watcher, builder, and gardener:

The name of deacon that is now appropriated to the lowest office in the church, was, in the time that the New Testament was written, used more promiscuously. For the apostles, the evangelists, and those whom the apostles sent to visit the church, are all called by this name. Generally in all those places where the word minister is in our translation, it is deacon in the Greek, which signifies properly a servant, or one who labours for another. Such persons are dedicated to the immediate service of God, and are appropriated to the offices and duties of the church. So this term both expresses the dignity and the labour of the employment.

The next order now is the name of presbyter or elder. Although at first it was applied not only to bishops, but to the apostles themselves, yet in the succeeding ages, it came to be appropriated to the second rank of the officers in the church. It either signifies a seniority of age, or of Christianity, in opposition to a neophyte or a novice, one newly converted to the faith. Later the title of counselor was appropriated to presbyter, after the pattern of the senate or a senator who by common practice were called counselors by reason of their age. Eventually the title presbyter became altered in pronunciation to be in English, priest. This presbyter or elder, being a term of respect, denotes the dignity of those to whom it belongs. St. Paul divides this title either into two different ranks, or into two different performances of the duties of the same rank: those that rule well, and those that labour in word and doctrine (1 Tim. 5:17). In this way presbyter has become a title that speaks both the dignity, and likewise the duty belonging to this function.

The title of bishop, meaning inspector or overseer, is now by the custom of many ages, given to the highest function in the church. It implies a dignity in him, as the chief of those who labour, so it does likewise express his obligation to care and diligence, both in observing, and overseeing the whole flock, especially in inspecting the deportment and labors of his fellow workers who are subordinate to him in the constitution of the church, yet ought to be esteemed by him as his brothers, his fellow laborers, and fellow servants, in imitation of the apostles. Next to the names of the sacred functions, I shall consider the other designations and figures, made use of to express them.

The most common is that of pastor or shepherd. It is to be remembered, that in the first simplicity of mankind for many ages, men looked after their own cattle, or employed their children in it. When they trusted that care to any one else, it was no small sign of their confidence, according to what Jacob said to Laban. The care of a good shepherd was a figure then so well understood that the prophet expresses God's care of his people by this figure of his feeding them as a shepherd, carrying his lambs in his bosom, and gently leading those that are with young (Is. 11:11). Christ also calls himself the good shepherd, who knew his sheep, and did not as a hireling fly away when the wolf came, but laid down his life for his sheep (John 10:11). This figure then, being so often employed in both Testaments, is an expression of the great trust committed to the clergy, which likewise supposes a great, a constant, and a tender care in looking to, feeding, instructing, watching over, and guarding the flock against errors and sins. It also assumes that clergy are ready to offer themselves to the first fury of persecution.

The title of stewards, or dispensors, which is the most honorable in a household, is also given to clergy. For stewards assign to every member his due share, both of labor and of provision. They watch over the others, and have the care of the domestic order assigned to them. So in this great family, of which Christ is the head, the stewards are not only in the position of great dignity, but also of much labour (1 Cor. 4:1,2). They ought to be observing the rest of this household, that they may be faithful in the distribution, and so encourage, admonish, reprove or censure as there is occasion for it.

Clergy are also called ambassadors, and this upon the noblest and most desirable premise. For their business is to treat of peace between God and man. To them is given the word and teaching of reconciliation. They are sent by Christ, and speak in God's name as if God himself were beseeching humanity through them, acting representatively on behalf of Christ who is the mediator, pressing all to be reconciled to God (2 Cor. 5:19,20)—words of a very high sound, of great trust and dignity, but which import likewise great obligations. An ambassador is very solicitous to maintain the dignity of his character and his master's honor, and chiefly to carry on that which is the main business that he is sent upon, which he is always contriving how to promote. So if the honour of this title affects us as it ought to do, with a just value for it, we ought at the same time to consider the obligations that accompany it, of living suitable to it, answering in some way the dignity and majesty of the King of kings that has committed it to us. It implies laboring with all possible diligence to effectuate the great design on which we are sent: reconciling sinners to God, the work having in itself a proportion to the dignity of him that employs us in it. . . .

Pastors are often called watchmen, (Ezek. 3:17), who used to stand on high towers, and were to give the alarm as they saw occasion for it. They were responsible for an attitude of constant attendance, watching in the night, as well as in the day. When this is applied to clergy, it suggests that they ought to be upon their watch-tower observing what dangers their people are exposed to, either by their sins which provoke the judgments of God, or by the designs of their enemies. The watchman does no good if by a false sense of respect he allows the people to sleep and perish in their sins. He must be willing to enunciate the judgments of God to them, even if it incurs their displeasure by their freedom being imposed upon, rather than permit them to perish in their security.

St. Paul also calls churchmen by the name of builders and gives to the apostles the title of master-builders (1 Cor. 3:10). This implies both hard and painful labour, and great care and exactness in doing it. If the building lacks precision, it will be not only exposed to the injuries of weather, but will quickly tumble down. This suggests that those who carry this title ought to study well the great design by which they must carry on the interest of religion, that so they may build up their people in their most holy faith so as to be a building fitly framed together.

Clergy are also called laborers in God's husbandry (1 Cor. 3:9), laborers in his vineyard and harvest, who are to sow, plant and water

(Mt. 20:1, 9:37, 38; 1 Cor. 3:6) and cultivate the soil of the church. This suggests a steady, continual return of daily and hard labour which is both painstaking pain and diligent. (Burnet, *Of the Pastoral Care*, pp. 44–49)*

These key metaphors for curacy define the realm in which pastoral care occurs and its manner of acting. They recur throughout the centuries of pastoral discussions. This preliminary view provides an overarching summary of a task whose specifics are to be subsequently elaborated.

IX. ❧ DIVINE CALL AND CHURCHLY CONFIRMATION: THE INWARD AND OUTWARD CALLING

It is incorrect to say either that one is properly called by God alone without the church, or properly called by the church alone without God. The pastoral writers have spoken often of the distinction between the immediate call of God, and that call of God which is mediated through ecclesial means and processes. Since prophets and apostles were called immediately, i.e., without mediation, they constitute an exception. After the original apostolic era, the calling to pastoral service is assumed to be mediated:

> God calls in two ways, either by means or without means. Today He calls all of us into the ministry of the word by a mediated call, that is, one that comes through means, namely, through man. But the apostles were called immediately by Christ Himself, as the prophets in the Old Testament had been called by God Himself. . . . Since the time of the apostles this [the mediated call] has been the usual method of calling in the world. (Luther, *Lectures on Galatians*, 1535, LW 26, pp. 17–18)

Human motivations and passions are by no means ignored by the pastoral writers, but these do not account for a calling, or in themselves qualify one to be sent as pastor. Luther distinguished two dimensions of one's being sent of God— primarily through God's own sending, and secondarily through the visible church's due recognition of God's own sending:

> The other way of sending is indeed also of God, but it is done through the instrumentality of man. It has been employed ever since God established the ministry with its preaching and its exercise of the Office of the Keys. This ministry will endure and is not to be replaced by any other. But the incumbents of this ministry do not remain; they die. This necessitates an ever-new supply of preachers, which calls for the employment of certain means. The ministry, that is, the Word of God, Baptism, and Holy Communion, came directly from Christ; but later Christ departed from this earth. Now a new way of sending was instituted, which works through man but is not of man. (Luther, "Sermons on the Gospel of St. John Chapters 3 and 4, 1539," LW 22, p. 482)

Chemnitz refined this distinction: Although the earliest apostles were called without means, (i.e., without an apparatus of examination and validation of one's inward calling), subsequent to apostolic times all calling to ministry is necessarily received through regularized, orderly means:

There is no legitimate or ordinary call to the ministry except from God, and it is two fold; either without means or through means.

What is a call without means, and how does it take place?

When someone is called and sent to the ministry neither by men nor through men as through regular means, but without means, by God Himself, and through God Himself, as God in this way called the patriarchs, prophets, and apostles, without any intervening human means. And they who have thus been called have the testimony of the Spirit and of miracles that they do not err in doctrine. . . . Is one, therefore, immediately to believe all fanatics when they claim that God has appeared to them, that the Lord has spoken to them, that the Father has given them this commission, and that they are thus stirred up and moved by the Spirit?

By no means. For God has forbidden this with an express warning. Jer. 14:14. But God endows those whom He calls without means either with the gift of miracles or with other testimonies of the Spirit with which to prove and confirm their call. . . . God at this time wants to call and send ministers to His church through a mediate (i.e., through means) call or regular means.

What, then, is a mediate call?

When any minister is called and appointed to the ministry of the church, indeed by God and divinely, but not without means, as the prophets and apostles [were], but through regular means, in a legitimate way. For a mediate call is as much from God as an immediate one, but they differ in the manner of the call. For God called the prophets and apostles immediately, through Himself. But God called and sent Titus, Timothy, Sosthenes, Silvanus, and others likewise, but not immediately, rather through means instituted and ordained by Himself for this purpose. . . . Timothy, bishop of the church at Ephesus, was not called immediately, but through Paul and the presbytery. 1 Tim. 4:14; 2 Tim. 1:6. . . . Paul likewise declares that God gives and places in the church not only apostles, who are called immediately, but also teachers and pastors, who are called mediately. Eph. 4:11; 1 Cor. 12:28. . . . Ministers are not the whole church, but only part of it (Eph. 4:11–12), and they are not lords of the church, but ministers and overseers (2 Cor. 1:24;4:5; Ezek. 33:7), therefore they neither can nor should seize to themselves alone the mediate call, with the other members of the church excluded; for not even the apostles did this, but drew the rest of the church in with themselves. Acts 1:15–16; 6:2–3; 14:23). (Chemnitz, *MWS*, Part 1, secs. 13–22, pp. 31–33)

Chemnitz provided a classical Protestant rationale for due process in ascertaining the authenticity of a call to ministry. The aim was to avoid fanatical individualism, to follow scriptural mandates, and to seek confirmation from the whole church of an inner sense of calling. Menno Simons, the leading theologian of the Anabaptist tradition and founder of the Mennonites, similarly argued:

Some are called by God alone without any human agent as was the case with the prophets and apostles. Others are called by means of the pious as may be seen from Acts 1:23–26. (Menno Simons, *Foundation of Christian Doctrine*, 1539, *CWMS*, p. 159)

Theories of mediated calling are primarily motivated by the desire to prevent fanaticism, the distortions of false prophets, erroneous teaching and low quality preparation for ministry. Although they have not always worked effectively so as to achieve unerringly their intended aim, they have doubtless served good purposes. No traditional church body ordains without some interpretation of the idea of mediated calling.

X. ❧ THE CALL OF GOD

The Christian teaching of the call of God to soul care has been worked out and reworked in many different generations of pastoral practice. However, its major features hinge on biblical mandates to which ministry in each cultural situation is seeking to respond. Here is Menno Simons' summary of these biblical mandates underlying the call to ministry:

"As the Father sent me, so I send you" (John 20:21). This Scripture remains unchangeable in the church of God. It means that all true teachers and preachers are sent of Christ Jesus, as He is sent of the Father. . . . This same Christ Jesus, the Bishop of bishops, and the Shepherd of shepherds, who was faithful in all things unto which He was sent of His heavenly Father, never sends to His members, children, and sheep to tend and protect them, any other bishops, teachers, shepherds, and laborers in the vineyard, than those who are of one body, spirit, and mind with Him, even as He is one with the Father. He sends those who by the divine word, which is Christ, are so renewed, converted, and changed that He may truly say of them, Behold, these are the children which God hath given me. . . . He sends such whose doctrine is a pungent salt; whose life is a shining light, who are patient, kind, generous, merciful, hospitable, not avaricious nor selfish, nor desirous of filthy lucre, not hateful, bloody, or contentious, well spoken of among those who are outside, ruling their own house well, having a virtuous wife, the gift of purity, and obedient children. Yes, in all things they are chaste, sober, unblamable, having the Spirit, fear, and love of God (1 Tim. 3:1ff). They are so minded in all things that they can truly say with Paul to their entrusted sheep, "Follow my example, as I follow Christ's" (1 Cor. 11:1). (Menno Simons, The Calling of Ministers, *CWMS*, pp. 440–442, NEB)*

It is not God who sends unfaithful ministers. If false teachers appear, they are by their false fruits proven to be not sent of God. Ministers sent of God are recognizable by their fruits, especially habituated behaviors of patience, kindness, mercy, and love.

Baxter brusquely warned that a holy calling will not save an unholy character:

We preached so many sermons of Christ, while we neglected him; of the Spirit, while we resisted him; of faith, while we did not ourselves believe; of repentance and conversion, while we continued in an impenitent and unconverted state; . . . . God is no respecter of persons; he saveth no men for their coats or callings; a holy calling will not save an unholy man. (Baxter, *RP*, p. 32)

The call to ministry is intrinsically connected with pivotal notions of apostolicity, compassion, and divine entrustment. It is from this awareness that its courage and diligence is derived:

Paul says, Rom. 10:15: "How shall they who are not sent preach" (namely in such a way that faith is engendered by hearing)? . . . The assurance of a divine call stirs up ministers of the Word, so that each one, in his station, in the fear of God, performs his functions with greater diligence, faith, and eagerness, without weariness. And he does not let himself be drawn or frightened away from his office by fear of any peril or of persecution, since he is sure that he is called by God and that that office has been divinely entrusted to him. (Chemnitz, *MWS*, Part 1, sec. 11, p. 30)

Aptness to teach (1 Tim. 3:2; 2 Tim. 2:24) is a crucial premise of the call to ministry:

May one seek or undertake the ministry of the church who has neither learned the fundamental Christian doctrine, nor understands [it], nor has the gift to teach others? By no means. for Paul commands Timothy and Titus to entrust the ministry to faithful and able men. 2 Tim. 2:2; 3:2; Titus 1:9.

Should, then, one who is somewhat endowed with those gifts, on his own initiative and personal judgment, without a special and legitimate call, undertake and claim for himself the office of teaching in the church? By no means. Rom. 10:15; Jer. 23:21; Heb. 5:4. (Chemnitz, *MWS*, Part 1, sec. 5–6, p. 28)

Those who imagine that eloquence or good verbal capacity is the essential qualification for ministry do well to listen to this unsparing caveat:

These will never gather fruit in the vineyard of the Lord, no matter how eloquent they may be, how esteemed and equipped. All that they attempt is wasted effort. They will rise too early or go out too late; their harangue is without power; their service is vain, their labor without fruit, yes, it is nothing but sowing by the seashore and reaping the wind. For no one can serve in this high and holy office conformable to God's will, except he whom the Lord of the vineyard has made capable by the Spirit of His grace. (Menno Simons, Foundation of Christian Doctrine, 1539, *CWMS*, p. 162)

One may, like Jonah, attempt to dodge the divine address, but according to Baxter, that may prove more difficult than imagined:

What an obligation, then, is laid upon us, by our call to the work! If our commission is sent from heaven, it is not to be disobeyed. When the apostles were called by Christ from their secular employments, they immediately left friends, and house, and trade, and all, and followed him. When Paul was called by the voice of Christ, he "was not disobedient to the heavenly vision" (Acts 26:19). Though our call is not so immediate or extraordinary yet it is from the same Spirit. It is no safe course to imitate Jonah, in turning our back upon the commands of God. If we neglect our work, he has a spur to quicken us; if we run away from it, he has messengers enough to overtake us, and bring us back, and make us do it; and it is better to do it at first than at last. . . . Do you think so basely of the Church of God, as if it deserved not the best of your care and help? Were you the keepers of sheep or swine, you would scarcely let them go, and say, They are not worth the looking after; especially if they were you own. And dare you say so of the souls of men? (Baxter, *RP*, pp. 130–131)*

A highly particularized calling may occur, as in the case of St. Patrick of Ireland, who even against his inclinations believed that he heard the voices of the Irish crying to him:

And there I saw in the night the vision of a man, whose name was Victoricus, coming as it were from Ireland, with countless letters. And he gave me one of them, and I read the opening words of the letter, which were, "The voice of the Irish"; and as I read the beginning of the letter I thought that at the same moment I heard their voice—they were those beside the Wood of Voclut, which is near the Western Sea—and thus did they cry out as with one mouth: "We ask thee, boy, come and walk among us once more." (Patrick, Works, Bk. I, sec. 23, ACW 17, p. 28)

Are there reliable behavioral evidences and visible fruits that may help people recognize pastors sent of God? Although the following passage may seem somewhat idealized, it provides a familiar pattern that is often repeated in the pastoral tradition:

> The shepherds who are sent of God and have been rightly called, teach the Word of God unfalsified, keep in its holy ordinances, live unblamably in their little power, for they are born of God, are taught and moved by His Holy Spirit; they seek neither gold nor possessions, neither an easy life nor praise of men on earth. They perform their assigned duties with all diligence. They fear God from their hearts and seek their fellow men with great fidelity. They are armed with the weapons of righteousness on the right hand and on the left. Rom. 6:7. They deal without respect to persons. The powerful sharp sword of the divine Word cuts from their lips. The shining lanterns are in their hands. They are taught in righteousness, and are full of spiritual wisdom. They divide the good from the evil, the holy from the unholy, and the clean from the unclean. In brief, they shine in doctrine and life, even as from the beginning to the present time it has been written and observed of all true prophets, apostles, and servants of God.
>
> O dear Lord, how lovely are those pastors and teachers who seek nothing but the extension of the kingdom of God; who preach the word of repentance and grace aright, so that they may win many souls, and that at the risk of name and fame, house and property, person and life.
>
> These are they who with Christ the Chief Shepherd gather and feed His sheep. (Menno Simons, Foundation of Christian Doctrine, 1539, *CWMS*, p. 168)

Although some may assume that the call to ministry is to be quietly received and not publically acknowledged, others have argued, using Paul as their example, that the calling is to be publicly stated and used as a key reference point for preaching:

> Therefore let the preacher of the Gospel be sure that his calling is from God. It is perfectly proper that he should follow Paul's example and exalt this calling of his, so that he may gain credence and authority among the people. In the same way the king's emissary elevates his office and calling. (Luther, "Lectures on Galatians Chapters 1 to 4, 1535," LW 26, p. 16)

The metaphor of ambassadorship is revealing, for no ambassador would come to a country unannounced, or fail to show credentials.

That vocation to ministry may develop slowly and become only gradually interpreted through a process that moves from opaque to clearer vision, is seen in Bonaventure's account of the call of St. Francis of Assisi:

God implanted in the heart of the youthful Francis a certain open-handed compassion for the poor. *Growing from his infancy* (Job 31:18), this compassion had so filled his heart with generosity that even at that time he determined not be deaf to the Gospel but *to give to everyone who begged* (Luke 6:30), especially if he asked "for the love of God." On one occasion when Francis was distracted by the press of business, contrary to his custom, he sent away empty-handed a certain poor man who had begged alms for the love of God. As soon as he came to his senses, he ran after the man and gave him a generous alms, promising God that from that moment onward, while he had the means, he would never refuse those who begged from him for the love of God. . . . Up to this time, however, Francis was ignorant of God's plans for him. He was distracted by the external affairs of his father's business and drawn down toward earthly things by the corruption of human nature. . . . he met a certain knight who was of noble birth, but poor and badly clothed. Moved to compassion for his poverty, Francis took off his own garments and clothed the man on the spot. . . . The following night, when he had fallen asleep, God in his goodness showed him a large and splendid palace full of military weapons emblazoned with the insignia of Christ's cross. Thus God vividly indicated that the compassion he had exhibited toward the poor knight for love of the supreme King would be repaid with an incomparable reward. And so when Francis asked to whom these belonged, he received an answer from heaven that all these things were for him and his knights. When he awoke in the morning, he judged the strange vision to be an indication that he would have great prosperity; for he had no experience in interpeting divine mysteries. (Bonaventure, *The Life of St. Francis*, CWS, pp. 186–188)

We conclude with a powerful meditation on the call of God provided by St. Ignatius Loyola. He proposed a well-defined method of assessing the circumstances under which wise vocational choice must be made. Three occasions of being drawn nearer no one's calling are examined: following grace, discerning of spirits, and tranquillity. Two methods are provided for working through a hard choice. The first one is a step by step approach to making a vocational choice; and the second one is an imaginative meditation upon giving up lesser loves and receiving the greatest perfection possible, while remembering death and judgment. Rightly followed, the meditation takes several hours:

The first occasion is when God our Lord moves and attracts the will so that the devout soul, without question and without desire to question, follows what has been manifested to it. St. Paul and St. Matthew did this when they followed Christ our Lord.

The second occasion is present when one has developed a clear understanding and knowledge through the experience of consolations and desolations and the discernment of diverse spirits.

The third occasion is in a time of tranquillity. Here one considers first for what purpose man is born, which is to praise God our Lord and to save his soul. Since he desires to attain this end, he chooses some life or state within the bounds of the church that will help him in the service of God our Lord and the salvation of his soul. I said "a time of tranquillity," when the soul is not agitated by diverse spirits and is freely and calmly making use of its natural powers.

If a choice has not been made on the first or second occasion, below are given two methods of making it during the third occasion.

The first method of making a wise and good choice contains six points:

The first point: To place before my mind's eye the thing on which I wish to make a choice. It may be an office or a benefice to be accepted or refused, or anything else that is the object of a mutable choice.

The second point: I must have as my aim the end for which I am created, which is the praise of God our Lord and the salvation of my soul. At the same time I must remain indifferent and free from any inordinate attachments so that I am not more inclined or disposed to take the thing proposed than to reject it, nor to relinquish it rather than to accept it. I must rather be like the equalized scales of balance, ready to follow the course which I feel is more for the glory and praise of God our Lord and the salvation of my soul.

The third point: I must ask God our Lord to deign to move my will and to reveal to my spirit what I should do to best promote His praise and glory in the matter of choice. After examining the matter thoroughly and faithfully with my understanding, I should make my choice in conformity with His good pleasure and His most holy will.

The fourth point: I will use my reason to weigh the many advantages and benefits that would accrue to me if I held the proposed office or benefice solely for the praise of God our Lord and the salvation of my soul. I will likewise consider and weigh the disadvantages and dangers that there are in holding it. I will proceed in like manner with the other alternative, that is, examine and consider the advantages and benefits as well as the disadvantages and dangers in not holding the proposed office or benefice.

The fifth point: After having thus weighed the matter and carefully examined it from every side, I will consider which alternative appears more reasonable. Acting upon the stronger judgment of reason and not on any inclination of the senses, I must come to a decision in the matter that I am considering.

The sixth point: After such a choice or decision has been reached I should turn with great diligence to prayer in the presence of God our Lord and offer Him this choice that His Divine Majesty may deign to accept and confirm it, if it be to His greater service and praise.

The second method of making a wise and good choice contains four rules and a note:

The first rule is that the love which moves me and causes me to make this choice should come from above, that is from the love of God, so that before I make my choice I will feel that the greater or lesser love that I have for the thing chosen is solely for the sake of my Creator and Lord.

The second rule is to consider some man that I have never seen or known, and in whom I wish to see complete perfection. Now I should consider what I would tell him to do and choose for the greater glory of God our Lord and the greater perfection of his soul. I will act in like manner myself, keeping the rule that I have proposed for another.

The third rule is to consider that if I were at the point of death, what form and procedure I would wish to have observed in making this present choice. Guiding myself by this consideration, I will make my decision on the whole matter.

The fourth rule is to examine and consider how I shall be on the day of judgment, to think how I shall then wish to have made my decision in the present matter. The rule which I should then wish to have followed, I will now follow, that I may on that day be filled with joy and delight. . . .

Take, O Lord, and receive all my liberty, my memory, my understanding, and my entire will, all that I have and possess. Thou hast given all to me, to Thee O Lord, I return it. All is Thine; dispose of it according to Thy will. Give me Thy love and Thy grace, for this is enough for me. (Ignatius Loyola, *Spiritual Exercises*, pp. 84–87, 103–104)

All of the selections of Part One revolve around the issue of the definition, clarification, and significance of the pastoral calling, the vocation to soul care. They define personal qualities requisite to soul care, that enable sufficient trust that care can be received. They show that pastoral care has for almost two millennia been a distinctive and well-defined vocation and discipline of study. The pastoral office is grounded in the awareness of personal and social need, and capacity for identification with the hurt and alienated. To the pastoral office is assigned responsibility for the ministry of word, sacrament, and pardon, a spiritual arena distinguishable from civil or business interests. Resistance to the pastoral calling is a perennial dimension of seriousness about it. The pastoral office is decisively shaped by a series of metaphors that define the calling that is grounded in biblical mandates and mediated through due ecclesiastical process.

2 The Shepherding Metaphor

NO IMAGE HAS INFLUENCED the practice of pastoral care more than its chief formative metaphor, the good shepherd caring for the vulnerable flock amid a perilous world. This central matrix of imagery has served as the foundation for other images of the pastor— guardian of tradition, guide through hazard, and physician of the flock. It is only on the basis of this axial metaphor that the pastor can reflect rightly upon due authorization to ministry and upon *diakonia*. It constitutes an important link in the correlation of Christ's shepherding with contemporary shepherding.

I. ❧ THE SHEPHERD OF SOULS

The shepherding metaphor reveals the care-giver in the role of a steady companion and patient guide of the soul, who constantly provides healthy nourishment for the soul. It is a consoling and refreshing image that combines and integrates diverse elements: nurture, wholesome feeding, leading, protecting and guarding the flock at rest. Origen painted the metaphor beautifully in his commentary on the Song of Songs, where the Chief Shepherd was understood as Christ himself:

The Good Shepherd makes it His business to seek for the best pastures for His sheep, and to find green and shady groves where they may rest during the noonday heat. . . . "He makes me lie down in green pastures, and leads me beside the waters of peace" (Ps. 23:2), thus making it clear that this Shepherd provides His sheep with water that is not only plentiful, but also wholesome and pure and utterly refreshing. (Origen, *The Song of Songs*, Bk. 2, ACW 26, pp. 122–123, NEB)*

The metaphor functions intricately at several levels. The shepherd does not care for every member of the flock in precisely the same way:

Keep an eye out for all parts of your flock, lest any one stumble by your negligence, and thereby perish. For the layman watches out only for himself, but you watch out for all. You carry a burden for all, a heavier load. For it is written: "The Lord said to Aaron, 'You, your sons and your father's family are to bear the responsibility for offenses

41

against the sanctuary, and you and your sons alone are to bear the responsibility for offenses against the priesthood' " (Num. 18:1, 2). Since you are called to give an account of each one of the flock, take care of each one. Preserve those that are sound, warn those that fall. When you have assigned them fasting, give them ease by remission. When with tears the offender begs readmission, receive him, and let the whole Church pray for him. When by imposition of your hand you have admitted him, permit him to remain afterwards in the flock. But for the drowsy and the careless, endeavour to convert and confirm, to warn and cure. (*Constitutions of the Holy Apostles*, Bk. II, Ch. XVIII, Sec. III, ANF VII, p. 403–404, NIV)*

The flexibility of the shepherding metaphor permits it to become imaginatively mixed and interwoven with other emergency metaphors and helping images, such as pilot or firefighter, as in Cyprian's letter to Pomponius:

The Lord speaks and says: "And I will appoint over you shepherds after my own heart, who will shepherd you with instruction." (Cf. Jer. 3.15). . . . . The ship must vigilantly be delivered from dangerous places lest it be broken among the cliffs and rocks. The bundle must be drawn out quickly from the fire before it is burned up by the oncoming flames. No one close to danger is safe for a long time. Nor will the servant of God who has entangled himself in the snares of the enemy be able to escape . . . . Therefore, dearly beloved Brother, take heed that the undisciplined be not consumed and perish, that you rule the brotherhood as far as possible with salutary counsels, and that you counsel each one for his salvation. Steep and narrow is the way through which we enter into life. (Cyprian, *Letters*, 4, sec. 2, 5, FC 51, pp. 11, 14; cf. ANF V, p. 357f)*

The shepherd is fully responsible for guiding the flock to good pastures. If the flock is negligently exposed to hazardous situations, the shepherd is fully accountable. Schismatic teachers seek to divide the flock:

As children of the light (Eph. 5:8) of truth, flee from division and wrong teaching. Wherever the shepherd goes, follow there as his sheep (John 10:10–12). For there are many specious wolves who by evil design take captive those who are seeking after God. . . . If anyone follows a maker of schism he "will not inherit the kingdom of God" (1 Cor. 6:9,10). (Ignatius of Antioch, *To the Philadelphians*, sec. 2–3, AF, pp. 104–105)*

The shepherd, in the ancient metaphor, was also a veterinarian, providing physical remedies for the ailments and sicknesses of the flock, and protecting each one from the risk of illness. Although pastoral writers employed this dimension of the metaphor, the analogy was admittedly imprecise, as Chrysostom revealed, because human beings cannot be treated like sheep. The shepherd's doctoring of sheep is different than the pastor's spiritual remedies amid personal crises:

Shepherds have full power to compel the sheep to accept the treatment if they do not submit of their own accord. It is easy to bind them when it is necessary to use cautery or the knife, and to keep them shut up for a long time when that is the right thing, and to introduce different kinds of food one after another, and to keep them away from water. And all other remedies the shepherds think will promote the animals' health they apply with perfect ease.

But human diseases in the first place are not easy for a man to see. "For who among men knows the thoughts of a man except the man's spirit within him?" (1 Cor. 2:11). How, then, can anyone provide the specific remedy for a disease if he does not know its character and often cannot tell whether the person is even ill? When it later becomes apparent, then it has become all the more intractable. You cannot treat human beings with the same authority with which the shepherd treats a sheep. Here too it is possible to bind and to forbid food and to apply cautery and the knife, but the decision to receive treatment does not lie with the one who administers the medicine but actually with the patient. (John Chrysostom, *On the Priesthood*, Ch. II, sec. 2, pp. 55–56)*

The tradition was aware of the limits of its lead metaphor—shepherd of souls—since people are not really sheep. The sheep doctor binds and coerces. The soul doctor has only the power of persuasion, not coercion. The metaphor best functions with an awareness of its limits.

II. ❧ Accountability of the Shepherd

The shepherd metaphor conflates several helping images: birthing, nurturing, feeding, guiding, and healing. In all of these it connotes radical responsibility for others. The assumption underlying this care is that the shepherd is finally accountable to God for whatever level of accountability he is specifically charged in ministry to others. The pastoral writers reflected deeply upon the unusual extent to which pastors are responsible for others:

As you pipe, so they dance; as you teach, so they believe; as you proceed, so they follow. Therefore, woe unto you if you teach erroneously; if you destroy and do not gather; if you deceive and do not shepherd; if you corrupt and do not convert! Receive eyes of wisdom, that you may rightly teach and lead others. (Menno Simons, Brief and Clear Confession, 1544, *CWMS*, p. 453)

Unlike other professionals who can flee when danger comes, soul care is committed to sharing the danger of those in its charge. One cannot walk away from the flock, particularly during a moment under attack. One of the most critical questions that pastoral writers had to decide in the earliest centuries of Christianity was to what extent it is conscienable for a pastor to abandon a flock when danger comes. This became an urgent, practical question of soul care during the years of persecution through which Tertullian lived. He was among a group of pastoral writers that took a rigorous view against "flight in time of persecution":

When those in authority—I mean deacons, priests, and bishops—take flight, how is the mere layman to understand the sense in which it was said: "Flee from city to city?" When the leaders run away, who of the common crowd can hope to persuade anyone to stand firm in battle? Without a doubt, the good shepherd lays down his life for his sheep. . . . He is a wicked shepherd who flees when he sees the wolf and leaves the flock to be devoured. . . . And against them Ezechiel and Jeremias thunder with similar recriminations, in that they have not merely depended upon their sheep and fattened themselves, but they have themselves dispersed the flock and, without a leader to guide them, left them the prey to all the beasts of the field. (Cf. Ezech. 34.2 Jer. 23.1ff). For, this is what happens when the church is deserted by the clergy in time of persecution. . . . Those who have been given charge over the Church cannot flee in time of persecution. If however, the flock were obliged to flee, then the shepherd would not be obliged to stand his ground. In that case, there would be no reason for him to stay "to protect his flock," since, as a matter of fact, they would have no need of protection, as a result of their liberty, of course, to flee. (Tertullian, *Flight in Time of Persecution*, Ch. 11, secs. 1–3, FC 40, pp. 296–298)*

The analogy is basically misconceived if one imagines that the shepherd is responsible only to the flock. Rather the shepherd is responsible *to* God *for* the flock. Chrysostom concluded that the most hazardous test of pastoral service is the divine assessment at the last judgment when one is called to account for one's care of the flock. The historical risks that may be encountered with predators or thugs are nothing by comparison. The shepherding metaphor is best kept in this eschatological frame of reference in order to see its compelling force:

A man who loses sheep through the ravages of wolves or the attacks of robbers or through pestilence or some other accident, might perhaps meet with a measure of pardon from the owner of the flock. Even if he is called upon to pay compensation, the penalty stops at money. But anyone entrusted with human beings, the rational souls of the flock of Christ, risks a penalty not of money but of his own soul for the loss of the sheep. Moreover, he has a far greater and more difficult struggle. His fight is not with wolves; his fear is not of robbers; his care is not to protect the flock from pestilence. Well then, against whom is the war? With whom is the battle? Listen to St. Paul. He says, "Our wrestling is not against flesh and blood, but against the principalities, against powers" (Eph. 6:12). (John Chrysostom, *On the Priesthood*, Ch. II, sec. 2, p. 54)*

The Apostolic Constitutions, compiled in the fourth century from previous strands of oral and written tradition, summarized the accountability of the pastoral shepherd with and for the laity. Lay persons are rationally accountable, and cannot blame the shepherd for disaster if warnings and guidance have been rightly given:

God says to the shepherds: "Ye shall be judged for your unskilfulness, and for destroying the sheep" (Ezek. 34:2). That implies that God will judge not only between one bishop and another, and between one guide and another, but also between one lay person and another, for each has some level of responsibility. For the sheep of whom we speak are none of them irrational animals, but rational creatures. This is said in order to prevent persons from later on saying, "I am just a sheep, not a shepherd. I have no concerns beyond myself. Let the shepherd be vigilant, for he alone will be required to give an account for me." For any sheep that will not follow a good shepherd will be exposed to wolves and to destruction. Likewise, any sheep who follow a bad shepherd will also be exposed to unavoidable death, since his shepherd will devour him. Care must be taken to avoid destructive shepherds. (*Constitutions of the Holy Apostles*, Bk. II, Ch. XX, sec. III, ANF VII, pp. 404–405)*

In Augustine's letter to his friend Alypius, bishop of Tagaste, we have a case study of a pastoral crisis with an unruly congregation. The episode revealed the seriousness of Augustine's view of the accountability of the shepherd, and of the danger to the congregation that refused to follow. The situation: In the year 395 A.D., Augustine had been preaching on a special occasion in Hippo, the anniversary of the birth of Leontius. Over a period of several days during this festive occasion, the crowd had become drunk and disorderly, threatening to mar the worship services. His letter to Alypius picks up the story:

Some were becoming openly violent, and declaring that they could not submit to the prohibition (intimated while you were here) of that feast which they call Laetitia, vainly attempting to disguise ther revels under a fair name. It happened most opportunely for me, by the hidden foreordination of the Almighty God, that on the fourth holy day that chapter of the Gospel fell to be expounded in ordinary course, in which the words occur: "Give not that which is holy unto the dogs, neither cast ye your pearls before swine" (Matt. 7:6). I discoursed therefore concerning dogs and swine in such a way as to compel those who clamour with obstinate barking against the divine precepts, and who are given up to the abominations of carnal pleasures, to blush for shame. . . .When, however, this discourse was, according to the ability and zeal of each, made known abroad by those who had heard it, it found many opponents. But when the morning of Quadragesima came round, and a great multitude had assembled at the hour of exposition of Scripture, that passage in the Gospel was read in which our Lord spoke of those sellers who were driven out of the temple. . . . I added to it an argument to prove with how much greater anger and vehemence our Lord would cast forth drunken revels. . . .

They wanted to fill the whole area of so large a place of worship, if they were permitted, with crowds of revellers and drunkards; and yet would not present to God those fruits of the Spirit which, by the authority of scripture, and by my groans, they were called to yield, and by the offering of which they would most suitably celebrate the saints' days.

This being finished, I returned the manuscript, and being asked to speak, I set before their eyes with all my might, as the danger itself constrained me, and as the Lord was pleased to give strength, the danger shared by them who were committed to my care, and by me, who must give account to the Chief Shepherd. . . .

Next morning, however, when the day dawned, which so many were accustomed to devote to excess in eating and drinking, I received notice that some, even of those who were present when I preached, had not yet desisted from complaint. . . . I resolved that after reading in Ezekiel's prophecy that the watchman has delivered his own soul if he has given warning, even though the persons warned refuse to give heed to him, I would shake my garments and depart. But then the Lord showed me that He leaves us not alone, and taught me how He encourages us to trust him; for before I had time to ascend to the pulpit, the very persons whose complaint . . . . I had heard came to me. Receiving them kindly, I by a few words brought them round to a right opinion. (Augustine, *Letters*, XXIX, To Alypius, A.D. 395, secs. 6–8, NPNF 1, I, p. 255)

Augustine understood himself to be responsible not merely to the congregation, but to the One who had entrusted their care to him. In this way, the pastor is responsible to God, and the congregation is responsible to the pastor. This structure of accountability cannot be treated cavalierly:

Hear what St. Paul says, or rather, not Paul but Christ who speaks in him: "Obey them that have the rule over you and submit to them; for they watch in behalf of your souls, as they that shall give account."

(Heb. 13:17). Is the fear of this threat trivial? We dare not say it is. (John Chrysostom, *On the Priesthood*, Ch. III, sec. 18, p. 103)

John Wyclif set forth three levels of accountability of the pastoral office—feeding, healing, and guarding:

Therefore, the first condition of the pastor is to cleanse his own spring, that it may not infect the word of God. . . . The pastor has a threefold office: first, to feed his sheep spiritually on the Word of God, that through pastures ever green they may be initiated into the blessedness of heaven. The second pastoral office is to purge wisely the sheep of disease, that they may not infect themselves and others as well. And the third is for the pastor to defend his sheep from ravening wolves, both sensible and insensible. (Wyclif, The Pastoral Office, Part 2, sec. 1, LCC XIV, p. 48)

The depth of this burden of responsibility makes it all the more necessary for the pastor to pray for grace and mercy in carrying out this ministry, as Luther aptly prayed:

Lord God, You have placed me in your church as overseer and pastor. You see how unfit I am to administer this great and difficult office. Had I previously been without help from you, I would have ruined everything long ago. Therefore I call upon you. I gladly offer my mouth and heart to your service. I would teach the people and I myself would continue to learn. To this end I shall meditate diligently on your Word. Use me, dear Lord, as your instrument. Only do not forsake me; for if I were to continue alone, I would quickly ruin everything. Amen. (Luther, "Lectures on Genesis, Chapters 26 to 30, 1542," LW 5, p. 123; WLS 2, p. 926; cf. WA 43, p. 513)

III. ❧ The Negligence of Shepherds

When spiritual directors default on their accountability and in the duty of corrective love, not only the church but the society as well is likely to suffer systemically from this neglect. John Chrysostom thought that the abuses of ministry were unparalleled in his time, unlike some self-giving models of ministry in his recent memory:

These virtues one shall not see these days, even in teachers. They are all gone and perished. The cause: love has grown so cold that sinners go uncorrected. Hear what the Apostle says writing to Timothy: "As for those who persist in sin, rebuke them in the presence of all, so that the rest may stand in fear" (1 Tim. 5:20). This is spoken to spiritual guides who are in a sickly state. For if the head be not sound, how can the rest of the body maintain its vigor? But mark how great is the present disorder: . . . . Plagues teeming with untold mischiefs have settled upon the Churches. Chief offices have become saleable. So numberless evils are springing up for which there is no one to redress, and no one to correct them. The disorder has even taken on a kind of systemic method and consistency. . . . One will have no difficulty finding persons who practise augury, who make use of charms, omens, incantations, who have committed fornication, adulterers, drunkards, and revilers—and the covetous, I am unwilling to add, lest I should hurt the feelings of any of those who are standing here. What more? Suppose any one should make scrutiny into all the communicants in the world, what kind of transgression is there which he would not detect? (John Chrysostom, *Homilies on Ephesians*, Hom. VI, NPNF 1, XIII, p. 8f, RSV)*

It is just because the pastoral office has such extraordinary potential influence, that it also is potentially subject to such great abuse. At times the level of anxiety about abuses seems extremely high and the rhetoric exaggerated by the pastoral writers, but their concern is to protect the faithful from being wantonly misled. The biblical themes recur:

God spoke in this way to Jeremiah; "Many shepherds have ravaged my vineyard and trampled down my field" (Jer. 12:10). And in another passage: "My anger is turned against the shepherds, and I will visit with punishment the leaders of the flock" (Zech. 10:3). And elsewhere Malachi spoke of "you priests who despise my name" (Mal. 1:6). . . . If the overseer himself is an offender, how will he be able any longer to prosecute the offense of another? (*Constitutions of the Holy Apostles*, Bk. II, Ch. XV, sec. III, ANF VII, p. 402, NEB)*

Jeremiah and Ezekiel were the main biblical sources for images of the negligent shepherd:

What risks that pastor runs who is negligent in caring. Ezekiel spoke in this way to those pastors who fail to care for the people: "You shepherds, these are the words of the Lord God: How I hate the shepherds of Israel who care only for themselves! Should not the shepherd care for the sheep? You consume the milk, wear the wool, slaughter the fat beasts, but you do not feed the sheep. You have not encouraged the weary, tended the sick, bandaged the hurt, recovered the straggler, or searched for the lost. . . . Because my shepherds have not asked after the sheep but have cared only for themselves and not for the sheep—therefore, you shepherds, hear the words of the Lord. These are the words of the Lord God: I am against the shepherds and will demand my sheep from them. I will dismiss those shepherds" (Ezek. 34:2–10). And he also adds, speaking to the people: "I will judge between one sheep and another. You rams and he-goats! Are you not satisfied with grazing on good herbage, that you must trample down the rest with your feet? . . . They shall know that I, the Lord their God, am with them, and that they are my people Israel, says the Lord God. You are my flock, my people, the flock I feed" (Ezek. 34:30, 31). . . . As to good shepherds, let lay persons honor them, love them, revere them. . . . For whoever hears Christ hears through them. (*Constitutions of the Holy Apostles*, Bk. II, Ch. XVIII, sec. III, ANF VII, p. 404, NEB)*

Exceptional caution has been at times required in order to determine whether a shepherd/pastor has been trustworthy. The political situation faced by Menno Simons, the founder of the sixteenth century Anabaptist movement, was analogous to underground operations during a tyrannical occupation. Amid these hazardous conditions, he was troubled that there were so few genuine shepherds available to guide the flocks, and so many pretending to be genuine. He dealt with the same themes of pastoral accountability from the prophets Ezekiel and Jeremiah:

Beloved in Christ Jesus, I am deeply troubled about you, for I hear that you hunger and thirst after righteousness and that there are so few dispensing it to men—persons who correctly cut the bread of the divine Word for their hungry consciences—so few shepherds who pasture the sheep of Christ aright; so few builders and masons to place the living stones in the temple of the Lord; so few watchmen who guard the city, the new Jerusalem, and blow the trumpet; so few fathers to beget the children of God and so few mothers to nourish these begotten ones. . . . Concerning the shepherds who pose as shepherds of Christ, who pasture the sheep for what they get out of it, as Ezek. 34:8 has it, pasturing themselves—you see how little they bother themselves about the sheep, whether they have pasture or not. Just so they get the wool and the milk, then they are satisfied. They pose as shepherds but they are deceivers. They are very different from the shepherds of which we read in Jeremiah, shepherds after His heart whom the Holy Spirit has sent. These other shepherds have not the love of Christ which Peter had and therefore Christ's commandment to pasture His lambs does not apply to them. They are not commanded, that is, if they are not sent how then can they preach? As you see, they are not God-sent shepherds who lead the sheep into the green pastures of the divine Word. Instead they let them starve. They are not the shepherds who lead them to the sparkling waters, but to the muddy pools which they have prepared with their feet, that is, by their glosses and human notions. (Menno Simons, Admonition to the Amsterdam Melchiorites, c. 1545, *CWMS*, pp. 1021–1022)

The early pastoral writers sought to teach laity to recognize and not collude with the twisted motivations of negligent and unreliable shepherds. The major clue was their pretentiousness:

Many foolish persons entertain false teachers so great an admiration, as if they could learn from them something more precious than the truth itself! That expression of Scripture, "Seek, and ye shall find," (Matt. 7:7) they interpret as spoken with this view, that they should discover themselves to be above the Creator, styling themselves greater and better than God. (Irenaeus, *Against Heresies*, Bk. II, Ch. xxx, sec. 2, ANF I, pp. 403–404)*

IV. ❧ The Attentiveness of the Shepherd

Ministries of care at times make massive demands upon one's time. Even under ordinary circumstances they may require exceptional emotive and physical energy. The pastoral writers have marvelled at the multiple levels of consciousness needed to perform the work of ministry well:

So the shepherd needs great wisdom and a thousand eyes to examine the soul's condition from every angle. . . . The priest, therefore, must not overlook any of these considerations, but examine them all with care and apply all his remedies appropriately for fear his care should be in vain. . . . If a man wanders away from the right faith, the shepherd needs a lot of concentration, perseverance, and patience. He cannot drag by force or constrain by fear, but must by persuasion lead him back to the true beginning from which he has fallen away. (John Chrysostom, *On the Priesthood*, Ch. II, sec. 4, p. 58)

Constancy is the watchword of the shepherd. The care-giver must take in variable signals, and absorb multiple levels of information, perceptions, nuances, from all angles. Yet the practical means of influence in ministry are extremely limited and modest, consisting essentially of language and persuasion. The soul cannot be forced. Not only intensive awareness but energetic activity and intelligence is required to combat demonic forms of temptation. The Anglican martyr, Hugh Latimer (d. 1555), wrote with relish and amusement of the most diligent prelate in the country:

There is one that surpasses all others, and is the most diligent prelate and preacher in all England. And would you like to know who it is? I will tell you—it is the Devil. He is the most diligent preacher of all. He is never out of his diocese; he is never from his cure: you shall never find him unoccupied; he is ever in his parish; he keeps residence at all times; you shall never find him out of the way; call for him when you will, he is ever at home. He is the most diligent preacher in all the realm. He is forever at his plough. No lording nor loitering can hinder him. He is ever applying his business. You shall never find him idle, I warrant you. His work is to hinder religion, maintain superstition, and set up idolatry. . . . St. Peter said of him: "Your enemy the devil, like a roaring lion, prowls round looking for someone to devour" (1 Pet. 5:8). I would have this text well viewed and examined, every word of it: "He prowls round," in every corner of his diocese. He goes on visitation daily. He leaves no place of his cure unvisited. He walks round about from place to place, and ceases not. "Like a lion," that is, strongly, boldly, and proudly; stately and fiercely, with haughty looks, with his proud countenances, with his stately braggings. "Roaring"; for he does not let any occasion go by to speak or roar out when he sees he has an opportunity. "Looking for someone to devour," and not sleeping, as our bishops do; but he seeks diligently, he searches out all corners where he might find his prey. He roves about in every place of his diocese. He does not stand still. He is never at rest, but always has his plough in hand pressing forward. There was never such a preacher in England as he is. (Hugh Latimer, "The Busy Bishop," OCC 1, p. 54–55)*

In the fourth century, John Chrysostom had similarly treated the theme of the unceasing struggle of the Enemy for souls. The constant combat with demonic temptation is compared with a battlefield, and the vigilant shepherd as a combatant:

The duration of a battle is short and even in that short period there are many respites; the approach of night, weariness of slaughter, time taken for food, and many other things naturally bring the soldier to a standstill, and so he is able to strip off his armour, enjoy a brief respite, refresh himself with food and drink, and revive his former strength in various other ways. But when facing the Evil One you must never lay down your arms; you must never take any sleep if you want to remain for ever unhurt. You must do one of two things: either take off your armour and so fall and perish, or stand always armed and watchful. For he always stands with his forces marshalled, waiting for our moments of inadvertence, and he takes more trouble to damn our souls than we take to save them. (John Chrysostom, *On the Priesthood*, Ch. VI, sec. 13, pp. 158–159)

The theme of constant watchfulness is intrinsically built into the role of shepherding. There is no set quitting time for the shepherd as if a bell rang and then one were no longer in charge of the flock. Rather, even in the late evening, the shepherd will still be softly piping:

Let the shepherd cease not to play the pipe of exhortation when his sheep are grazing, and especially when they are settling down to sleep, for there is nothing which the wolf so fears as the tones of the shepherd's pipe. (John Climacus, *To the Shepherd*, p. 236)

V. 🕭 ACTIVE CURACY AND CONTEMPLATIVE SOLITUDE

Two strains of interpretation of full time religious vocation have developed side by side in the Christian tradition: those who withdrew from the world in monastic prayer, and those who engaged in the world in active curacies. Soul care developed differently in these two contexts: persons in religious orders submitted themselves to intensive spiritual direction under an abbot or spiritual guide, while parish congregations were under the care of the pastor. Our subject in this study is far more the latter than the former. Yet it is clear that active ministries of parish care have often owed profound debts to the monastic tradition of spiritual guidance in refining, sharpening, and experimenting with the depth dimensions of soul care.

A close reading of the classical pastoral texts will reveal the recurrent hunger of those in active pastoral ministries for a more contemplative life. Yet this is often balanced by the even stronger affirmation of the vitality, challenge, and meaningfulness of care of a parish. Human values and spiritual growth may be actualized in curacy that would have been less likely under the conditions of monastic withdrawal, and vice versa. John Chrysostom thought that the active life of parish leadership required even greater spiritual preparation than a secluded environment:

> Even hermits living in the desert, far away from city and market-place and the distractions they cause, although they continually enjoy a haven and a calm sea, are unwilling to rely on the security of that way of life, but add innumerable other safeguards, and hedge themselves in all round. They take care to be very precise in all they say and do, on purpose to be able to approach God with frankness and with spotless purity, as far as a man can do so. How much ability, then, and how much strength do you suppose the priest needs to enable him to keep his soul from every contamination and preserve its spiritual beauty unimpaired? He needs far greater purity than they do. And since he has the greater need, he is a prey to more temptations, which can defile him unless he makes his soul inaccessible to them by the practice of unremitting self-denial and strict self-discipline. (John Chrysostom, *On the Priesthood*, Ch. IV, sec. 1, p. 137).

Gregory the Great recognized and described well the temptation that pastors experience in their profound desire to find a quiet place:

> There are some, as we have said, enriched with great gifts, who, while they are ardent for the studies of contemplation only, shrink from serving to their neighbour's benefit by preaching; they love a secret place of quiet, they long for a retreat for speculation. With respect to which conduct, they are, if strictly judged, undoubtedly guilty in proportion to the greatness of the gifts whereby they might have been publicly useful. (Gregory the Great, *BPR*, Bk. I, Ch. V, NPNF 2, X, p. 4)

Ambrose affirmed both monastic and parish life. Aware of strengths and limitations in each, he reflected on their complementarity:

> Who doubts that in stricter Christian devotion these two qualities are the more excellent: the duties of clerics and the customs of monks? The one is a discipline which trains for courtesy and morality, the other for abstinence and patience; the one as on an open stage, the other in secrecy; the one is observed, the other is hidden from sight. . . . The one life, then, is in the arena, the other in a cave; the one is opposed to the confusion of the world, the other to the desires of the flesh; the one subdues, the other flees the pleasures of the body; the one more agreeable, the other safer; the one ruling, the other reigning in self; yet each denying herself that she may be Christ's. . . . The one, therefore, struggles, the other withdraws; the one overcomes enticements, the other flees them; for the one the world is a triumph, to the other a place of exile; to the one the world is crucified and itself to the world, to the other it is unknown; the one has more trials, and so a greater victory; the other falls less often, and keeps guard more easily. (Ambrose, *Letters*, Letters to Priests, FC 26, pp. 347–349)

In Part One we set forth qualities requisite for soul care, defined the pastoral office and principal acts of ministry, distinguished the inward from the outward call of God to pastoral service. In Part Two we have explored the shepherding metaphor that undergirds all other pastoral metaphors, the accountability of the pastor before God for the flock, the constant attentiveness that characterizes shepherding, concluding with the rhythm of prayer and service—inward nurture and outward activity—that characterizes the pastoral life. Now we turn to some of the thornier questions of proper authorization for soul care.

3 Authority for Soul Care

WHENEVER CARE OF SOULS tries to proceed without examining its proper authorization, it is prone to becoming mired in deep confusions about itself. Several issues clamour at this point: By whom and by what means is pastoral service rightly authorized? How could the *servant* image of ministry be consistent with the fact that pastors exercise *power* of a sort, and are expected to express appropriate influence, while yet remaining servants? These issues cannot be duly assessed without also asking how contemporary ministry is dependent upon apostolic ministry and historic ministries, and above all upon Jesus' own ministry.

I. ⧼ SERVANT MINISTRY

The most frequently used Greek and Latin words for ministry (*diakonia* and *ministerium*) are rooted in the notion of service. To minister is to serve. Yet the extraordinary influence of the soul guide, when functioning well, has given the office of ministry the semblance of power. Thus it has become necessary for the pastoral writers to sort out questions concerning the proper *power, influence, authorization, and authority of the pastoral office in the light of its fundamental definition as service*. We begin with Luther's rigorous disclaimer that the pastoral office does not imply or carry with it any sort of temporal or coercive power:

> My office, and that of every preacher and minister, does not consist in any sort of lordship but in serving all of you, so that you learn to know God, become baptized, have the true Word of God, and finally are saved. Never do I claim worldly power; princes and lords, mayors and judges, are to establish and provide for that. My office is merely a service which I am to give to everyone freely and gratuitously, nor should I seek from it either money or goods, either honor or anything else. (Luther, "Sermon on Matt. 20:24–28, 1537," WA 47, p. 368; WLS 2, pp. 923–924)

Ministry is paradoxically thought of as a leadership role, yet one which serves by patiently facilitating the nurture and growth of the soul. Some have thought of ministry as an exalted office of legitimated spiritual power, yet these images are best grounded in the undergirding notion of ministry as service.

Catherine of Siena viewed the mystery of service paradoxically:

Oh! My beloved ones, they made themselves subjects, being prelates, they made themselves servants, being lords, they made themselves infirm, being whole and without infirmity and the leprosy of mortal sin, being strong they made themselves weak, with the foolish and simple they showed themselves simple, and with the small insignificant. And so with love they knew how to be all things to all men, and to give to each one his nourishment. . . . They put themselves in the midst of the thorns of tribulation, and exposed themselves to every peril with true patience, offering incense odoriferous with anxious desires, and humble and continual prayers. With tears and sweat they anointed the wounds of their neighbour. (Catherine of Siena, *A Treatise of Prayer*, p. 254)

When candidates for ministry nurse an idealized fantasy that they will do unusual good works in ministry, there may yet remain at unexamined levels the egocentric desire to exercise direct influence on others' lives. Gregory asked with due gravity: How are those to be treated pastorally, who desire ordination but do not yet understand its heart as service?

But for the most part those who covet pastoral authority mentally propose to themselves some good works besides, and though desiring it with a motive of pride, still muse how they will effect great things: and so it comes to pass that the motive suppressed in the depths of the heart is one thing, another what the surface of thought presents to the muser's mind. For the mind itself lies to itself about itself. . . . One can by no means learn humility in a high place who has not ceased to be proud while occupying a low one. . . . Wherefore from his past life let every one discover what he is. . . . Even an unskilful person guides a ship along a straight course in a calm sea; but in one disturbed by the waves of tempest even the skilled sailor is confounded. . . . What is to be held to, except that one who abounds in virtues should accede to government under compulsion, and that one who is void of virtues should not, even under compulsion, approach it? (Gregory the Great, *BPR*, Ch. IX, NPNF 2, X, p. 6)

II. ❧ AUTHORITY IN MINISTRY

Pastoral care is essentially a service done for the good of the soul, not a coercive office that wields temporal power, external influence, or secular authority. It is out of this assumption that the classic pastoral writers have proceeded to designate the peculiar authority given in ministry:

You are not to rule as the rulers of the nations, but as a servant ministering to them, as a father to the oppressed, visiting them as a physician, guarding them as a shepherd,—in short, taking all care for their salvation? (Clementina, *Homilies*, Hom. III, ANF VIII, p. 250)

It should not be assumed by this, however, that ministry thereby disavows all influence or authority or legitimation of its proper office. The Zacchaeus and Peter of the following account are imaginatively projected by an unknown Ante-Nicene writer imaginatively back upon the scriptural account (Luke 19:1ff). "Peter" is speaking:

Peter: "Of those present, whom shall I choose but Zacchaeus, to whom also the Lord went in and rested, judging him worthy to be redeemed?" Having said this, Peter laid his hand upon Zacchaeus, who stood by, and asked him to sit down in his own chair. But Zacchaeus, falling at his feet, begged that he would permit him to decline the task of spiritual guidance, promising at the same time that "Whatever the guide is required to do, I will do; only please relieve me of the burden of being called a guide. For I am afraid of assuming the name of guide since it teems with bitter envy and danger."

Then Peter said: "If you are afraid of this, then you do not have to be known as a *guide*, but you are permitted simply to be called *the one appointed*. This was allowed by the Lord when he pronounced as blessed that one who is appointed to minister to his fellowservants (Luke 12:42). But if you wish it to be altogether unknown that you have authority of administration, you seem to me to be ignorant that the acknowledged authority of the president has great influence as regards the respect of the multitude. For every one obeys him who has received authority, having conscience as a great constraint. (Clementina, *Homilies*, Hom. III, ANF VIII, p. 250)*

This pseudonymous writing, attributed to Clement of Rome but probably collected in the fourth century from oral and written traditions of the second and third century, reveals how serious was the debate in early Christianity on the proper definition of pastoral authority. While paradigms like guidance or rulership do not fully grasp the essence of pastoral authority, nonetheless any attempt to disavow authority altogether is disallowed. One dare not let it remain completely unknown that one is duly authorized for the ministry of preaching, pastoral care, and sacrament. The shepherd of the Christian flock in a given parish is an honorable office whose intrinsic dignity may be properly identified and should not be surreptitiously hidden:

You shall honor the one who speaks to you the word of God. Recollect his words day and night. Revere him, not as the author of the new birth, but as one that has been made the occasion of your increased well-being. For where right teaching about God lives, there God is present. You do well to seek the presence of those who are mature in faith every day, that their words may guide you. (*Constitutions of the Holy Apostles*, Bk. VII, sec. I, ANF VII, p. 467)*

Adequate authorization for ministry rests on a firm, explicit connection with the apostolic witness. Any individualistic appeal to the Holy Spirit that runs contrary the apostolic tradition has been viewed as suspect:

No preachers on earth have testimony that equals the apostles. All others are hereby commanded to follow in the footsteps of the apostles, to remain loyal to their teaching, and to teach nothing additional or different. And yet the true token whereby this message of the Holy Spirit is to be known and tested is also indicated here when He says: "The Holy Spirit will testify of Me" (John 15;26). This indicates that the Spirit will preach of nothing except this Christ. (Luther, "Sermon on John 15:26–16:41," WA 21, p. 426; WLS 1, p. 41)*

Ambrose employed a finely balanced trinitarian view to speak of proper authorization for ministry:

The Spirit gives the same things as the Father gives, as the Son also gives. Let us now receive more expressly what we touched upon above, that the Holy Spirit also enjoins the same duty as the Father and the Son, and appoints the same, for Paul said: "Keep watch over yourselves and over all the flock of which the Holy Spirit has given you charge, as shepherds of the church of the Lord" (Acts 20:28).

Therefore, oneness of authority, oneness of establishment, oneness of bestowing. For, if you separate establishment and power, what cause was there for God the Father establishing and the Holy Spirit establishing those whom Christ had established as apostles, unless, perchance, as if sharing a possession or a right they, like men, feared prejudice, and so the operation was divided, and the authority distributed? (Ambrose, "The Holy Spirit," FC 44, p. 150–151; cf. NPNF 2, X, Bk. II, Ch. xiii, pp. 134f.)

According to most pastoral writers, some sort of ordered ministry is God's own intention. God's care is mediated to us by God's own design through human hands and words, through appointed ministries. Constant direct revelation is not God's way of communicating. One need not presumptuously expect recurrent direct revelation as if it easily could circumvent scripture, tradition, and ordered ministry:

He wants us to go and hear the Gospel from those who preach it. There and nowhere else are we to find it. The enthusiasts ignore the ministry and meanwhile sit in a corner awaiting the Holy Spirit. But they will find a nice reception! In place of the lovely Dove they will find a black raven, the devil himself. (Luther, "Sermon on Acts 9:1–22, 1534," WA 52, p. 615; WLS 2, p. 946)

Alleged pastoral authority that ignores or circumvents the apostolic witness is suspect. As early as the second century, Irenaeus was combatting gnostic views of individualistic inspiration disconnected from the apostolic tradition as the basis for ministry:

Some allege that the truth is not delivered to them by means of written documents, but through a living voice . . . But when we refer them to that tradition which originates from the apostles, and which is preserved by means of the successions of presbyters in the Churches, they object to tradition, saying that they themselves are wiser not merely than the presbyters, but even than the apostles, because they have discovered the unadulterated truth. For they maintain that the apostles intermingled the things of the law with the words of the Saviour; and that not the apostles alone, but even the Lord Himself, spoke at one time as from the Demiurge, at another from the intermediate place, and yet again from the Pleroma, but that they themselves, indubitably, unsulliedly, and purely, have knowledge of the hidden mystery. . . . It comes to this, therefore, that these men do now consent neither to Scripture nor to tradition. (Irenaeus, *Against Heresies*, Bk. III, Ch. ii, sec. 1–2, ANF I, p. 415)*

A medieval scholastic definition of authority in ministry was set forth by Jean of Paris (d. 1306). Spiritual power was understood primarily as power to give and withhold sacraments:

Since Christ intended to withdraw his physical presence from his Church it was necessary for him to institute ministers who would administer these sacraments to men. These ministers are called *sacerdotes*, sacred ones, because they confer sacred things, because they are leaders in the sacred order, because they teach sacred truths. In all this they are intermediaries between God and man. It was necessary then that these ministers should not be angels but men, men having a spiritual power, as the Apostle says: "For every high priest is taken from among men and appointed their representative before God" (Heb. 5:1). This was to be appropriate both with the instrument they employ (the sacraments) wherein is a spiritual power under an element of the sense-order, and also with the principal cause of the salvation of men, namely the incarnate Word, who inasmuch as he is both God and man, effects our salvation by his own power and authority. From what has been said this definition can be formulated: the priesthood is the spiritual power, given by Christ to the ministers of his church, of administering the sacraments to the faithful. (Jean de Paris, *On Royal and Papal Power*, Ch. 2, pp. 82–83, NEB)*

According to the Apostolic Constitutions, it is the purity of heart manifested by the leader and congregation sharing in Christ's body that gives moral power and authority to ecclesial admonitions:

If the offender sees that the bishop and deacons are innocent and blameless and the flock pure, he will not venture to despise their authority . . . . For when he looks round the whole church one by one, and can spy no blemish either in the bishop or in the people who are under his care, he will be put to confusion, and pricked at the heart. (*Constitutions of the Holy Apostles*, Bk. II, sec. III, ANF VII, p. 399)*

III. 🙢 APOSTOLICITY AND SUCCESSION

Christian care of souls does not exist apart from the apostolic tradition that awakens, informs, and energizes it. Pastoral care is an extension of the apostolic ministry. Since the human condition is prone to forgetfulness, pastoral writers have stressed the intrinsic connection of apostolicity and soul care.

One of the earliest writers of the pastoral tradition, Clement of Rome, anticipated the problem of succession that would in time become acute: After the first generation of apostles and their immediate successors died, who would carry on the witness to Christ's presence in the world? How could such witnesses be authenticated? When they differed, how could they again become unified? How might an appropriate succession of witnesses be engendered over many generations? How might criteria be devised to determine whether a pastor is authentically representative of and accountable to the unique witness of the original apostles to God's own care for humanity in Christ?

Similarly, our Apostles knew, through our Lord Jesus Christ, that there would be dissensions over the title of bishop. In their full foreknowledge of this, therefore, they proceeded to appoint the ministers I spoke of, and they went on to add an instruction that if these should fall asleep, other accredited persons should succeed them in their office. (Clement of Rome, *To the Corinthians*, sec. 44, ECW, p. 46)

According to Clement, writing in the last decade of the first century (immediately after the Domitian persecution, about 96 A.D.), this was not a later accretion of the pastoral tradition, but a feature that developed at its early stages. It was determined that the successors to the apostles would duly examine and appoint ministers to continue faithfully the apostolic witness and the caring ministry of Jesus. This process, Clement argued, was in accord with established Jewish tradition. Clement wrote of the period immediately following Jesus' resurrection:

When they had received their orders and had been filled with confidence by the resurrection of our Lord Jesus Christ, and confirmed in faith by the word of God, they went out in the confidence of the Holy Spirit, preaching the gospel, that the Kingdom of God was about to come. So, preaching in country and city, they appointed their firstfruits having tested them by the Spirit, to be bishops and deacons of those who should afterwards believe. And this was no novelty for long ago it had been written concerning bishops and deacons. For the Scripture says in one place: "I will make peace your governor and righteousness your ruler" (Isa. 60.17). (Clement of Rome, *To the Corinthians*, Ch. xlii, ANF I, 16, NIV)*

Numerous catalogues of succession of bishops are found among early Christian writings. They were of more than incidental importance for this reason: to guarantee to the congregations that the Word delivered now through preaching and counsel would be the same as that of the earliest apostles.

It is most apparent by the testimonies of all Antiquity, Fathers, and Ecclesiastical Histories, that all the churches in Christendom that were planted and governed by the Apostles, and by whatever coadjutors or apostolical persons to whom the Apostles had fully communicated their apostolical authority, did think that after the death either of any of the Apostles who ruled among them, or of any other the Bishops ordained by the Apostles, it was the meaning of the Holy Ghost, testified sufficiently by the practice of the Apostles, that the same order and form of ecclesiastical government should continue in the Church for ever. And therefore upon the death of any of them, either Apostles or Bishops, they, the said Churches, did always supply the most worthy and eminent persons among them to fill their places; who, with similar power and authority that their predecessors had, did ever succeed them. Thus in every city and episcopal see where there were various priests and ministers of the Word and Sacraments and but one Bishop only, the catalogues of the names, not of their Priests but of their Bishops, were very carefully kept from time to time, together with the names of the Apostles or Apostolical persons, the Bishops their predecessors, from whom they derived their succession. (John Overall, The Convocation Book of 1606, sec. 4, pp. 147f.; *Angl.*, p. 371)*

According to the Apostolic Constitutions, and numerous other early sources, all proper ordination to Christian soul care was thought to exist in linear, direct, historical succession from the Apostles:

By our Saviour were we apostles, thirteen in number, ordained; and by the Apostles I, James, and I, Clement, and others with us, were ordained, that we may not make the catalogue of all those bishops over again. And in common, presbyters, and deacons, and sub-deacons, and readers, were ordained by all of us. (*Constitutions of the Holy Apostles*, Bk. VIII, sec. V, ANF VII, p. 500)

The motive for securing the succession of the apostolic witness through ordination was to guarantee the authenticity of the earliest eyewitnesses. This is why the lists of successions played such a prominent role in early pastoral writings:

Now concerning those bishops which have been ordained in our lifetime, we let you know that they are these:—James the bishop of Jerusalem, the brother of our Lord; upon whose death the second was Simeon the son of Cleopas; after whom the third was Judas the son of James. Of Caesarea of Palestine, the first was Zacchaeus, who was once a publican; after whom was Cornelius, and the third Theophilus. Of Antioch, Euodius, ordained by me Peter; and Ignatius by Paul. Of Alexandria, Annianus was the first, ordained by Mark the evangelist; the second Avilius by Luke, who was also an evangelist. Of the church of Rome, Linus the son of Claudia was the first, ordained by Paul; and Clemens, after Linus' death, the second, ordained by me Peter. Of Ephesus, Timotheus, ordained by Paul; and John, by me John. Of Smyrna, Aristo the first; after whom Strataeas the son of Lois; and the third Aristo. Of Pergamus, Gaius. Of Philadelphia, Demetrius, by me. Of Cenchrea, Lucius, by Paul. Of Crete, Titus. Of Athens, Dionysius. Of Tripoli in Phoenicia, Marathones. Of Laodicea in Phrygia, Archippus. Of Colossae, Philemon. Of Borea in Macedonia, Onesimus, once the servant of Philemon. Of the churches of Galatia, Crescens. Of the parishes of Asia, Aquila and Nicetas. Of the church of Aeginae, Crispus. These are the bishops who are entrusted by us with the parishes in the Lord. (*Constitutions of the Holy Apostles*, Bk. VII, sec. IV, ANF VII, pp. 477–478)

It is doubtless a literary devise of a fourth century redactor that has various apostles speaking above, but the purpose of such a list is to establish in the mind of the reader that current ministry is grounded in faithfulness to apostolic ministry to which each minister enjoys a direct connection. Note also that specific territories or parishes were defined under the guidance of particular bishops. Hence authorization and territoriality were from a primitive period very closely linked.

It remained a recurrent theme of early pastoral literature that congregations owed a duty of obedience to pastors duly authorized by episcopal guidance in apostolic succession. This commissioning is in fantasy reenacted by this fourth century redactor:

Peter therefore ordered the letter to be read to the people; and after the reading of it, he addressed them and gave them full instructions

about everything, but especially that they should obey Zacchaeus, whom
he had ordained bishop over them. Also he commended the presbyters
and the deacons to the people, and not less the people to them. (Clementina, Recognitions of Clement, Bk. III, Ch. lxxiv, ANF VII, p. 133)

However one might assess the historical validity of such oral traditions, it is
clear that the early pastoral tradition took very seriously its rootage in the apostolic tradition, usually defined historically and mediated by a succession of
ordinations. In this way personal opinion was strictly to be distinguished from
apostolic authority. By the time of Origen, a debate was apparently proceeding
as to whether portions of the apostolic writings were to be considered on the
same level with the Old Testament revelation, and whether distinguishable levels of authority exist even within the New Testament. Origen thought that Paul
himself provided a pattern for distinguishing Paul's own opinion from divine
inspiration:

> The apostolic writings are to be pronounced wise and worthy of belief, and that they have great authority, but that they are not on the
> same level with "says the Lord" (2 Cor. 6:18). Consider on this point
> the language of St. Paul. When he declares that "every inspired scripture has its use for teaching the truth and refuting error" (2 Tim. 3:16),
> does he include his own writings? Or does he not include his dictum,
> "I say this, as my own word, not as the Lord's" (1 Cor. 7:12); and "That
> is what I teach in all our congregations" (1 Cor. 7:17) and he speaks of
> all that he went through "at Antioch, at Iconium, at Lystra" (2 Tim.
> 3:11), and similar things which he writes in virtue of his own authority,
> and which do not quite possess the character of words flowing from
> divine inspiration. (Origen, *Commentary on John*, Bk. I, sec. 5, ANF X,
> p. 299, NEB)*

Despite a strong tradition of episcopal succession, there was nonetheless an
equally strong tradition of appeal to consensus among church leaders in making appointments to ministries. Thus Ignatius, Bishop of Antioch at the end of
the first century or beginning of the second, appealed to Polycarp to "summon
a council" to appoint a missionary to Syria:

> It is fitting, Polycarp most blessed by God, to summon a council most
> fit for God which will appoint someone whom you regard as especially
> dear to you and zealous, someone who can be called God's courier, and
> will judge him worthy to go to Syria and glorify your zealous love to
> the glory of God. (Ignatius of Antioch, *Letter to Polycarp*, sec. 7, AF, pp.
> 118–119)*

IV. ❧ THE APOSTOLIC TRADITION

Christian care of souls is diminished when viewed non-historically as if the premodern experience of God's care had never occurred, or anti-traditionally as if there were no memory of that care, or individualistically as if it were concerned about one lone individual helping another lone individual apart from a community of prayer, praise and celebration. These misunderstandings are averted when current soul care views itself as rigorously grounded in the apostolic tradition of soul care as it was historically preserved and transmitted. According to the Epistle of Barnabas, the delivered tradition is not to be amended:

Keep the traditions you have received, without making any additions or deductions of your own. (*Epistle of Barnabas*, sec. 19, ECW, p. 218)

The apostles clearly intended that the original teaching of eyewitnesses to Jesus be accurately passed on intergenerationally, as the basis of care of souls:

I am not talking of anything novel or strange, or raising any new questions. Although I am an instructor of the Gentiles now, I was a pupil of the Apostles once; and what was delivered to me then, I now minister faithfully to students of the truth. How can anyone, who has been rightly taught and learnt to love the Word, not wish to be told the precise nature of the revelations which that Word so openly made to His disciples? Visibly present among them, the Word made His disclosures to them in the plainest of language; though unrecognized by the unbelieving, He discoursed without reserve to the disciples; and because they were reckoned faithful by Him, they came to know the mysteries of God. (*Epistle to Diognetus*, sec. 2, ECW, p. 182)

It was no insignificant point to the African theologian, Tertullian, writing about 200 A.D., that the apostolic tradition had survived intact during all those preceding generations to serve the guidance of souls in his own time:

Come now, you who would indulge a better curiosity, if you would apply it to the business of your salvation, run over the apostolic churches, in which the very thrones of the apostles are still pre-eminent in their places, in which their own authentic writings are read, uttering the voice and representing the face of each of them severally. Achaia is very near you, (in which) you find Corinth. Since you are not far from Macedonia, you have Philippi; (and there too) you have the Thessalonians. Since you are able to cross to Asia, you get Ephesus. Since, moreover, you are close upon Italy, you have Rome, from which there comes even into our own hands the very authority (of apostles themselves). How happy is its church, on which apostles poured forth all their doctrine along with their blood! where Peter endures a passion like his Lord's! where Paul wins his crown in a death like John's! where the Apostle John was first plunged, unhurt, into boiling oil, and thence remitted to his island exile! See what she has learned, what taught, what fellowship has had with even (our) churches in Africa! One Lord God does she acknowledge, the Creator of the universe, and Christ Jesus (born) of the Virgin Mary, the Son of God the Creator; and the Resurrection of the flesh; the law and the prophets she unites in one volume with the writings of evangelists and apostles, from which she drinks in her faith. This she seals with the water (of baptism), arrays with the Holy Ghost, feeds with the Eucharist, cheers with martyrdom, and against such a discipline thus (maintained) she admits no gainsayer. . . . Even the rough wild-olive arises from the germ of the fruitful, rich, and genuine olive; also from the seed of the mellowest and sweetest fig there springs the empty and useless wild-fig. In the same way heresies, too, come from our plant, although not of our kind; (they come) from the grain of truth, but, owing to their falsehood, they have only wild leaves to sow. (Tertullian, *On Prescription Against Heretics*, Ch. XXXVI, ANF III, pp. 260–261)

Tertullian was writing only a century and a half after Jesus' ministry, perhaps seven or eight generations after the death of Jesus. Here we find a picture of cohesive unity of a far-flung Christian witness, resonating with what he believed to be accurately transmitted reports of Jesus' ministry and its significance. The chief means by which the apostolic tradition was preserved through hazardous times were ordination and apostolic teaching:

After the death of the apostles there were Guides and Rulers in the churches. Whatever the apostles had committed to them and they had received from them, they continued to teach to the multitude through the whole time of their lives. They too, again, at their deaths committed and delivered to their disciples after them precisely what they had received from the apostles; also what James had written from Jerusalem, and Simon from the city of Rome, and John from Ephesus, and Mark from Alexandria, and Andrew from Phrygia, and Luke from Macedonia, and Judas Thomas from India: that the epistles of an apostle might be received and read in the churches that were in every place, just as the achievements of their Acts, which Luke wrote, are read; that hereby the apostles might be known, and the prophets, and the Old Testament and the New; that all may recognize that one truth was proclaimed in them all: that one Spirit spoke in them all, from one God whom they had all worshipped and had all preached. Widely different cultures received their teaching. Everything, therefore, which had been spoken by our Lord by means of the apostles, and which the apostles had delivered to their disciples, was believed and received in every country, by the operation of our Lord, who said to them: "I am with you, even until the world shall end" (Matt. 28:20). . . . And by ordination to the priesthood which the apostles themselves had received from our Lord, did their Gospel wing its way rapidly into the four quarters of the world. And by mutual visitation they ministered to one another. (The Teaching of the Apostles, ANF VIII, pp. 670–671)*

It is no small thing for a pastor to abandon the apostolic tradition:

A small thing is not small when it leads to something great; and it is no small matter to forsake the ancient tradition of the Church which was upheld by all those who were called before us, whose conduct we should observe, and whose faith we should imitate. (John of Damascus, On the Divine Images, First Apology, sec. 2, NPNF 2, IX, p. 14)

A tradition of consensual interpretation of scriptures gradually developed through ecumenical councils, which guided soul care. The statements of these councils were at times distorted by unscrupulous teachers, but on the whole have remained reliable guides to ministry:

For cutting out certain of the things which the holy Fathers had written, and placing with them and mixing up certain false things of their own, they have tried by a letter of Cyril of holy memory as though from a testimony of the Fathers, to free from anathema the aforesaid impious Theodore: in which very passages the truth was demonstrated, when the parts which had been cut off were read in their proper order and the falsehood was thoroughly evinced by the collation of the true. . . . Having thus detailed all that has been done by us, we again confess that we receive the four holy Synods, that is, the Nicene, the Constantinopolitan, the first of Ephesus, and that of Chalcedon, and we have taught, and do teach all that they defined respecting the one faith. (Second Council of Constantinople, A.D. 553, The Sentence of the Synod, The Seven Ecumenical Councils, NPNF 2, XIV, pp. 309–310)

V. 🕭 Cohesion and Catholicity amid Diverse Ministries

It is precisely because the care of souls has been so far-flung in varied cultural situations, speaking many languages, addressing diverse historical challenges with flexible means, that all the more energy has been given to ensuring its fundamental unity, its direct continuity with the ministry of Jesus, its cohesion in apostolic teaching. This required a continuing battle with views different from (*haeresis*) the ancient apostolic witness. It also required a steady commitment to nurture in each new historical situation a living sense of participation in the one body of Christ. There was profound pastoral meaning in the early church's search for catechetical coherence, for catholicity, for unity in Christ:

The Church, then, is called Catholic because it is spread through the whole world, from one end of the earth to the other, and because it never stops teaching in all its fulness every doctrine that men ought to be brought to know: and that regarding things visible and invisible, in heaven and on earth. It is called Catholic also because it brings into religious obedience every sort of men, rulers and ruled, learned and simple, and because it is a universal treatment and cure for every kind of sin whether perpetrated by soul or body, and possesses within it every form of virtue that is named, whether it expresses itself in deeds or words or in spiritual graces of every description. The Church is well named Ecclesia because it calls everyone out and assembles them together. (Cyril of Jerusalem, *The Catechetical Lectures*, Lect. XVIII, LCC IV, p. 186)

Christian soul care reaches out for every class, every culture, every historical and social situation, yet maintaining its unity in Christ. Others who developed novel or different views (*haeresis*) that were inadmissible within the assumptions of apostolic teaching had to be answered. These views were named according to their inventors:

Those who followed Marcion, were called Christians no more, but henceforth Marcionites. Similarly Valentinus also, Basilides, Manichaeus, and Simon Magus, have imparted their own name to their followers, and therefore are known as Valentinians, Basilidians, Manichees, or as Simonians. Cataphrygians derive from Phrygia, and from Novatus Novatians. So too Meletius, when ejected by Peter the Bishop and Martyr, called his party, no longer Christians, but Meletians. So too when when Alexander of blessed memory had cast out Arius, those who remained with Alexander, remained Christians; but those who left with Arius were subsequently called Arians. Mark well also that those who after Alexander's death communicate with his successor Athanasius, and those with whom Athanasius communicates, are instances of the same rule. None bear his name, nor is he named from them, but all similarly are called Christians. For though we have a succession of teachers and become their disciples, yet, because we are taught by them the things of Christ, we both are, and are called, Christians all the same. But those who follow the other than apostolic teachings, though they have innumerable successors in their heresy, yet for certain bear the name of him who devised it. Thus, though Arius be dead, and many of his party have succeeded him, yet those who think with him, as being known from Arius, are called Arians. (Athanasius, *Discourses Against the Arians*, sec. 3, LF, VIII, pp. 181–182)

The essential cultural pluralism of ecumenical pastoral care was early and repeatedly affirmed. Many cultures, languages, and classes (all in intent) were cared for, but amid all this variety, there was a rigorous commitment to the unity of the body of Christ under apostolic teaching, and a strong resistance to doctrinal pluralism:

Where diversity of doctrine is found, there must be some corruption either of the Scriptures or expositions thereof. (Tertullian, *On Prescription Against Heretics*, Ch. XXXVII, ANF III, p. 261)*

This unity was constantly being challenged by false teachers and misleading mentors. For this reason it was at times thought questionable even to give them access to the teaching of the apostles since they would inevitably be prone to distort it:

> For as they are heretics, they cannot be true Christians, because it is not from Christ that they get that which they pursue of their own mere choice, and from the pursuit incur and admit the name of heretics. Thus, not being Christians, they have acquired no right to the Christian Scriptures; and it may be very fairly said to them, "Who are you? When and whence did you come? As you are none of mine, what have you to do with that which is mine? Indeed, Marcion, by what right do you hew my wood? By whose permission, Valentinus, are you diverting the streams of my fountain? By what power, Apelles, are you removing my landmarks? This is my property. Why are you, the rest, sowing and feeding here at your own pleasure? This (I say) is my property." (Tertullian, *On Prescription Against Heretics*, Ch. XXXVII, ANF III, p. 261)

Heterodoxies are by definition self-chosen. They are deliberate decisions individuals make in defiance of the delivered apostolic tradition:

> Indeed, in almost every epistle, when enjoining on us the duty of avoiding false teachings, Paul sharply condemns unapostolic views. The practical effects of false teachings are false choices. They are called in Greek heresies, a word used in the special sense of that deliberate choice that someone makes when one either teaches them to others or takes up with them for himself. It is for this reason that he calls such persons self-condemned, because each has chosen for himself that for which he is judged. . . . In the Lord's apostles we possess our authority; for even they did not of themselves choose to introduce anything, but faithfully delivered to the nations the doctrine which they had received from Christ. (Tertullian, *On Prescription Against Heretics*, Ch. VI, ANF III, p. 245)*

This does not imply that all diversity of liturgical practice is forbidden. An irenic German cardinal, Nicolas of Cusa, (c. 1400–1464), argued in this way for varieties of worship within the apostolic tradition:

> Harmony will be found in stessing these common elements, and the Christian religion will be approved insofar as in its observation it retains in both these sacraments that simplicity that in the estimate of others is most praiseworthy. . . . What about fastings, ecclesiastical duties, abstinence in the matter of food and drink, formulae for prayers, and such matters? . . . . Where it is impossible to maintain conformity, then, provided that faith and peace are preserved, the various nations should be permitted their own devotions and ceremonies. As a matter

of fact, I think that this diversity would bring about an increase in devotion. For each individual nation will endeavor to make its own ritual more splendid, that they might surpass others and, in this way, they will achieve greater praise from both God and man. (Nicholas De Cusa, "De Pace Fidei," Ch. xviii, *Unity and Reform*, p. 236)

Those who have once followed a false faith may learn through it how better to proclaim true faith, according to the Council of Chalcedon:

For then indeed is the true faith defended with the best results, when a false opinion is condemned even by those who have followed it. (Chalcedon, A.D. 451, The Tome of St. Leo, The Seven Ecumenical Councils, NPNF 2, XIV, p. 258)

Admittedly there are astonishing varieties of soul care in the two millennia of Christian pastoral tradition. So numerous are they that appear to call into question the essential validity and unity of the tradition altogether. The Thirty-nine Articles of the Church of England of the sixteenth century succinctly stated a wise path toward the celebration of the variety of pastoral traditions within the history of Christianity:

It is not necessary that Traditions and Ceremonies be in all places one, or utterly like; for at all times they have been divers, and may be changed according to the diversity of countries, times, and men's manners, so that nothing be ordained against God's Word.

Whosoever, through his private judgment, willingly and purposely, doth openly break the Traditions and Ceremonies of the Church, which be not repugnant to the Word of God, and be ordained and approved by common authority, ought to be rebuked openly (that others may fear to do the like), as he that offendeth against the common order of the Church, and hurteth the authority of the Magistrate, and woundeth the consciences of the weak brethren. (Anglican Thirty-nine Articles, *CC*, Art. xxxiv, pp. 277–278)

Accordingly, one need not be intimidated by the variety of traditions. Rather they are all to be measured and tested in relation to scripture. Luther thought some early pastoral writers were distinctly more reliable and usable than others.

Bonaventura is the best among the scholastic teachers. Among the ecclesiastical teachers Augustine holds the first place, Ambrose the second, Bernard the third. Among the teachers of the church Tertullian is a vertable Carlstadt. Cyril has the best ideas. Cyprian is a holy martyr but a very weak (*imbecillus*) theologian. Among teachers Theophylact is the best interpreter of Paul. (Luther, *Table Talk*, W-T 1, #683; WLS 1, p. 313)

Protestant writers did not hesitate to look to patristic councils for authoritative guidance on pastoral care. The Lutheran scholastic teacher, Martin Chemnitz, commended the early Ecumenical Councils and to the patristic writers to those preparing for care of souls:

First carefully test and examine them as to whether they are legitimately called, whether they rightly hold the fundamentals of salutary doctrine and reject fanatic opinions, whether they are endowed with the gifts necessary to teach others sound doctrine and whether they can prove their lives to be honorable, so that they can be examples to the flock; for this concern we have the very solemn precept of Paul. 1 Ti 5:22; 2 Ti 2:2. The older councils therefore decreed many things regarding examination of those who are to be ordained; these things are found in Gratian, Distinct. 23, 24, and 81. And canon 4 of the 4th council of Carthage, at which Augustine was present, decreed thus: Let one who is to be ordained be ordained when he has, in an examination, been found to be rightly instructed. And the canon of Nicaea, Distinct. 81, says: If any are promoted (to be) presbyters without examination, church order does not recognize them, because they are ordained contrary to the rule. (Chemnitz, *MWS*, Introduction, sec. 3, pp. 26–27)

The major ecumenical councils of the first five centuries were affirmed by most Protestant theologians and Confessions, and held to be reliable witnesses to scripture. The Protestant pastoral tradition sought to provide guarantees that ordinands would have read classical ecumenical theology as a basis for their practice of pastoral care.

VI. ✿ The Visibility of Church and Ministry

There is in the minds of classical pastoral writers an intrinsic connection between church and ministry: There is no church without ministry, and no ministry without church. Some sought to define more substantially how ecclesiology requires care of souls, and how a fundamental doctrine of ministry assumes and commends the *ecclesia* that it serves. Pastoral care came to assume an operational distinction between invisible and visible church. For ministry serves a visible community which nonetheless transcends any particular time and place:

The visible Church, which is also catholic or universal under the gospel (not confined to one nation as before under the law) consists of all those, throughout the world, that profess the true religion, and of their children; and is the kingdom of the Lord Jesus Christ, the house and family of God, out of which there is no ordinary possibility of salvation.

Unto this catholic visible Church Christ hath given the ministry, oracles, and ordinances of God, for the gathering and perfecting of the saints, in this life, to the end of the world: and doth by his own presence and Spirit, according to his promise, make them effectual thereunto.

This catholic church hath been sometimes more, sometimes less visible. And particular churches, which are members thereof, are more or less pure, according as the doctrine of the gospel is taught and embraced, ordinances administered, and public worship performed more or less purely in them.

The purest churches under heaven are subject both to mixture and error; and some have so degenerated as to become no churches of Christ, but synagogues of Satan. Nevertheless, there shall be always a Church on earth to worship God according to his will. (Westminster Confession, Ch. XXV, sec. ii-v, *CC*, p. 222)

The way one defines the church is all-important in shaping the way one defines ministry, as in the Anglican Articles of Religion:

The visible Church of Christ is a congregation of faithful men, in the which the pure Word of God is preached, and the Sacraments be duly ministered according to Christ's ordinance, in all those things that of necessity are requisite to the same. (Anglican Thirty-nine Articles, *CC*, Art. xix, p. 273)

A cluster of biblical metaphors (vineyard, inheritance, propitiatory sacrifice) assisted the writers of the Apostolic Constitutiions in defining the essence of the church:

The Catholic Church is the planting of God, and His beloved vineyard. It contains those who have believed in His unerring divine religion; who are the heirs by faith of His everlasting kingdom; who are partakers of His divine influence, and of the communication of the Holy Spirit; who are armed through Jesus, and have received His holy reverence into their hearts; who enjoy the benefit of the sprinkling of the precious and innocent blood of Christ; who have free liberty to address the Almighty God personally as Father, since they are fellow-heirs and joint-partakers of His beloved Son. (*Constitutions of the Holy Apostles*, Bk. I, sec. I, ANF VII, p. 391)*

The worshipping community is praying, in this Anglican collect, for a ministry that reflects the fundamental reality of the church:

Almighty God, our Heavenly Father, Who hast purchased to Thyself an Universal Church by the precious Blood of Thy dear Son, Mercifully look upon the same, and at this time so guide and govern the minds of Thy servants, the Bishops and Pastors of Thy flock, that they may lay hands suddenly on no man, but faithfully and wisely make choice of fit persons to serve in the sacred Ministry of Thy Church. And to those which shall be ordained to any holy function give Thy grace and heavenly benediction; that both by their life and doctrine they may set forth Thy glory and set forward the salvation of all men;

through Jesus Christ our Lord. Amen. (Book of Common Prayer, 1662; *Angl.*, pp. 636–637)

Despite difficult historical crises, the church's witness will not cease, according to Luther, because God has promised the Word to the world:

It must be granted that faith has not disappeared since the time the Word of God came to the woman, for the Word has not been suspended or silenced. The Christian Church must always remain, though only two human beings were to exist on earth; for only for the sake of those who believe does God let the Word go forth. Therefore there is no doubt that the church has never yet entirely disappeared. At times, however, it suffers abatement. Yet it remains standing. (Luther, "Sermon on Genesis Four, 1523," WA 24, p. 149; WLS 1, p. 280)

VII. ❧ THE ORGANISMIC METAPHOR: WHOLE BODY OF CHRIST

The community of faith is like a body with members in which each part is affected by the whole, and the whole by each part. The whole community shares in the pain and joy of any one of its members, according to the metaphor of an integrated bodily organism. As a result the tradition of pastoral care has been strongly shaped by a vision of corporate health that cannot abstract a particular individual out of community. The corollary premise is that corporate sickness strongly affects the dysfunction of any member.

Who can hurt any part of the body without hurting the whole body? What pain can we feel in the tip of the toe that is not felt in the whole body? Or what honor can be shown to the feet in which the whole body will not rejoice? but we are one body. Whatever another suffers, that I suffer and bear; whatever good befalls him, befalls me. So Christ says that whatsoever is done unto one of the least of His brethren, is done unto Him. If a man partake of the smallest fragment of the bread of the altar, is he not said to have partaken of the bread? If he despise one crumb of it, is he not said to have despised the bread?

When we, therefore, feel pain, when we suffer, when we die, let us turn hither our eyes, and firmly believe and be sure that it is not we, or we alone, but that Christ and the Church are in pain, are suffering, are dying with us. For Christ would not have us go alone into the valley of death, from which all men shrink in fear; but we set out upon the way of pain and death attended by the whole Church. (Luther, *The Fourteen of Consolation*, Ch. VI, WML I, p. 166–167)

The organic or bodily metaphor placed the emphasis upon the integration and equilibrium of the whole social organism, not exclusively upon a single individual's functioning. This metaphor has powerful implications for political justice:

even the smallest, weakest, most neglected member of the community is important:

When someone steps on the smallest toe, the entire body is affected, the eyes look displeased, the nose wrinkles, the hand grabs for the toe, and every member wonders and asks what has happened. For it is characteristic of this oneness that no piece or part lives and feels for itself alone without having the life and the feeling of all the others, that is, of the entire body. When the lowliest member of Christendom suffers, the entire body at once feels it and is astir so that all come together, complain, and cry. (Luther, "Sermon on John 17:11," WLS 1, p. 275)

If a pastor gives inordinate attention to only the influential or wealthy in a congregation, then pastoral care becomes distorted, lacking full awareness of the whole-body metaphor:

What is more harmful in a minister of the Word of God than for him to act differently toward persons of rank and riches from the way he acts toward lowly folk and paupers when he is sent for the purpose of serving all, flattering no one, and despising no one? (Luther, "Sermon on Psalm 8," WA 5, p. 288; WLS 2, p. 930)

The whole body with many members aims toward complete, full-functioning, health. Each member grows through activity toward a perfection that can only be eschatologically conceived:

To understand what the apostle means when he says that we shall all come to a perfect humanity, we must consider the connection of the whole passage, which says: "And these were his gifts: some to be apostles, some prophets, some evangelists, some pastors and teachers, to equip God's people for work in his service, to the building up of the body of Christ. So shall we all at last attain to the unity inherent in our faith and our knowledge of the Son of God—to mature manhood, measured by nothing less than the full stature of Christ." (Eph. 4:11–13) . . . . So "Let us speak the truth in love; so shall we fully grow up into Christ. He is the head, and on him the whole body depends. Bonded and knit together by every constituent joint, the whole frame grows through the due activity of each part, and builds itself up in love." (Eph. 4:15–16). Behold what the perfect humanity is—the head and the body, which is made up of all the members, which in God's own time shall be perfected. But new additions are daily being made to this body while the Church is being built up, to which it is said, "Now you are Christ's body, and each of you a limb or organ of it" (1 Cor. 12:27). (Augustine, *The City of God*, Bk. XXI, Ch. 19, NPNF 1, II, p. 496, NEB)*

Since Christ is the head of the body, it is not appropriate to view a pastor as unambiguously "head" of a congregation, but more appropriately as steward and proclaimer of the headship of Christ:

A bishop, pastor, or preacher should not be called the head of the church but a minister and steward, as St. Paul says: "Let a man so account of us as of the ministers of Christ and stewards of the mysteries of God" (1 Cor. 4:1). St. Peter calls himself a fellow elder and a witness of the sufferings of Christ and says: The elders should feed the flock of Christ and not lord it over the people (1 Peter 5:1–3). (Luther, "Sermon on Colossians 1:18–20, 1537," WA 45, p. 310; WLS 2, p. 930)

VIII. ❧ PASTORAL REALISM CONCERNING THE REFORMABILITY OF THE CHURCH

It is understandable that a new pastor will come to a parish with significant hopes of growth, improvement, and the increase of the love of God and humanity. But when these expectations become perfectionistically exaggerated, or are thought to be too easily accomplished, a crisis may ensue for both pastor and parish. Not every parish is easily malleable even with the best intentions and efforts. It is better if a pastor views the task realistically, yet with confidence in God's empowerment.

The fantasies of some pastors about the human capacity for vast and immediate change is sometimes self-defeating:

Usually ministers, especially when they are brand-new and have recently entered their office, imagine that when they speak, they should gain their purpose promptly and that everything should happen and change quickly. But this is far from being the case. The prophets and Christ Himself failed to achieve this. Things go as men proverbially say: You are too young to make old rogues pious. (Luther, "Exposition on Habakkuk 1:3," WA 19, p. 357; WLS 2, p. 927)

On the unusual occasion in 1660 of the simultaneous consecration of seven Anglican bishops, William Sancroft stated these realistic sentiments:

Blest be the mercies of God, we are at last returned, and Titus is come back into Crete; and there are elders ordained for every city. But *hic Rhodus, hic Saltus.* Reverend Father, this is your Crete, adorn it as you can. The province is hard, and the task weighty and formidable, even to an Angel's shoulders. That we mistake not, Titus was not left behind in Crete to take his ease, or to sleep out the storm which soon after overtook St. Paul at sea. . . . As in Crete new founded, so in England new restored, there must needs be many things wanting, and much amiss, not so easily to be supplied or amended. (William Sancroft, Sermon, 1660; *Angl.*, p. 773)

Luther warned that the pastor had best not expect constant expressions of gratitude for the good he has accomplished. It is best to be realistic about the limits of parishioners' ability to receive care:

If someone renders people the greatest and most helpful service, the Enemy sets them against him, with the result that they do not requite his friendship and that he has only bought enemies for himself, as Ecclus. 29:6 says, and has bred a serpent in his bosom. Furthermore, the Enemy makes people weary and disgusted, with the result that because of such ingratitude and malice nobody is willing to do any favors and to give any help. Then they all turn out to be just like Timon. This gives rise to proverbial sayings like "Bread given to strange dogs and to strange children is lost." (Luther, "Sermons on the Gospel of St. John Chapter 15, 1537," LW 24, p. 267)*

It is commendable to continue faithfully in one's office even when things tend to go badly wrong, according to Luther, because if one has been duly called and appointed, God's purpose will manifest itself in due time. God's word will not return void.

He who will not be satisfied with his ministry until he has converted and Christianized all will never find peace. Abraham found contempt of God everywhere: yet he did not become broken in spirit, but he and his family continued in the true religion and instructed others. So you should not lose courage either but should continue in the office assigned to you by God. Let Him worry about the success of the Word. (Luther, "Sermon on Isaiah 51," WA 25, p. 316; WLS 2, p. 952)

Where the pastor meets no opposition, care of souls has been defaulted. The Word faithfully presented awakens opposition:

If ministers of the Word desire to be accounted faithful and prudent on the Day of Christ, they must be very sure that St. Paul did not speak empty words or prophesy in vain when he said; "There must be heresies among you that they which are approved may be made manifest among you" (1 Cor. 11:19). Let the minister of Christ know, I say, that as long as he preaches Christ purely, there will be no lack of perverse folk, even among our own people, who will disturb the church. (Luther, *Lectures on Galatians*, WA 40, p. 37; WLS 2, p. 931)

The pastor who seeks an easily perfectable church is in for trouble. In even more trouble is the pastor who looks for one already perfected:

He who would have, and is in search of, a church in which no dissension and no difference exist among preachers, no insincerity against the First Table, and no outrage and wickedness against the Second Table, will never find his church. (Luther, "Sermons on Psalm 72, 1540," WA 49, p. 41; WLS 1, p. 288)

Bishop William Laud wrote this prayer for the patient amendment and correction of the church:

Gracious Father, I humbly beseech Thee for Thy Holy Catholic Church. Fill it with all truth, in all truth, with all peace. Where it is corrupt, purge it. Where it is in error, direct it. Where it is superstitious, rectify it. Where anything is amiss, reform it. Where it is right, strengthen and confirm it. Where it is in want, furnish it. Where it is divided and rent asunder, make up the breaches of it, O Thou Holy One of Israel. (Laud, Book of Common Prayer, 1662; *Angl.*, p. 638)

IX. ❧ THE EXEMPLARY MINISTRY OF JESUS OF NAZARETH

Contemporary pastoral care seeks to reflect God's care for humanity as made known in Jesus. Current ministries are authenticated only insofar as they express and embody Jesus' continuing presence. This is why pastors are called to study Jesus' pattern of ministry.

In the light of contemporary New Testament studies, it may seem that unprecedented clouds of questioning have been raised about the historical memory concerning Jesus, which for some diminish confidence in statements about Jesus. But as we will see, these doubts, questions and challenges have been vexing Christian pastoral care from its earliest times. There has never been a century of Christian pastoral care in which no serious questions have been raised about the adequacy of our available knowledge of Jesus. Some of the earlier questioners doubted that Jesus was ever born at all, some thought that he was not flesh but spirit only, some thought that he was not of God, some questioned whether the reports about Jesus were accurate, some thought the resurrection was dubious, some questioned the accuracy of the transmission of the early tradition. So all these issues that still continue as historical critical issues of textual criticism, historical criticism, form-criticism of the oral tradition, and redaction criticism of the editors of early documents—all these issues were primordially present and rudimentarily explored in the first three centuries of the church's life. What follows are a few select quotes that will give the reader the gist of how the early Christian pastoral writers were thinking about the question of the possibility of knowledge of Jesus' ministry, upon whom our ministries of care in each new generation radically depend.

Do we have an accurate record of Jesus' ministry? Do the New Testament gospels, such as Mark, give us an accurate picture and recollection of Jesus' mode of ministry? Papias (c.60–c.130), bishop of Hierapolis, and one who is reported by Irenaeus to be "a hearer of John, a companion of Polycarp," answered as follows:

Mark having become the interpreter of Peter, wrote down accurately whatsoever he remembered. It was not, however, in exact order that he related the sayings or deeds of Christ. For he neither heard the Lord nor accompanied Him. But afterwards, as I said, he accompanied Peter, who accommodated his instructions to the necessities [of his hearers], but with no intention of giving a regular narrative of the Lord's sayings. Wherefore Mark made no mistake in thus writing some things as he remembered them. For of one thing he took especial care, not to omit anything he had heard, and not to put anything fictitious into the statements. (Papias, Fragments, ANF I, pp. 154–155)

Why was Papias concerned to point out that Mark took special care not to omit anything he had heard, and not to exaggerate or falsify any report? Doubtless because the question of the authenticity of Mark's report was already under some question. This demonstrates that the early pastors were intensely concerned with the accuracy of evidence. Otherwise why would Papias go so far as to provide his reader in this passage with a deliberate rationale for why Mark's order in reporting the events of Jesus' ministry does not correspond precisely with other available accounts? This is hardly evidence of carelessness, but rather of Mark's avid interest in accuracy in reporting Peter's witness as it had become adapted through preaching to various audiences.

Yet if reports of Jesus' ministry do not precisely agree, how are they to be trusted? Origen provided a widely-shared rationale, hinging on the diversity of the intention and audience of the various evangelists:

If the discrepancy between the gospels is not solved, we must give up our trust in the gospels, as being true and written by a divine spirit, or as records worthy of credence, for both these characters are held to belong to these works. . . . There are many other points on which the careful student of the Gospels will find that their narratives do not agree. . . . The student, staggered at the consideration of these things, will either renounce the attempt to find all the Gospels true, and not venturing to conclude that all our information about our Lord is untrustworthy, will choose at random one of them to be his guide; or he will accept the four, and will consider that their truth is not to be sought for in the outward and material letter.

We must, however, try to obtain some notion of the intention of the Evangelists in such matters. . . . They use in the same way His sayings, and in some places they tack on to their writing, with language apparently implying things of sense, things made manifest to them in a purely intellectual way. I do not condemn them if they even sometimes dealt freely with things which to the eye of history happened differently. . . . They proposed to speak the truth where it was possible both materially and spiritually, and where this was not possible it was their intention to prefer the spiritual to the material. (Origen, *Commentary on John*, sec. 2–4, ANF X, pp. 382–383)

Were autograph copies of original apostolic writings preserved as late as the fourth century, to guarantee the authenticity of the apostolic writers? Bishop Peter of Alexandria, (d. 311), a scholar who had served as head of Christianity's most famous catechetical school at Alexandria, clearly believed that such copies had survived the two hundred or more years since they had been written, since they were so carefully protected by those to whom these revered writings were entrusted:

Now it was the preparation, about the third hour, as the accurate books have it, and the autograph copy itself of the Evangelist John, which up to this day has by divine grace been preserved in the most holy church of Ephesus, and is there adored by the faithful. (Peter of Alexandria, Fragments, Sec. V, ANF VI, p. 283)

Eusebius went so far as to argue that something of the character of Jesus could be known through the persons who have truly followed him, since his spirit has shown transparently and accurately through their lives. He takes special pains to note that women as well as men authentically manifest his spirit. For they care deeply about the soul:

And if in the widest sense you wish to deduce from the character of His followers the character of their leader, you have today a myriad disciples of the teaching of Jesus, great numbers of whom actively resist being tyrannized by bodily pleasures in order that they might guard their minds against being numbed by brute passions, so that by the time they grow mature in temperance, they provide bright evidence of the nurture of His words. And not men only live the life of wisdom in this way for His sake, but innumerable myriads of women too, throughout the world. They are like priestesses of the Supreme God, embracing the highest wisdom, enraptured with the love of heavenly wisdom. . . . spending all their care on the soul. (Eusebius, *The Proof of the Gospel*, Bk. III, Ch. 6, p. 148)*

X. ❧ JESUS' MINISTRY AND OURS

The pastor's care for the Christian community constitutes a finite attempt to reflect God's infinite care for the world. When persons are sent to minister, Christ preceeds; when they reach out for the hungry and sick, Christ is already present incognito in the needy neighbor; when they preach rightly, God's own self-disclosure in Christ is being expressed through fragile language. At every turn, the church has no ministry except that of manifesting, embodying, and pointing to the presence of the living Christ in the real world. This raises a constellation of questions about the intrinsic relation of our efforts at ministry and Christ's own ministry.

In his meditation on the Lord's petition to "give us this day our daily bread," Luther prayed for Christ himself to sustain day by day the church's caring ministry:

Give Thy grace to all preachers, that they may preach Thy Word and Christ, to profit and salvation, in all the world. Help all who hear the preaching of Thy Word to learn Christ, and honestly to better their lives thereby. Graciously drive out of the Holy Church all strange preaching and teaching from which men do not learn Christ. Have mercy upon all bishops, priests, clergy and all that are in authority, that they may be enlightened by Thy grace to teach and govern us aright by precept and example. Preserve all that are weak in faith, that they may not stumble at the bad example of their spiritual guides.

Preserve us from heretical and apostate teachers, that we may remain one, partaking of one daily bread—the daily doctrine and word of Christ. Graciously teach us to regard aright the sufferings of Christ, receive them into our hearts, and form them in our lives, to our salvation.

Do not permit us at our last hour to be deprived of the true and holy body of Christ. Help all priests to use and administer the holy sacrament worthily and savingly, to the edification of the whole Church. Help us and all Christians to receive the Holy Sacrament at its proper season, with Thy grace and to our salvation. (Luther, *Brief Explanation*, WML II, pp. 380–381)*

When pastoral counsel is at its best, the living Christ is actively counseling, instructing the believer through the Spirit. Athanasius spoke of Christ as "living Counselor" to active faith:

For that about which one counsels, one must understand. And that about which one has gained understanding is that about which one counsels. Certainly the saviour himself has made them correspond, as being cognate, when he says, "Counsel is Mine and security; Mine is understanding, and Mine strength" (Prov. 8:14). . . . The Son of God then, is the Word and the Wisdom. He is the Understanding and the Living Counsel. In him is the good pleasure of the Father. (Athanasius, Four Discourses Against the Arians, III, Ch. XXX, sec. 65, NPNF 2, IV, p. 429)*

Those called into the new covenant will be sustained by grace through challenges and obstacles, according to the Westminster Confession. For it is Christ's own ministry that is promised continuance:

To all those for whom Christ has purchased redemption, he certainly and effectually applies and communicates that redemption: making intercession for them, and revealing to them, in and by the Word, the mysteries of salvation; effectually persuading them by his Spirit to believe and obey; and governing their hearts by his Word and Spirit; overcoming all their enemies by his almighty power and wisdom, in such manner and ways as are most consonant to his wonderful and unsearchable dispensation. (Westminster Confession, Art. viii, *CC*, p. 295)*

Christ's living presence in the church and ministry is not fully grasped under the analogy of moral example, imitation, or following Christ's footsteps. As Anglican Joseph Hall pointed out, not all of Christ's actions were intended for direct or simple imitation. It is not a slavish, legalistic repetition of Jesus' external deeds that are commended for contemporary ministry, but rather sharing with others the same spirit of mercy that God through Christ shared with humanity:

> Neither Christ nor His Apostles did all things for imitation. I speak not of miraculous acts. We need not be silent before a judge, as Christ was. We need not take a towel, and gird ourselves and wash our servants' feet, as Christ did. We need not make tents for our living, as Paul; nor go armed, as Peter. (Joseph Hall, Epistles, Works, VI, p. 242)

Yet the compassion of Jesus for the poor, sick, and alienated remains the primary pattern for all ministries of compassion, care, healing and outreach:

> When the elders had set before him a woman who had sinned and left the sentence to him and went away, our Lord, the Searcher of hearts, inquired of her whether the elders had condemned her, and when she answered No, he said to her: "Go thy way therefore, for neither do I condemn thee." Listen bishops: This Jesus, our Saviour, our King, and our God, ought to be set before you as your pattern. Him you ought to imitate in being meek, quiet, compassionate, merciful, peaceable, without passion, apt to teach, and diligent to convert, willing to receive and to comfort. (*Constitutions of the Holy Apostles*, Bk. II, sec. III, Ch. XXV, ANF IV, p. 408)

Eusebius wove together a brilliant pattern of biblical images to speak of how Christ himself is the prototypical pastoral counselor, minister, priest, physician of souls, shepherd. According to Eusebius, Jesus' very name assigned to him the role of care-giver:

> He is called Sun of Righteousness, and True Light, carrying out and co-operating in His Father's commands. He is also known as servant of the Father and Creator. . . . He has received the care of the Universe, and is Priest to the Father on behalf of all who are responsive, who make himself known as favourable and merciful to all. He is called as well Eternal High Priest. . . . He is named Shepherd of the Sheep, and since he promises to care for sick souls, He would rightly be called Saviour and Physician. This of course is the meaning of the name "Jesus" in Hebrew. . . . So, then, God the Word was called the Son of Man, and was named Jesus, because He made His approach to us to

cure and to heal the souls of men. (Eusebius, *The Proof of the Gospel*, Bk. IV, Ch. 10, pp. 184–185)*

The selections in Part Three have sought to clarify the right basis for authorization for pastoral care. Pastors are expected to exercise influence, but under the constraint of the servant image, distinguishable from the coercive exercise of temporal power, external influence, or secular authority. Such influence is constantly to be viewed in relation to the apostolic tradition that awakens, informs, and energizes it. Viewed non-historically or individualistically, the authorization to pastoral care is diminished and misunderstood. There is profound pastoral intent and meaning in the church's search for unity, catechetical coherence, ecumenical consensus, and catholicity that reaches out for all types and conditions of humanity in each emergent historical period. The pastor cares for a visible community which nonetheless transcends every particular place and time. Each member of the body of Christ affects the whole body, and is affected by the sickness or health of the body. The realistic assessment of the church as a community embracing both wheat and tares will help avert the dangers of perfectionistic and compulsive reformism. Contemporary pastoral care seeks to reflect God's care for humanity as made known in Jesus.

4 The General Ministry of the Whole Church and the Sacred Ministry

THE LIFE OF FAITH active in love is the gift and task of the whole church. The office of care of souls is given to some few who are called to represent the whole church in the crucial situations of preaching, sacramental adminstration, church order and pastoral care. The sacred ministry is not to be affirmed in such a way that the ministry of the laity is neglected or denied, but affirmed and enhanced. On the other hand, the general ministry of the whole church is not to be asserted in such a way that the ordained ministry is disenfranchised or diminished. To hold these complementary parts in creative tension has been a problem of pastoral thinking from the outset.

I. ⁊ THE PRIESTHOOD OF ALL BAPTIZED CHRISTIANS

All baptized believers are recipients of the grace of baptism. In this sense, the whole church, and not ordained ministry alone, is the recipient of spiritual gifts. Thus every believer is gifted in some particular way for the ministry of the whole church.

There is no one who has believed in God through Christ, that has not received some spiritual gift. (*Constitutions of the Holy Apostles*, Bk. VIII, sec. I, ANF VII, p. 480)*

All baptized believers belong to this "royal priesthood," a way of speaking of the whole Christian community:

As many of us as have been baptised are all priests without distinction, as indeed we all are. Yet to some has been committed public ministry with our consent. They must learn that they they have no right to rule over us except in so far as we freely concede it. For thus it is written in I Peter 2:9, "You are a chosen race, a royal priesthood, a holy nation, God's own people." Therefore we are all priests, as many of us as are Christians. But the priests, as we call them, are ministers chosen from among us, who do all that they do in our name, and the priesthood is nothing but that ministry of which we learn in I Corin-

81

thians 4:1, "This is how one should regard us, as servants of Christ and stewards of the mysteries of God." It follows from this that whoever does not preach the Word, called by the Church to this very thing, is no priest at all. And further, that the sacrament of ordination can be nothing else than a certain rite of choosing preachers in the Church. (Luther, *The Babylonian Captivity*, WML II, p. 279, RSV)*

Sacred ministry, therefore, is a service to the whole community, done representatively for the whole. As governors would be superfluous without a people to govern, so clergy are superfluous, and need not exist, without the laity:

A governor should not despise his subordinates, nor should a leader his followers. For where there are none to be guided, the guides would be superfluous, just as where there are no designated leaders, the government would not stand. So the bishop must not act contemptuously toward presbyters and deacons, nor presbyters against the people. For the survival of the congregation depends on their mutuality. Bishops and presbyters are only priests in relation to the people; and likewise the laity are the laity in relation to the clergy. (*Constitutions of the Holy Apostles*, Bk. VIII, sec. I, ANF VII, p. 480)*

Baptism does not make everyone baptized a pastor or representative minister. But it does, according to Luther's interpretation of I Peter 2, make the whole believing community, in a sense, participants in the priestly role. Luther thought it highly significant that the New Testament did not normally use the Greek word for priests to designate ecclesiastical officers:

In the New Testament the Holy Spirit carefully avoids giving the name *sacerdos*, priest, to any of the apostles or to any other office. Rather He applies this name to the baptized or Christians, as their birthright and hereditary name from Baptism. For in Baptism none of us is born an apostle, preacher, teacher, pastor; but there all of us are born solely priests. Then we take some from among these born priests and call and elect them to these offices that they may discharge the duties of the offices in the name of all of us. (Luther, "Private Mass and the Consecration of Priests, 1533," WLS 3, p. 1140, WA 38, 230; cf. LW 38, p. 188)

The idea of the general priesthood of all is found not only in Protestant sources, but also in patristic writings. Peter Chrysologus (c. 400–450), Bishop of Ravenna, developed the theme that the believer is called to radical sacrifice, analogous to priestly sacrifice:

Let us now hear the contents of the Apostle's exhortation. "I exhort you to present your bodies" (Rom. 12:1). By requesting this, the Apostle has raised all men to a priestly rank. "To present your bodies as a living sacrifice." O unheard of function of the Christian priesthood, inasmuch as man is both the victim and the priest for himself! . . . Be, O man, be both a sacrifice to God and a priest. Do not lose what the divine authority gave and conceded to you. Put on the robe of sanctity, gird yourself with the belt of chastity. (Peter Chrysologus, *Sermons*, 108, FC 17, pp. 168–169)

II. ❧ REPRESENTATIVE MINISTRY

The doctrine of general ministry does not threaten or challenge ordained ministry. Nor does the fact that priesthood belongs to the whole body of Christ imply that every baptized member is called or qualified to preach or counsel:

For although we are all priests, this does not mean that all of us can preach, teach, and rule. Certain ones of the multitude must be selected and separated for such an office. . . . This is the way to distinguish between the office of preaching or the ministry, and the general priesthood of all baptized Christians. The preaching office is no more than a public service which happens to be conferred upon someone by the entire congregation, all the members of which are priests. (Luther, "Commentary on Psalm 110, 1539," LW 13, p. 332)

The priesthood of all believers does not imply that anyone can individualistically arrogate to oneself a representative ministry:

We are all priests, and there is no difference between us; that is to say, we have the same power in respect to the Word and all the sacraments. However, no one may make use of this power except by the consent of the community or by the call of a superior. For what is the common property of all, no individual may arrogate to himself, unless he be called. And therefore this sacrament of ordination, if it have any meaning at all, is nothing else than a certain rite whereby one is called to the ministry of the Church. Furthermore, the priesthood is properly nothing but the ministry of the Word, mark you, of the Word—not of the law, but of the Gospel. (Luther, *The Babylonian Captivity*, WML II, p. 283)

Not every believer is called to sacred or public ministry, because of the special requirements of the teaching office and the celebration of sacraments:

All believers are called priests. Rv 1:6. 5:10: 1 Ptr 2:9. Have all, therefore, a general call to the ministry? All we who believe are indeed spiritual priests, but we are not all teachers. . . . Yet all Christians have a general call to proclaim the virtues of God, 1 Ptr 2:9, and especially family heads to instruct their households. Dt 6:7; 1 Co 14:35. . . . But the public ministry of the Word and of the Sacraments in the church is not entrusted to all Christians in general, as we have already shown,

1 Co 12:28; Eph 4:12. For special or particular call is required for this, Ro 10:15. (Chemnitz, *MWS*, Pt. 1, sec. 9–0, p. 29)

The public ministry is a service done by some on behalf of all. It is not given to all baptized Christians, but to those who are called. One cannot arbitrarily assign it to oneself:

No sound Christian makes all equal in the administration of Word and Sacraments, not only because all things ought to be done in the church decently and in order, but also because, by the special command of Christ, Ministers are ordained for that purpose. Therefore, as a special call is required, no one who is not called may take the honour upon himself. (Calvin, Antidote to the Council of Trent, Seventh Session, Canon X, *SW*, p. 216)*

The ordained ministry is set apart on behalf of the general ministry. One had best remain in private life who does not understand this set-apartness:

Great works as ours require greater grace. . . . Do not think that a heedless, careless course will accomplish so great a work as this. You must look to come off with greater shame and deeper wounds of conscience than if you had lived a common life. . . . We have seen some private Christians of good esteem, who, having thought too highly of their parts, and thrust themselves into the ministerial office, have proved weak and empty men, and have become greater burdens to the Church than some whom we endeavoured to cast out. They might have done God more service in the higher rank of private men. . . . As you may render God more service, so you may do him more disservice than others. The nearer men stand to God, the greater dishonour God has by their miscarriages. (Baxter, *RP*, pp. 77–78)*

The pastor has a representative function on behalf of the whole church. This was vividly grasped by early pastoral writers. Ignatius thought that the feeling and willing of the congregation were being concretely embodied and symbolically expressed through its pastoral leadership:

To the holy church at Tralles. . . . I know that you have understanding which is blameless and unwavering in endurance, not habitual but innate, as Polybius your bishop informed me when he was with me at Smyrna by the will of God and Jesus Christ, and he so warmly congratulated me—a prisoner in Christ Jesus—that I saw your whole congregation in him. I received your godly love through him. . . . I have received an embodiment of your love, and have it with me, in your bishop, whose demeanor is a great lesson and whose gentleness is his power. I think that even the godless revere him. (Ignatius of Antioch, *Letter to the Trallians*, sec. 1.2, 3.2, AF, pp. 92–93)

III. ❧ The Need for an Ordered Ministry

In order to protect the flock from unscrupulous guides and false teachers, the early pastoral tradition found it necessary to develop an ordered ministry. That implies due process for selecting care-givers, and careful procedures for authorizing pastoral care in a given territory. The following selections provide a glimpse of why the ordering of ministry has been thought so important. Any individualistic view of charismatic gifts that would proceed without scripture, without historical continuity with apostolic witnesses, without community, without accountability, or without order and ordination has been repeatedly rejected.

The metaphor of the hazards of the sea voyage helped establish the point of the necessity for ordered ministry:

The church is like a great ship carrying through a violent storm those from many places, who seek to live in the city of the good kingdom. Think of God as the shipmaster. Think of Christ as the pilot. If so, then imagine that the episcopal officer is like a mate, the deacons like sailors, the teacher like a midshipman. The passengers are the laity. The world is the sea. Temptations, persecutions, and dangers toss the ship about like cyclonic winds. Afflictions come in waves. The deceivers and false prophets are like uncertain winds and squalls. The jagged rocks and promontories await like judges in high places threatening terrible sentences. There are wild places where two seas meet. These are like unreasonable schismatics who doubt of the promises of truth. One must beware of pirates, the hypocrites. . . . If you are going to sail with a fair wind so that you will reach the harbor of the hoped-for city, pray so as to be heard. But prayers become audible by good deeds. . . . Let those sailing expect every tribulation, as travelling over a great and troubled sea, the world: sometimes disheartened, persecuted, dispersed, hungry, thirsty, naked, hemmed in; and at other times united, assembled and at rest. (Clementina, *The Epistle of Clement to James*, Ch. XIV-XV, ANF VIII, pp. 220–221)*

One gets the picture of a hazardous journey through dangerous waters that requires the careful ordering of diverse tasks, rationalization of limited resources, organization of competencies and assignments. The ship in storm does not survive by laborious democratic debate, but by prompt, well-planned action under strict guidance and accountability. Thus a radically populist polity or simplistic equalitarianism where every decision is subjected to popular vote has seldom been regarded as adequate to the mission of this vessel, the church.

If everybody wanted to hear confession, to baptize, to administer the Sacrament, how unseemly that would be! Again, if everybody desired to preach, who would listen? If we were all to preach at the same time, what a confused chattering that would be, such as you now hear among frogs!

Therefore it should be thus: the congregation chooses a suitable person, who administers the Sacrament, preaches, hears confession, and baptizes. To be sure, all of us possess this power; but no one except him who is chosen by the congregation to do so should presume to practice it publicly. In private I certainly may use this power. If, for instance, my neighbor comes and says: My friend, I am burdened in conscience; speak a word of absolution to me, then I am at liberty to do so. But in private, I say, this must be done. (Luther, "Exposition on John 20:19–31, 1526," WA 10 I, pp. 2239f.; WLS 1, p. 5)

Luther assumed a pivotal distinction between public and private acts of caring witness. If public, they must be duly authorized. This is why an ordered ministry is necessary and commendable:

It is necessary, therefore, that the Church, as a city built upon a hill, have an order approved of God, and good government. In particular, let the bishop, as chief, be heard in the things which he speaks; and let the elders give heed that the things ordered be done. Let the deacons, going about, look after the bodies and the souls of the brethren, and report to the bishop. Let all the rest of the brethren bear wrong patiently; but if they wish judgment to be given concerning wrongs done to them, let them be reconciled in the presence of the elders; and let the elders report the reconciliation to the bishop. (Clementina, *Homilies*, Hom. III, ANF VIII, p. 250)

Even in the experimental left wing of the reformation among such as Anabaptists led by Menno Simons there was strong resistance to unordained persons publicly preaching and admonishing:

No one is to undertake of himself to preach or admonish from church to church unless he be sent or ordained thereto by the congregation or the elders. (Menno Simons, The Wismar Articles of 1554, *CWMS*, p. 1042)

The relation between *laos* and *cleros* properly is one of complementary harmonization, analogous to a well-practiced symphonic choir:

Therefore it is fitting for you to run your race together with the bishop's purpose—as you do. for your presbytery—worthy of fame, worthy of God—is attuned to the bishop like strings to a lyre. Therefore by your unity and harmonious love Jesus Christ is sung. Each of you must be part of this chorus so that, being harmonious in unity, receiving God's pitch in unison, you may sing with one voice through Jesus Christ to the Father, so that he may both hear you and recognize you, through what you do well, as members of his Son (Ignatius of Antioch, *Letter to Ephesians*, 4:1, AF, p. 78)

IV. ❧ SET APART

The idea that ministry is set apart does not imply that it is designated for honor, but rather for service, for representative caring, for authentically proclaiming the good news in pastoral visitation and public worship, enabling the laity better to manifest Christ's presence in the world. Christian soul care contains perplexing layers of tensions: It is *in* yet not *of* the world; it serves within in a particular time, yet points beyond that time to the source and end of history; it shares fully in the body of Christ, yet is set apart in order to more fully activate the life of the body. The pastoral tradition has tried to articulate both sides of these tensions without losing one dimension when another is stated.

Numerous passages speak of the ways in which the life of the priest is to be separated and viewed as distinguishable from the laity. To make this point, Christian teaching frequently appealed to the Old Testament priestly tradition which sharply distinguished priest and people:

The command [was] given to Moses to ascend the mountain with the priests while the people stayed behind. God first separated the priests from the people and then commanded Moses to enter the cloud.

You see, then, the separation. See how among priests one looks for nothing of a vulgar nature, nothing ordinary, nothing in common with the interests and practice and character of the undisciplined multitude. The priestly dignity demands a prudent demeanor, different from that of the crowd, a serious mode of life, an especial sense of gravity. How can the priest expect the people to honor him if he possesses no quality different from the people? Why should a man admire you if he sees his own qualities in you; if he sees nothing in you which he does not discover first in himself; if he finds in you, whom he thinks he should respect, the very thing of which he is ashamed in himself?

Let us tread beyond the opinions of the common herd, and let us avoid the thoroughfares of ordinary living, and the routes of the beaten road. (Ambrose, *Letters*, To Irenaeus, 387 A.D., FC 26, p. 455)

Just as bread and altar are set apart for special use in holy consecrations, so is priesthood set apart for representative ministry, and for holiness of heart and life:

This holy altar, where we now stand, is in itself an ordinary stone slab, in no way different from other slabs with which our walls are built and our pavements are adorned. But since it has been consecrated for the service of God, and has received the blessing, it is a holy table, an undefiled altar, no longer touched by the hands of all, but only by the priests, and by them with reverence. Again, the bread is, to begin with, common bread, but when the sacramental act has consecrated it, it is called, and becomes, the body of Christ. So with the sacramental oil, and the wine; though things of small value before the blessing, after the sanctification by the Spirit each of them has its special effectiveness. Again, the same power of the word also makest revered and honourable, separated from community with the general public by the new quality given by the blessing. Yesterday he was one of the crowd, one of the people; he is suddenly made into a leader, a president, a teacher of religion, a guide into hidden mysteries: and he performs these functions without being changed in any way in bódy or in form. (Gregory of Nyssa, LCF, pp. 161–162)

What makes the slab of stone or the piece of bread different? It is that the Spirit has been invoked by the praying community that the ordinary might be consecrated to extraordinary purpose for the service of God. So it is with the priest. Ambrose set forth the reasons why the altar was regarded as a place of refuge and sanctuary, and how this reflects the basic idea of priesthood as departure and exile from the world:

Thus I must first explain properly the fact that it was the cities of the Levites that were given for a place of refuge. However, it is clear that the provision was a fitting one, because the Levites are those fleeing from this world to please God; they leave country, parents, children, and all their kin, to cleave to God alone. Indeed, it was said also to Abraham, "Leave your own country, your kinsmen, and your father's house" (Gen. 12:1). But perhaps you may say, "He was not a Levite." But he had Levi in his loins, as we read in the Letter to the Hebrews. And the Lord speaks to the Levites when He says to His disciples, that is, to the Apostles, "If anyone wishes to be a follower of mine, he must leave self behind; he must take up his cross and follow me" (Matt. 16:24). And yet it was then said to all, "But you are a chosen race, a royal priesthood, a dedicated nation, and a people claimed by God for his own way" (1 Pet. 2:9). The fullness has come, the remnant has departed. For Christ has called all men, the way of departure is open to all, that all may follow, and there has been set before all humanity a kingdom and life everlasting.

Therefore one who has God as his portion should care for nothing except God; else he may be hindered by the duty of providing for the other's need. For the time that is given to other duties is snatched away from the cultivation of religion and this, our proper duty. For the flight of the priest is really the renunciation of family, and a kind of alienation from dear ones, so that one who longs to serve God denies himself with regard to his own. Therefore it was right that a decree of the eternal law entrusted fugitives to fugitives; thus, those who have forgotten this world may receive those who condemn their own sinful works, seek forgetfulness of their earlier life, and desire to efface the worldly deeds they have performed. Therefore the minister of God's holy altar is one who is in flight from his own. For this reason the Lord, like a chief priest, gave an example for the Levites in His Gospel, when He said, "Who is my mother? Who are my brothers?" (Matt. 12:48). This means: I do not know my mother, I do not recognize my brothers, I am unacquainted with my near ones. "My mother and my brothers— they are those who hear the word of God and act upon it" (Luke 8:21). Therefore the minister knows the word of God only when he knows those in whom the word of God is at work. And so he is an exile from the world; fleeing from the body, fleeing from the passions, he deprives himself of all men to remain alone, even as Elias said, "I alone am left" (1 Kings 19:14). But he was not alone, for he had Christ with him. (Ambrose, *Flight From the World*, sec. 2.6–2.7, FC 65, pp. 284–285, NEB)*

Ambrose, who had served high political office as governor of Milan before becoming bishop, here develops the analogy between the fugitive from law and the fugitive from the world. The priest is like the fugitive. The set apart altar receives them both. The separation of priest from family is particularly poignant, for it reveals how one may love others, yet choose a love that transcends but embraces those others.

This set-apartness rightly intensifies accountability, since it is set in public light:

It was a saying of king Alphonsus, that "a great man cannot commit a small sin"; much more we say, that a learned man, or a teacher of others, cannot commit a small sin; or, at least, that the sin is great as committed by him, which is smaller as committed by another. You are more likely than others to sin against knowledge, because you have more than they; at least, you sin against more light, or means of knowledge. . . . Your sins have more hypocrisy in them than other men's, by how much the more you have spoken against them. . . . Every child that you baptized, and every administration of the supper of the Lord, did import your own renouncing of the world and the flesh, and your engagement to Christ. (Baxter, *RP*, pp. 76–77)

V.   SACRED MINISTRY

If sacred ministry is duly called and set apart to serve the general ministry, then it becomes necessary to ask what functions clergy perform that are not assigned to laity. An early prototype of this issue occurred in the question: Shall undesignated, unordained, unauthorized persons administer baptism or the Lord's Supper or ordination? This answer even in the fourth century echoed long precedent:

Neither do we permit the laity to perform any of the offices belonging to the priesthood; as, for instance, neither the sacrifice, nor baptism, nor the laying on of hands, nor the blessing, whether the smaller or the greater: for "nobody arrogates the honour to himself; he is called by God, as indeed Aaron was" (Heb. 5:4). (*Constitutions of the Holy Apostles*, Bk. II, sec. I.10, ANF VII, p. 429)

Early pastoral apologists argued that the administration of penitence, like that of baptism and the Supper, was not assigned generally to laity, but rather to those who are called to this duty. To the whole church the commandment is given to "judge not, lest you be judged" (Matt. 7:1), to be merciful amid our own need for mercy. But the special command is given to those set apart for shepherding to try to make good judgments about the care of the souls entrusted to them:

If you [as lay persons] judge your brother, you become a judge without being constituted such by anybody. For the priests only are entrusted with the power of judging, since it was to them that it is said, "judge fairly" (Deut. 1:16); and "dispense true justice" (Deut. 16:18); and again, "administer true justice" (Zech. 7:9). But to laity this is not entrusted. On the contrary it is said to those who are not magistrates or ministers: "Pass no judgement, and you will not be judged" (Luke 6:37). (*Constitutions of the Holy Apostles*, Bk. II, sec. V, ANF VII, p. 413)*

Rigorous behavioral expectations are applied to those who have been, in the mind of the church, set apart for sacred ministry. Consistency, empathy, even-handedness, and a steady temper are required for soul care:

The priestly virtue is of no ordinary kind, for he has to beware of taking part not only in more serious faults, but even in the least. He must be prompt to show mercy, not regret a promise, recall the fallen, have sympathy with pain, preserve meekness, love piety, repel or quell anger; let him be like a trumpet urging the people to devotion, and bring them to tranquility.

The old saying is: "Accustom yourself to being consistent, so that your life will set forth as it were a picture, always preserving the same likeness which it received." How can he be consistent who is at one time aflame with anger, at another seething with fierce indignation, now with face aglow, now changed to paleness, varying and changing color every moment? But, granted that it is natural to be angry, or that there generally is good reason therefore, it is one's duty to temper wrath; not to be carried away with the fury of a lion, not knowing how to be gentle; not spreading tales, nor eliciting family quarrels, for it is written; "A passionate man diggeth up sin" (Prov. 16:27). (Ambrose, *Letters*, To Priests, FC 26, p. 343)*

Ambrose appeals for excellent behaviors among those who hold the priestly office, behaviors such as mercy, encouragement, and gentleness. Does this imply a different moral standard for clergy than for laity? Any moral instruction which is given to the whole church, one expects the clergy to follow, Tertullian argued:

> Now listen to the subtle reasoning of our opponents. They say that the Apostle's permission to remarry is so general that he binds none but clerics to the obligation of monogamy. . . . Whence do we take our bishops and clergy? Is it not from among all of us? . . . The question under consideration concerned the qualities required in men who were to receive orders in the church. It was necessary, then, that the law which was meant for all should be shown forth in the persons of those who stand in the forefront of the Church so that in this way the binding force of the edict would, in some measure, be impressed upon all and so that the members of the laity might understand the better their own obligation to follow a way of life which conditions men for leadership; and the men in Orders were themselves not to beguile themselves into the belief that they were permitted to do as they pleased, as though by some special privilege of their position. (Tertullian, *On Monogamy*, sec. 12, ACW 13, p. 98)

There is not one standard for clergy and another for laity, but rather the clergy are merely asked to practice what they preach, to hold to the morality they proclaim, so that they will not be a scandal to the rest of the community seeking to embody the same moral claims. The rigor of life under orders does not imply a different morality than for laity, but it does seek to manifest a leadership style, and to prevent priests from thinking they can do as they please, as if the office itself granted license.

VI. ❧ PRIESTLY CARE

Our subject is pastoral care, but a significant part of that subject focuses on intercession, representative prayer for the whole community, liturgical action, and sacrificial action on behalf of the community. Early Christian pastoral writers appealed to the Jewish tradition of priesthood, interpreted in the light of Christ's priesthood. With few exceptions, priesthood remains in most pastoral writings an essential dimension of pastoral care.

Calvin provided a centrist Protestant definition of ministry as priesthood:

> What of the priesthood?
> It is the office and prerogative of appearing in the presence of God to obtain grace, and of appeasing his wrath by the offering of a sacri-

fice which is acceptable to him. . . . To what is the office of priest conducive?

First, by means of it he is the mediator who reconciles us to the Father; and, secondly, access is given us to the Father, so that we too can come with boldness into his presence, and offer him the sacrifice of ourselves, and our all. In this way he makes us, as it were, his colleagues in the priesthood. (Calvin, Catechism of the Church of Geneva, *SW*, p. 253)

The Greek word *presbuteros*, usually translated elder, is the root word of our English word "priest." It has had a somewhat confusing history, which Anglican Joseph Mede tried to sort out:

If it be well examined, "Priest" is the English of "Presbyter" and not of "Sacerdos," there being in our tongue no word in use for Sacerdos—"Priest," which we use for both, being improperly used for a Sacrificer, but naturally expressing a Presbyter, the name whereby the Apostles call both themselves and those which succeed them in their charge. For who can deny that our word Priest is corrupted of Presbyter? Our ancestors the Saxons first used Preoster, whence, by a farther contraction, came Preste and Priest. The High and Low Dutch have Priester, the French Prestre, the Italian Prete; but the Spaniard only speaks full Presbytero. (Joseph Mede, Diatribae, Bk. I, No. 5, on I Cor. 4:1; *Angl.*, p. 370)

The central priestly act—intercession—has far-reaching pastoral implications. It is a bold act of standing before God and by due consecration representing others. The intercessor receives authority to be representative through God's own calling and by due process of ordination. In doing so, the intercessor represents both the community of believers and the world. John Chrysostom stated this audacious point succinctly:

What sort of man ought someone to be, who is an ambassador for a whole city—no, not just a city: the whole world—and begs God to be merciful to the sins of all men, not only the living, but the departed too? I do not think that even the confidence of a Moses or Elijah is adequate for this great intercession. He approaches God as if he were responsible for the whole world, and himself the father of all men, praying that wars everywhere may end and tumults cease, supplicating for peace and prosperity, and a speedy release from all ills, peace and prosperity, and a speedy release from all ills, private or public, that threaten any man. (John Chrysostom, *On the Priesthood*, Ch. VI, sec. 4, p. 140)

Thomas Aquinas described this priestly, intercessory service in this way:

The priest is appointed mediator and stands, so to speak, between the people and God, as we read of Moses (Deut. 5:5), wherefore it belongs to him to set forth the Divine teachings and sacraments before the people; and besides to offer to the Lord things appertaining to the people, their prayers, for instance, their sacrifices and oblations. Thus the Apostle says (Heb. 5:1): "For every High Priest is taken from among men and appointed their representative before God, to offer gifts and sacrifices for sins." (Thomas Aquinas, *Summa Theologica*, II-II, Q. 86, Art. 2, Vol. II, p. 1559)

Most pastoral writers viewed the priestly office as divinely instituted, an expression of God's own intention and plan for the salvation of humanity, and therefore not finally explainable by social custom or historical accident:

The office of the priesthood is performed on earth, but it ranks among the heavenly things. And with good reason; for this ministry was set up not by an angel, or an archangel, or by any created power, but by the Paraclete himself. (John Chrysostom, LCF, p. 175)

There is a fourfold sense in which representative ministry is like salt, according to Alan of Lille:

To priests the Lord says: "You are the salt of the earth. If the salt loses it savor, how shall it be seasoned?" (Mt. 5:13). Salt has four properties: it makes the ground infertile; it flavors food; it protects meat from decay, and it keeps worms out of meat. These four come together in the spiritual salt, that is, in the priest, who should plough the earth of his people—that is, plough up their earthly thoughts with the ploughshare of his preaching—lest they sprout the thorns and thistles of the vices, and thus he should make the land infertile for evil works. His own land, that is, his own flesh, he is bound to make infertile to the vices and he must preserve his flesh from decay, that is, keep it free of dissipation and gluttony. . . . The salt of priesthood becomes tasteless in three ways: through ignorance, through negligence, through greed. . . . When the leaders have no-one above themselves to correct them, and those who are more prudent have no-one to instruct them, they are made tasteless through neglectfulness, for negligence produces indifference in all their works, and destroys the fruit of their works. There is no devotion in their psalms, no thoughtfulness in their reading, in their exhortations to penitence no diligence, no care in celebrating Mass; in their direction of their flocks no discretion; in their good words no effort. (Alan of Lille, *The Art of Preaching*, Ch. xliv, CFS 23, pp. 160–162)

Chrysostom, who praised and exalted the dignity of the office of priesthood as much as any writer of the pastoral tradition, thought that the influence of the priest, properly understood, was analogous to parental influence, and in its own distinctive way potentially greater than parental influence:

God has given greater power to priests than to natural parents, not only for punishment, but also for help. The difference between the two is as great as between the present and the future life. Parents bring us into this life; priests into the life to come. Parents cannot avert bodily death nor drive away the onset of disease; priests have often saved the soul that is sick and at the point of death, by making the punishment milder for some, and preventing others from ever incurring it, not only through instruction and warning, but also through helping them by prayer. (John Chrysostom, *On the Priesthood*, Ch. III, sec. 6, p. 74)

As one does not become a citizen by being elected judge, so one does not become a baptized Christian by being elected a priest. Before being a judge, one must already be a citizen; and so before becoming a priest, it is assumed that one is already a baptized believer, hence a member of the royal priesthood, the body of Christ.

The priestly office . . . . is the common property of all Christians. However, we deal with a different matter when we speak of those who have an office in the Christian Church, such as minister, preacher, pastor, or curate. These are not priests in the sense that Scripture commonly speaks of priests. They became priests before they received their office, in fact, when they were baptized. Hence they are not priests because of their calling or office. The Scripture calls them "servants" or "bishops," that is, overseers; the apostles speak of them as presbyters, that is, elders. The best, the most mature men, well-tried, learned, fit, and experienced, were chosen for this office. This is the reason why the term "presbyter" was used, for it means the same as "an old man." It is certainly fitting to choose such men for any administrative duty; in fact, Scripture commends this. Such people are to be chosen by the church only for the sake of the office. They are to be separated from the common mass of Christians in the same way as in secular government, where certain people of the citizenry or municipality are chosen and appointed as officials. One does not become a citizen by being elected burgomaster or judge, but one is elected to the office because one already possesses citizenship and is a member of the citizenry. (Luther, "Commentary on Psalm 110, 1539," LW 13, p. 331)

Although Luther's view cannot be claimed as one that would gain universal consent among pastoral writers, it is a view held by many. Luther argued that priesthood is given to the whole community of those who live in Christ, and among them are *presbuteroi* duly chosen to represent and embody that general ministry. If all Christians are priests, then would it not also be correct to say that all are also pastors? Luther strongly argued that although all baptized believers are in the general sense priests, not all can or should be pastors:

It does not help their case to say that all Christians are priests. It is true that all Christians are priests, but not all are pastors. For to be pastor one not only must be a Christian and a priest but must have an office and a field of work committed to him. This call and command make pastors and preachers. (Luther, "Exposition on Psalm 82, 1530," WA 3 I, p. 211; WLS 3, p. 1131)

VII. 🙠 PRIESTLY SACRIFICE UNDER THE OLD AND NEW COVENANT

The early Christian reconceptualization of priesthood emerged in constant dialogue with and dependence upon the Jewish priestly tradition. The pastoral writers took considerable pains to show that Christian pastoral care is both like and unlike the levitical priesthood:

You bishops are to your people priests and Levites, ministering to the holy tabernacle, the holy Catholic Church. For you stand at the altar of the Lord your God, and offer to Him reasonable and unbloody sacrifices through Jesus the great High Priest. You are to the laity prophets, rulers, governors, and kings, as mediators between God and His faithful people, who receive and declare His word, well acquainted with the Scriptures. You are the voice of God, and witnesses of His will who bears the sins of all. You intercede for all. If you hide the key of knowledge from those in your charge or fail to declare his word, you know very well that the word severely judges you, and you are liable to severe judgment. . . . As you are patterns for others, so have you Christ for your pattern. As He is concerned for all, so shall you be for the laity with whose care you are charged. (*Constitutions of the Holy Apostles*, Bk. II, sec. IV, ANF VII, p. 409)*

Since sacrifice was crucial to the Jewish idea of priesthood, the question arose early and was often debated as to whether or in what sense Christ and Christian priests offer sacrifice.

If the priesthood established by the law has come to an end, and the priest who is "in the order of Melchizedek" (Heb. 5:6) has offered his sacrifice, and has made all other sacrifices unnecessary, why do the priests of the new covenant perform the mystical liturgy? Now it is clear to those instructed in divinity that we do not offer another sacrifice, but perform a memorial of that unique and saving offering. For this was the Lord's own command: "Do this in remembrance of me"

(1 Cor. 11:26). So that by contemplation we may recall what is symbolized, the sufferings endured on our behalf, and may kindle our love towards our benefactor, and look forward to the enjoyment of the blessings to come. (Theodoret of Cyrus, LCF, pp. 276–277)

Christian priesthood is not fundamentally to be sought and acquired, but received subject to call:

Christ was to be the type of all priests. He took flesh, so that "in the days of his earthly life he offered up prayers and petitions, with loud cries and tears, to God who was able to deliver him from the grave. Because of his humble submission his prayer was heard: son though he was, he learned obedience in the school of suffering, and, once perfected, became the source of eternal salvation for all who obey him, named by God high priest in the succession of Melchizedek" (Heb. 5:7–10). At last, when His sufferings were completed, as though completed Himself, he gave health to all, He bore the sin of all.

So He Himself also chose Aaron as priest, in order that not man's will but the grace of God should have chief place in the election of a priest, not the voluntary offering of himself, nor the taking of it upon himself, but the heavenly call; thus he may offer gifts for sins who can compassionate sinners, since He Himself, he says, bears our weakness. No one ought take the honor to himself, but be called by God, as was Aaron. Thus, even Christ did not demand but received the priesthood. (Ambrose, *Letters*, FC 26, p. 338, NEB)*

The good priest seeks to embody a credible pattern or picture of trust in providence and holy love that could plausibly inspire others to holiness and love. This becomes especially credible when the laity behold the priestly servant amid suffering and danger where self-sacrificial acts are costly:

The Prophet David bids us be imitators of holy Aaron, for he set him among the saints of the Lord to be imitated by us, saying: "Moses and Aaron are among his priests, and Samuel among them who call upon his name" (Ps. 99:6). Plainly he is a man worthy of being set before all to be followed, for, when plague spread among the people because of stubborn persons, he offered himself between the living and dead so that he might restrain the plague and that no more persons should perish. Truly is he a man of priestly mind and spirit who with dutiful affection, like a good shepherd, offered himself for the flock of the Lord. Thus he broke the sting of death, checked its onslaught, refused it further course. Love assisted his merits, for he offered himself in behalf of those who were resisting him. (Ambrose, *Letters*, FC 26, p. 339)

Levitical priesthood is distinguishable from the Christ's priesthood as promise from fulfillment, as law from gospel:

The priests of the Law and the sanctuaries of the Law have gone. Let us draw near our new High Priest, to the throne of grace, the Guest of our souls, the Priest, made not according to the law of the carnal commandment, but chosen by the power [of the command] which cannot end. He did not take the honor to Himself, but He was chosen by the Father, as the Father Himself says: "Thou art a priest forever, in the succession of Melchizedek" (Ps. 110.4; Heb. 7.17). We see what the new Priest has offered. Other priests make offerings for themselves and their people. This one, having no sin of His own for which He should make offerings, offered Himself for the world and by His own Blood entered the Holy of Holies. He, then, is the new Priest and the new Victim, not of the Law but above it, the Advocate of the world, the Light of time, who said: "Behold I come, and he came." (Apoc. 32.7). Let us approach Him to adore Him in the fullness of faith and to hope in Him whom we do not see with our eyes, but whom we have in our heart. (Ambrose, *Letters*, 50, To Horontianus, FC 26, pp. 271–272, NEB)*

If ancient levitical sacrifice is no longer central to the definition of priesthood in the Christian tradition, then in what sense is sharing in Christ's ministry thought to be a priesthood?

Seeing then that sacrifice is now no part of the church's ministry, how should the name of priesthood be rightly applied to it? . . . The fathers of the Church of Christ with firm language usually call the ministry of the gospel priesthood in regard to that which in the gospel is proportionable to ancient sacrifices, namely the communion of the blessed Body and Blood of Christ, even though that is not now properly spoken of as a sacrifice. But when people now hear the term "priest," it does not any longer draw their minds to any thought of sacrifice, any more than the name of a senator or of an alderman causes them to think of old age or to imagine that every one so termed must necessarily be ancient because years were originally a criterion in the nomination of senators and aldermen.

Therefore with respect to being named, let them use what dialect they will, whether we call it a priesthood, a presbytership, or a ministry it makes little difference, although in truth the word presbyter does seem more fit, and a form of speech more agreeable than priest with the drift of the whole gospel of Jesus Christ. . . . What better title could there be given them than the revered name of presbyters or fatherly guides? The Holy Spirit does not anywhere in the body of the New Testament call them priests, even though much mention is made of them. (Richard Hooker, The Laws of Ecclesiastical Polity, Bk. V, Ch. lxxiii, sec. 2, 3; cf. *Angl.*, p. 369)*

It was early decided in canon law that Christian priesthood should not be thought of as restricted to those of priestly descent:

Since we know that, in the region of the Armenians, only those are appointed to the clerical orders who are of priestly descent (following in this Jewish customs); and some of those who are even untonsured are appointed to succeed cantors and readers of the divine law, we decree that henceforth it shall not be lawful for those who wish to bring any one into the clergy, to pay regard to the descent of him who is to be ordained; but let them examine whether they are worthy (according to the decrees set forth in the holy canons) to be placed on the list of the clergy, so that they may be ecclesiastically promoted, whether they are of priestly descent or not. (Quinisext Synod, A.D. 692, Canon XXXIII, The Seven Ecumenical Councils, NPNF 2nd, Vol. XIX, p. 381)

According to Hebraic tradition, priestly duty is wholly distinctive and unlike other duties:

We know that the Levites are not reckoned among the rest, but are preferred before all, for they are chosen out of all, and are sanctified like the firstfruits and the firstlings which belong to the Lord, since the payment of vows and redemption for sin are offered by them. "You shall not record the total number of the Levites or make a detailed list of them among the Israelites. You shall put the Levites in charge of the Tabernacle of the Tokens, with its equipment and everything in it. They shall carry the Tabernacle and all its equipment; they alone shall be its attendants and shall pitch their tents round it" (Num. 1:49–51). . . . Good Levites have ever preserved the mystery entrusted to them. (Ambrose, *Duties of Clergy*, Book I, sec. 259–260, NPNF 2nd, X, p. 42, NEB)*

Christian ministry is united in Christ's ministry. Luther, battling what he regarded as extreme abuses of the priesthood, argued that there is only one priest, Jesus Christ, and that the term for levitical-sacrificial priesthood in Greek, *hiereus*, is not characteristically used in the New Testament to describe the apostolic ministry:

The Christian Church knows of, and believes in, only one sacrifice whereby the sin of the world was put away and paid for. Just so it also knows and believes that there is only one Priest, the Son of the eternal God, born of Mary, Christ Jesus. God's Word directs to this faith. For the name "priest" (in Greek *hiereus*, a man so called because of the sacrifice he offers officially) is not applied to any man in the New Testament but only to the one, true Priest, Jesus Christ. Ministers of the church, on the other hand, have different names and are called apostles, evangelists, bishops, presbyters, shepherds, etc. Such names they bear, not because of any sacrificing but because of their preaching and other services which must be continued in the church. (Luther, Sermon on John 1, WA 52, 567; in WLS 3, p. 1142)

VIII. Charismata

Ministry itself is a gift (*charisma*) of the Spirit. The relationship of care of souls to special gifts has been variously treated by pastoral writers of differing traditions and centuries. Although there remain significant differences of opinion, particularly within Protestantism, concerning the meaning, diversity, and authority of charismatic gifts, there is generally a broad consensus on the assumption that ministry is recipient of gifts of the Spirit.

The discussion of gifts of the Spirit is complicated by several layers of issues: Are gifts given to the general ministry or to the sacred ministry? Are different gifts given to various levels of ministry? Were some gifts given only for the apostolic age, and not for subsequent ages? Once given, do the gifts remain? How is *glossolalia*, the gift of ecstatic utterance, to be understood? How are special gifts to be tested?

We begin with a passage in the *Didache* on testing special claims of charismatic gifts. If they show evidence of egocentric motivations under the guise of religious fervor, they are to be rejected:

> While a charismatist is uttering words in a trance, you are on no account to subject him to any tests or verifications; "every sin shall be forgiven, but this sin shall not be forgiven." Nevertheless, not all who speak in trances are charismatists, unless they also exhibit the manners and conduct of the Lord. It is by their behaviour that you can tell the imposter from the true. . . . If any charismatist, speaking in a trance, says, "Give me money (or anything else)," do not listen to him. On the other hand, if he bids you give it to someone else who is in need, nobody should criticize him. Everyone who comes "in the Name of the Lord" is to be made welcome, though later on you must test him and find out about him. You will be able to distinguish the true from the false. (*Didache*, sec. 11, ECW, p. 233)

This reasonable test can be applied to any alleged charismatic gift: Is it being applied for one's own or others' benefit?

The ordination and empowering to ministry is itself thought to be a *charisma*, a gift of the Spirit, which continues once given:

> Now, besides that the power and authority delivered with those words is itself *charisma*, a gracious donation which the Spirit of God bestows, we may most assuredly persuade ourselves that the hand which imposes upon us the function of our ministry does under the same form

of words so tie itself thereunto, that one who receives the burden is thereby forever warranted to have the Spirit with him and in him for his assistance, aid, countenance and support in whatever he faithfully does to discharge duty. (Richard Hooker, Laws, Bk. V, Ch. xxvii, 1ff., Works, II, pp. 455f.; *Angl.*, p. 346)*

Early in the tradition, some claimed the ecstatic gift of being able to "see" into the soul. Tertullian gives the impression that such reports were taken seriously and studied, perhaps something like reports of parapsychological phenomena might be studied today:

There is among us a sister who has been favored with wonderful gifts of revelation which she experiences in an ecstasy of the spirit during the sacred ceremonies on the Lord's day. She converses with the angels and, sometimes, with the Lord Himself. She perceives hidden mysteries and has the power of reading the hearts of men and of prescribing remedies for such as need them. In the course of the services, she finds the matter of her visions in the Scripture lessons, the psalms, the sermon, or the prayers. One time I happened to be preaching about the soul when she became rapt in ecstasy. After the services were over and the laity had left, we asked her as is our custom, what visions she had had. (All her visions are carefully written down for purposes of examination.) "Among other things," she reported, "I have seen a soul in bodily shape and a spirit appeared to me, not an empty and flimsy thing, but an object which could be taken in the hands, soft and light and of an ethereal color, and in shape altogether like a human being. That was my vision." (Tertullian, *On the Soul*, Ch. 9, sec. 4, FC 10, p. 197)

Similarly studies of paranormal phenomena today concern auras, psychic coloration, trance states in which "revelations" occur, psychic diagnosis, out of body experiences, etc. It is noteworthy that such reports were being written down, and presumably collected and studied, seventeen hundred years before the modern study of parapsychology began.

The Anglican Articles forbade public prayer in a tongue not understood by the people:

It is a thing plainly repugnant to the word of God, and the custom of the Primitive church, to have public Prayer in the church, or to minister the sacraments, in a tongue not understanded of the people. (Thirty-nine Articles, Art. xxiv, *CC*, p. 274)

The Apostolic Constitutions argued that the spiritual gifts were not limited to the apostolic age, but continue to be given as the Spirit wills, not with wooden uniformity or predictability, in succeeding generations of belief:

"Now these signs shall follow them that have believed in my name: they shall cast out devils; they shall speak with new tongues; they shall take up serpents; and if they drink any deadly thing, it shall by no means hurt them: they shall lay their hands on the sick, and they shall recover." (Mark 16:17,18). These gifts were first bestowed on us the apostles when we were about to preach the Gospel to every creature, and afterwards were of necessity afforded to those who had by our means believed. They were not intended for the advantage of those who perform them, but for the conviction of the unbelievers, that those whom the word did not persuade, the power of signs might put to shame. For signs are not for us who believe, but for the unbelievers, both for the Jews and Gentiles. . . . It is not therefore necessary that every one of the faithful should cast out demons, or raise the dead, or speak with tongues; but such a one only who is vouchsafed this gift. (*Constitutions of the Holy Apostles*, Bk. VIII, sec. I.1, ANF VII, p. 479)*

Those claiming the gift of prophecy must be tested as to whether their prophetic understanding is consonant with previous prophetic tradition:

Without a doubt the prophets studied Moses; the later prophets studied the former ones and recorded their good thoughts, inspired by the Holy Spirit, in a book. For they were not people like the spirits and sectarians, who have flung Moses aside, devised their own visions, and preached their own dreams. (Luther, "Annotations on the Penteteuch, 1543," WA 54, pp. 3f.; WLS 3, p. 1145)

The selections in Part Four distinguish between the general ministry of the laity and the sacred ministry of word, sacrament, and order. Sacred ministry is best affirmed in such a way that the ministry of the laity is not denied but enabled. Every baptized believer is gifted in some way for the ministry of the whole church, a ministry which the set-apart ministry is seeking to equip and enable. Public acts of representative ministry must be rightly ordered, duly authorized, and decently enacted. The priestly act of intercession reflects Christ's own prototypical intercession for the church. Levitical priesthood is distinguishable from Christ's priesthood as promise from fulfillment, law from gospel.

5 Ordination

EACH STEP THUS FAR TAKEN in clarifying the pastoral office leads toward the moment of public confirmation of the call to pastoral service in the rite of ordination. The earnest candidate for ministry will engage in searching self-examination, study of the church's ordinal prayers, and classical ordinal admonitions.

I. ❧ AVOIDING UNFIT OR PREMATURE ORDINATIONS

It is the responsibility of both the ordinand and those who ordain to proceed with caution toward the rite of ordination. The crucial injunction to "not be over-hasty in laying on hands" comes from First Timothy:

> Listen to what St. Paul says to his disciple Timothy, his true and beloved child: "Do not be over-hasty in laying on hands in ordination, or you may find yourself responsible for other people's misdeeds" (1 Tim. 5:22). . . . It will not help those who appoint a man to say that they did not know the man they appointed. The fault is all the greater because they promoted someone they did not know. What seems to be an excuse actually increases their guilt. Is it not peculiar that, when people want to acquire a servant, they . . . make inquiries of neighbours, and after all this still lack confidence, and demand a long trial period; yet when they are going to admit a man to this great ministry, they make a careless and random choice without further examination, if someone or other sees fit to vouch for him, to please or spite other people?
>
> Who then will intercede for us at the hour when those who should stand up for us themselves need others to stand up for them? Certainly anyone who is going to confer an appointment should make a careful inquiry; but the one who is to be appointed should be more careful still. (John Chrysostom, *On the Priesthood*, Ch. IV, sec. 1, pp. 110–111, NEB)*

Ill-prepared ordinations may jeopardize the health of the Christian community. This is why the advice and consent asked of all relevant parties in ordination is taken so gravely:

If anyone gives to a man who wants to ruin the church the power to
do so, he will himself be to blame for the outrages of his nominee. . . .
Why is it that when a decision has to do with war or commerce or
farming or other worldly business, a farmer would never agree to sail,
nor a soldier to plough, nor a skipper to lead an army, even if he were
threatened with all kinds of death? Obviously because each one of them
foresees the danger of inexperience. (John Chrysostom, *On the Priesthood*, Ch. IV, sec. 2, pp. 111–112)

Classic pastoral writers often spoke of the direct link between disorder in the
church and disorder in the ministry:

Tell me, where do you think all the disorders in the churches origi-
nate? I think their only origin is in the careless and random way in
which the prelates are chosen and appointed. (John Chrysostom, *On the
Priesthood*, Ch. III, sec.10, p. 79)

Recommendations by elders of ordinands for lifetime pastoral service is not to
taken lightly, as if it were primarily a popularity contest or political campaign.
Those who recommend an unfit person for ministry bear responsibility for
subsequent undesired consequences:

[Pastors must take care] in the testimonials they sign in favour of
those that come to be ordained. Many have confessed to me that they
had signed these upon general reports or urgent requests, though the
testimonial assumes personal knowledge. . . . A Bishop must depend
upon them; for he has no other way to be certainly informed: and
therefore as it is a lie, passed with the solemnity of hand and seal, to
affirm any thing that is beyond one's own knowledge, so it is a lie made
to God and the Church; since the design of it is to procure Orders. So
that if a Bishop trusting to that, and being satisfied of the knowledge
of one that brings it, ordains an unfit and unworthy one, they that
signed it, are deeply and chiefly involved in the guilt of his laying hands
suddenly upon him: therefore every Priest ought to charge his conscience in a deep particular manner, that so he may never testify for
any one, unless he knows his life to be so regular, and believes his
temper to be so good, that he does really judge him a person fit to be
put in Holy Orders. (Burnet, *Of the Pastoral Care*, Ch. VIII, *SC*, p. 104)*

Not all ordinations are in the deepest sense valid, if unfit candidates are un-
wisely recommended and ordained. Some ordinations are indeed regrettable:

Marcian had promoted to the rank of presbyter a converted Jew
named Sabbatius, who nevertheless continued to retain many of his
Jewish prejudices; and moreover he was very ambitious of being made
a bishop. . . . Under pretext of more ascetic austerity, he privately
withdrew from the church, saying that "he was grieved on account of

certain persons whom he suspected of being unworthy of participation in the sacrament." It was however soon discovered that his object was to hold assemblies apart. When Marcian understood this, he bitterly censured his own error, in ordaining to the presbyterate persons so intent on vain-glory; and frequently said, "That it had been better for him to have laid his hands on thorns, than to have imposed them on Sabbatius." (Socrates Scholasticus, *Ecclesiastical History*, Bk. V, Ch. XXI, NPNF 2, II, p. 129)

Here is a case in point of an unwise ordination, and how it was dealt with by Augustine:

Timotheus was ordained a subdeacon at Subsana against my advice and desire, at the time when the decision of his case was still pending as the subject of deliberation and conference between us. Behold me still grieving over this, although he has now returned to you; and we do not regret that in our consenting to his return we obeyed your will.

May it please you to hear how, by rebuke, admonition, and prayer, we had even before he went away from this place, corrected the wrong which had been done, lest it should appear to you that up to that time nothing had been corrected by us because he had not returned to you. By rebuke, addressing ourselves first to Timotheus himself, because he did not obey you, but went away to your Holiness without consulting our brother Carcedonius, to which act of his the origin of this affliction is to be traced; and afterwards censuring the presbyter (Carcedonius) and Verinus, through whom we found that the ordination of Timotheus had been managed. When all of these admitted, under our rebuke, that in all the things alleged they had done wrong and begged forgiveness, we would have acted with undue haughtiness if we had refused to believe that they were sufficiently corrected. For they could not make that to be not done which had been done, and we by our rebuke were not expecting or desiring to do more than bring them to acknowledge their faults, and grieve over them. By admonition: first, in warning all never to dare again to do such things, lest they should incur God's wrath; and then especially charging Timotheus, who said that he was bound only by his oath to go to your Grace, that if your Holiness, considering all that we had spoken together on the matter, should, as we hoped might be the case, decide not to have him with you, out of regard for the weak for whom Christ died, who might be offended, and for the discipline of the Church, which it is perilous to disregard. . . . By prayer, moreover, we had laboured to correct ourselves commending both the guidance and the issues of our counsels to the mercy of God, and seeking that if any sinful anger had wounded us, we might be cured by taking refuge under His healing right hand.

Behold how much we had corrected by rebuke, admonition, and prayer! (Augustine, *Letters*, Letter to Severus, LXIII, NPNF 1, I, p. 320)

Some pastoral writers were realistic enough to recognize and acknowledge that political partisanship may inordinately influence certain ordinations. John Chrysostom felt this problem keenly in the fourth century:

One man says, "Reject him, because he is young"; another says, "Because he has not learnt how to flatter," another, "Because he has offended so-and-so." Or again, someone says, "Reject him in case so-and-so should be hurt to see his own nominee rejected and this man appointed"; another says, "Reject him because he is good and just"; another, "Because sinners fear him"; and another gives some other such reason. They have ready to hand all the pretexts they require. Even the number of existing clergy is sufficient argument, when they have no better. (John Chrysostom, *On the Priesthood*, Ch. III, sec. 15, p. 92)

Vows once taken must not be taken lightly and later disavowed:

Happy are those who have the faithful fulfillment of an agreement as a trait of character, and no tendency to lie. It is clearly better not to promise than to withhold what was pledged. By not promising a man may be branded as stingy, but he is not burdened with the sin of guileful circumvention. . . . The charm of a preferred gift is lost when the receiver must ask for it over and over again. The man who must reluctantly give what he promised really offered nothing by his promises. We read in scripture: "When you make a vow to the Lord your God, do not put off its fulfillment; otherwise the Lord your God will require satisfaction of you and you will be guilty of sin. If you choose not to make a vow, you will not be guilty of sin; but if you voluntarily make a vow to the Lord your God, mind what you say and do what you have promised" (Deut. 23:21–13). Therefore, dearly beloved, I warn anyone who knows he has vowed a gift to the Lord to fulfill it promptly. If anyone is not certainly able to pay a vow, let him not make it. (Valerian, *Homilies*, Hom. 4, secs. 4–5, FC 17, pp. 323–324, NEB)*

II. ❧ The Ordinal Examination

Orthodox, Catholic and Protestant traditions have all given considerable attention to examination for ordination preparatory to due authorization to care for souls. Although these examinations have differed in content and approach, in all traditions it has been considered important that candidates be meaningfully and rigorously examined. Here is a Protestant view of the ordinal examination:

The examination contains two parts, of which the first concerns doctrine—to ascertain whether the candidate for ordination has a good and holy knowledge of Scripture; and also whether he be a fit and proper person to communicate it edifyingly to the people.

Further to avoid all danger of the candidate holding some false opinion, it will be good that he profess his acceptance and maintenance of the doctrine approved by the Church.

To know whether he is fit to instruct it would be necessary to proceed by interrogation and by hearing him discuss in private the doctrine of the Lord.

The second part concerns life, to ascertain whether he is of good habits and conducts himself always without reproach. The rule of procedure in this matter which it is needful to follow is very well indicated by Paul. (Calvin, *Draft Ecclesiastical Ordinances*, LCC XXII, p. 59)

Clement of Alexandria thought that a reasonable level of discernment was required for soul care, and had to be assessed by those examining candidates for ministry:

To those, then, who are not gifted with the power of discernment, and are not inclined to knowledge, the word is not entrusted. Otherwise it would be like the ravens who imitate human voices, yet have not the slightest understanding of what they say. (Clement of Alexandria, *The Stromata, or Miscellanies*, Bk. VI, Ch. XII, ANF II, p. 516)*

Admittedly, the calling, examining, and selection process for pastoral service does not always work with perfect fairness. Some have been left out that should have been included:

Some are enlisted in the ranks of the clergy to prevent their siding with the enemy, and others because of their bad character, to stop them causing a lot of trouble if they are overlooked! . . . They not merely choose the unworthy; they reject those who are suitable. . . . For I think it is as bad to keep out the capable as to bring in the useless. (John Chrysostom, *On the Priesthood*, Ch. III, sec. 15, pp. 90–91)

Careful, sensitive, and compassionate inquiry into the life commitments, behavioral patterns, and beliefs of the ordinand is clearly pertinent to the ordination process. There can be no appeals to absolute privacy if the behavior and integrity of the pastor is a central part of the assessment of competency for pastoral service.

Let examination also be made whether he be unblameable as to the concerns of this life; for it is written: "Search diligently for all the faults of him who is to be ordained for the priesthood." (*Constitutions of the Holy Apostles*, Bk. II, Sec. I, Ch. ii, ANF VII, p. 397)

These age restrictions were set for clergy in the seventh century:

Let the canon of our holy God-bearing Fathers be confirmed in this particular also; that a presbyter be not ordained before he is thirty years of age, even if he be a very worthy man, but let him be kept back. For our Lord Jesus Christ was baptized and began to teach when he was thirty. In like manner let no deacon be ordained before he is twenty-five, nor a deaconess before she is forty. (Quinisext Synod, A.D. 692, Canon XIV, The Seven Ecumenical Councils, NPNF 2, XIX, p. 372)

III. 🙌 BEHAVIORAL EXCELLENCES OF ORDINANDS

The ordinal examination attempts to assess not only doctrinal adequacy, but sufficiency of development of personal, interpersonal, and behavioral qualities required for the care of souls. Given the importance of the office of pastor, it is appropriate that the Christian community seek out leadership fit for ministry among those especially well-suited temperamentally for it, who show early evidence of high aptitudes for care of souls. A profile of desired behaviors of ordinands has often been implicitly assumed and from time to time has become explicitly stated. Several different types of profiles and perspectives have developed over twenty centuries. Luther summarized these excellences in this way:

To begin with, he must be apt to teach; he should have a good head; be eloquent; should have a good voice; a good memory; should know how to stop; should be industrious in his work; should hazard life and limb in his work; should let himself be plagued by everybody. Finally, he should patiently bear the fact that nothing is seen more easily and quickly in preachers than their faults. (Luther, *Table Talk*, W-T 2, #2580; WLS 3, #3545, pp. 1109–1110)

Knowing "how to stop" is no easy thing for those who are vocationally drawn to the sound of language. A striking point in Luther's list is the vulnerability assumed in the willingness to "let oneself be plagued by everybody." This assumes a capacity to listen, become involved, be accessible, and be addressed by pain— not everyone has this capacity, a crucial pastoral quality. Assessment of character traits, such as the tendency to avarice, thus may become an important function of ordinal examination.

You are to ordain bishops worthy of the Lord, and presbyters and deacons who are prayerful, righteous, meek, free from the love of money, lovers of truth, approved, holy, who do not discriminate among persons, who are able to teach religious truth and rightly divide the doctrines of the Lord. (*Constitutions of the Holy Apostles*, Bk. VII, sec. II, ANF VII, p. 471)*

An example of the way in which the pre-Nicene church actively sought out leadership is found in the Clementine literature. It contained a moving appeal to a promising leader to take on episcopal pastoral oversight. In this case the pseudonymous writer attributed this speech to "Peter" addressed to "Clement," yet the material is doubtless of much later date. More important is the *form* of the appeal, which is likely of third century origin.

"Since, as . . . the day of my death is approaching, I lay hands upon this Clement as your bishop; and to him I entrust my chair of discourse." . . . While he thus spoke, I [Clement] knelt before him, and entreated him, declining the honour and the authority of the chair. But he answered: "Please do not ask me about this. For it has seemed to me good that it be this way, and all the more good if you decline it. For this chair has no need of a presumptuous person who is ambitious to occupy it. Rather the one needed must be upright in conduct and deeply skilled in the word of God. But show me one better than yourself, who has travelled more with me, who has heard more of my discourses, or learned better the regulations of the Church, and I shall not force you to do something good against your will. But it will not be in your power to show me your superior. For you are the choice first-fruits of the multitudes redeemed through our mission. However, consider this further, that if you do not undertake the administration of the Church because you fear falling into sin, you may be sure that you sin more, when you have it in your power to help the godly, who are as it were, at sea and in danger. . . . The sooner, therefore, you consent, so much the sooner will you relieve me from anxiety.

But I myself also, O Clement, know the griefs, anxieties, dangers, and reproaches that are destined to come to you from the uninstructed multitudes. These you will be able to bear nobly, looking to the great reward of patience bestowed on you by God. But also please consider this fairly with me: When does Christ have need of your help—now or in eternity? Does Christ need you now, when the Enemy has sworn war against His bride; or moreso in the time to come, when He shall reign victorious having no need of further help? Is it not evident to any one who has even the slightest understanding that it is now? Therefore please hasten with all good-will in this present time of necessity to do battle on the side of this good King whose character it is to give great rewards after victory. Therefore take the oversight gladly, and furthermore, take it without delay." (Clementina, *The Epistle of Clement to James*, Ch. II-IV, ANF VIII, pp. 218–219)*

This passage provides a classic example of the modest refusal of the episcopal office (*nolo episcopari*), which was thought to further attest the modesty and excellence of the candidate. It may rightly be viewed as as a prototypical argument made to a candidate for pastoral oversight after he had once declined the office, asking him to "take oversight gladly." The complex, ritualized interaction had six steps: (1) the request to take office; (2) the decline of authority;

(3) the argument for acceptance, which is all the more validated by the readiness to decline it; (4) the challenge to the individual to find another better suited; (5) the expression of sympathy for the burdens involved; and (6) the immediate need placed in eschatological context.

Although attitudes toward the marriage of ordinands has changed from time to time, it is clear that from early times the requirements for ordination have taken into account candidates' sexual ethics and marital status. In the pre-Nicene period it was thought that the unmarried ordinand should not later marry, or if married not remarry:

We have already said, that a bishop, a presbyter, and a deacon, when they are constituted, must be but once married, whether their wives be alive or whether they be dead; and that it is not lawful for them, if they are unmarried when they are ordained, to be married afterwards; or if they be then married, to marry a second time, but to be content with that wife which they had when they came to ordination. (*Constitutions of the Holy Apostles*, Bk. VI, sec. III, Ch. xvii, ANF VII, p. 457)

Such restrictions may seem wooden or invasive of privacy to modern individualistic consciousness, but the principle value upheld in such a maxim is spiritual contentment, i.e., being content and accepting the state one is in, whether married or single. One had best not assume that one's happiness will necessarily come from a change in the domestic state out of which one entered sacred ministry.

IV. 🔖 ORDERS

Although the definition of levels or grades of ministry has been much debated in the pastoral tradition, there is wide agreement that at least three primary terms are used in the New Testament to describe types of pastoral service: *diakonos, presbuteros, and episkopos.* How these types or "orders" of ministry mutually cohere and complement each other is the subject of the following texts.

Each of the three tasks or "orders" has distinguishable responsibilities: insuring that right doctrine is taught (*episkopos*), that the people are properly counseled and guarded from sin (*presbuteros*), and that through service the discipline of the community is maintained (*diakonos*).

Hear [the bishop] therefore with all attention, and receive from him the doctrine of the faith; and from the presbyters the monitions of life; and from the deacons the order of discipline. (Clementina, *Recognitions of Clement*, Bk. III, Ch. lxvi, ANF VIII, p. 132)

A much later (sixteenth century Anglican) account of these three degrees of ecclesial order was set forth by Richard Hooker. He stressed the continuity of consensus about the three orders from apostolic times:

The most ancient of the Fathers mention those three degrees of ecclesiastical order specifically and no more. "When your captains," said

Tertullian, "that is to say the Deacons, Presbyters and Bishops flee away, who shall teach the laity that they must be constant?". . . . I may securely therefore conclude that there are at this day in the Church of England no other than the same degrees of ecclesiastical order—namely Bishops, Presbyters, and Deacons—which had their beginning from Christ and His blessed Apostles themselves. (Richard Hooker, *Laws of Ecclesiastical Polity*, Bk. V, Ch. xxviii, Works, II, pp. 455–482; *Angl.*, pp. 347–348) *

Ignatius emphasized that the authenticity of leadership in the church depended upon apostolicity insured by the *episkopos*:

Do nothing apart from the bishop, but be subject also to the presbytery as to the apostles of Jesus Christ, our hope [cf. 1 Tim. 1:1]; for if we live in him we shall be found in him. Those who are deacons of the mysteries of Jesus Christ [cf. 1 Cor. 4:1] must please all men in every way [cf. 1 Cor. 10:33]. For they are not ministers of food and drink but servants [cf. 1 Cor. 4:1] of the church of God [cf. 1 Cor. 10:32]; therefore they must guard themselves from accusations as from fire [cf. 1 Cor. 3:15].

Similarly all are to respect the deacons as Jesus Christ and the bishop as a copy of the Father and the presbyters as the council of God and the band of the apostles. For apart from these no group can be called a church. (Ignatius of Antioch, *Letter to Trallians*, sec. 2–3, AF, pp. 92–93)

The Ignatian letters of very early date assumed a tradition that had already been established, which focussed on the connection of all clergy with a bishop in the apostolic tradition. If that connection holds and is confirmed by the Spirit, the church can continue, with deacons serving and *presbuteroi* guiding:

I send you my greetings in the Blood of Jesus Christ, wherein is joy eternal and unfailing; all the more so when men are at one with their bishop—and with their clergy and deacons too, whose appointment with him is approved by Jesus Christ, and confirmed and ratified, according to His will, by His Holy Spirit. (Ignatius of Antioch, *To the Philadelphians*, Salutation, ECW, p. 111)

Clement of Rome argued that bishops and deacons were not only present from the outset in the apostolic ministry, but in fact had their roots in Jewish tradition:

Now, the Gospel was given to the Apostles for us by the Lord Jesus Christ; and Jesus the Christ was sent from God. That is to say, Christ received His commission from God, and the Apostles theirs from Christ. The order of these two events was in accordance with the will of God. So thereafter, when the Apostles had been given their instructions, and all their doubts had been set at rest by the resurrection of our Lord Jesus Christ from the dead, they set out in the full assurance of the Holy Spirit to proclaim the coming of God's kingdom. And as they went through the territories and townships preaching, they appointed their first converts—after testing them by the Spirit—to be bishops and deacons for the believers of the future. This was in no way an innovation, for bishops and deacons had already been spoken of in Scripture long before that. (Clement of Rome, *To the Corinthians*, sec. 42, ECW, p. 45)

The responsibilities of each order have been clearly defined. According to Clement, each order of ministry does well to stay within its appointed bounds of responsibility:

Let each of you, brethren, in his own order give thanks to God, with a good conscience, not exceeding the fixed rule of his ministration, and with reverence. (Clement, 1st Epistle to Corinthians, NE, sec. xli, 1, p. 11)

Bonaventure argued that a principal reason for setting apart priests was to provide a fit means of providing the remedies of the sacraments, in order that they not be offered by all everywhere, but by some in ways appropriate to their original purpose:

Because for our salvation the restorative principle, namely, the incarnate Word, as God and man, has instituted the remedies of the sacraments ordinately, distinctly, and powerfully to accord with the dictates of His goodness, wisdom, and power, He entrusted to men the remedies of the sacraments to be dispensed not in any way whatever but in the way which order, discretion, and power dictate. Some persons ought to be distinguished and separated to carry out this office, and this power should be given to them by a proper law. . . . And because this dignity rests principally in orders, the sacrament ought not to be dispensed except with great discretion and solemnity, and accordingly neither by everyone nor to everyone nor in every place nor at an indiscriminate time, but rather to literate persons, honorable, and free from all unsuitable irregularities, to one fasting, in a sacred place, during Mass, and at times set by ecclesiastical order. (Bonaventure, *Breveloquium*, pp. 208, 210)

V. ❧ ANCILLARY ORDERS

While there was general agreement throughout most of the classic pastoral tradition on three primary orders of ministry, there were diverse speculations about other ancillary orders of ministry, such as subdeacons and archdeacons.

The idea of a seven-fold order of ministry may be found in the Athanasian canons:

> Upon seven pillars has Wisdom rested her house. So seven are the good spirits of God in the church: the bishops and presbyters and deacons and halfdeacons and readers and singers and doorkeepers. These Zechariah has called the seven eyes of God, of whom God has said: "Whoever touches you touches the apple of my eye" (Zech. 2:8). For the seven orders that we have named, the same are the seven eyes of the church. And what is the church's head but Christ? They are the seven pillars upon which the church is founded, of which the wise Solomon said that Wisdom has built her an house and established it upon seven pillars (Prov. 9:1). . . . Be assured O bishop, that the church is established not upon you alone, but also upon the other six orders in the church. Do not reject or despise them. Rather honor them, for they are your fellows and ministers with you. . . . The bishop that despises the doorkeeper or deacon or singer, cannot rightly guide their orders. For how can the bishop celebrate the mysteries and at the same time keep the doors, or sing and receive of the mysteries? A body that has a head also needs feet. (*Athanasian Canons*, pp. 20–21, NIV)*

These seven orders: bishop, presbuter, deacon, half or subdeacon, reader, singer, and doorkeeper, recur in this or similar forms in classical discussions of major and minor orders. The number seven resonated with other analogous speculations about perfections appearing in sequences of seven.

An early Anglican view of the major and minor orders was set forth by Joseph Mede, who distinguished two principle types of order (guides and servants) which could then be further broken down into sub-categories, so that a bishop is a type of presbyter, and a reader is a type of deacon.

> There are properly but two orders ecclesiastical, *Presbyteri* and *Diaconi*—the one the Masters, Priests; the other the Ministers, Deacons. The rest are but divers degrees of these two. As Bishops are a degree of Presbyters of Divine ordinance, to be as heads, chiefs, and presidents, of their brethren, so Subdeacons, Lectors, and indeed any other kind of ecclesiastical ministers, whether *in ecclesia* or *Foro ecclesiastico* (I mean whether they attend Divine duties in the Church, or jurisdiction in Ecclesiastical Courts) are all a kind of Deacons, being to the Presbyters, either single or episcopal, as the Levites were to the Sacerdotes in the Old Testament, namely to minister unto or for them. Thus, when we say Bishops, Presbyters, and Deacons, we name but two Orders, yet three degrees. (Joseph Mede, Diatribae, Bk. I, No. 5; *Angl.*, p. 348)

One of the minor orders is that of reader. An early (pre-Nicene) view of the ordination of readers is seen in this ordinal prayer from the Apostolic Constitutions. Using the biblical prototype of Esdras (Ezra the scribe), the salient petition is that the Spirit be given to this ministry. The text also reveals that reader was viewed as a transitional order leading toward the presbuteral office:

Ordain a reader by laying thy hands upon him, and pray unto God, and say: O Eternal God, who art plenteous in mercy and compassions, who hast made manifest the constitution of the world by Thy operations therein, and keepest the number of Thine elect, do Thou also now look down upon Thy servant, who is to be entrusted to read Thy Holy Scriptures to Thy people. Give him Thy Holy Spirit, the prophetic Spirit. Thou who didst instruct Esdras Thy servant to read Thy laws to the people, do Thou now also at our prayers instruct Thy servant, and grant that he may without blame perfect the work committed to him, and thereby be declared worthy of an higher degree, through Christ, with whom glory and worship be to Thee and to the Holy Ghost for ever. Amen. (*Constitutions of the Holy Apostles*, Bk. VIII, sec. II, ANF VII, p. 493)

Calvin expressed an opinion about how these ancillary orders evolved:

It is likely that subdeacons were at first assigned to deacons to assist them in poor relief; but that distinction was gradually confused. Moreover, archdeacons began to be created when the wealth of possessions demanded a new and more exact kind of administration, although Jerome relates that they already existed in his day. (Calvin, Inst., LCC, Bk. IV, Ch. IV, p. 1073)

VI. ❧ THE PATH TO ORDINATION

Ordination is not conferred exclusively by human agency, but by divine grace through human agency. The pastoral tradition has thought carefully about how ordination is to be properly authorized, transmitted, guaranteed, and authenticated.

Ordination, according to Ignatius, is not sought, but given; not assertively pursued but divinely blessed:

Your bishop's office, which exists for the good of the whole community, was never obtained by his own efforts, as I know very well, nor by any other mere human agency, still less in any spirit of self-glorification; but it was conferred upon him by the love of God the Father and the Lord Jesus Christ. (Ignatius of Antioch, *Letter to the Philadelphians*, sec. 1, ECW, p. 111)

Since the succession of the apostolic witnesses is a crucial notion underlying ordination to curacy, the act of ordination has been ordinarily administered by clergy rather than laity (excepting congregational polities). The Christian way to ordination, in this sense, followed Levitical precedent. Ambrose argued that

the seriousness of the process by which one becomes a pastor must be consonant with the seriousness of ministry itself:

A priest must consecrate a priest, and he himself clothe him with the
vestments, that is, with priestly virtues; then, if he sees that he lacks
none of the priestly garments, and all things are in good order, he
admits him to the sacred altars. One who is to make supplication for
the people should be chosen by the Lord and approved by the priests,
so there may be nothing which may give serious offence in him whose
duty it is to intercede for the offences of others. (Ambrose, *Letters*, FC
26, p. 342)

A similar maxim appeared in the Apostolic Constitutions:

We do not permit presbyters to ordain deacons, or deaconesses, or
readers, or ministers, or singers, or porters, but only bishops; for this
is the ecclesiastical order and harmony. (*Constitutions of the Holy Apostles*,
Bk. III, sec. II, Ch. xxii, ANF VII, p. 430)

Consequently, if one is ordained by another who is not fully authorized to
ordain, then one's ordination may be questioned:

By what means then did Ischyras become a Presbyter? Who was it
that ordained him? Was it Colluthus? For this is the only supposition
that remains. But it is well known, and no one has any doubt about the
matter, that Colluthus died a Presbyter, and that every ordination of
his was invalid, and that all that were ordained by him during the schism
were reduced to the condition of laymen, and in that rank appear in
the congregation. (Athanasius, *Defence Against The Arians*, NPNF 2, IV,
p. 107)

Although it was hoped that ordination by due process would be approved by
the *laos*, it was not generally assumed that ordination would be subjected to
popular lay vote. Lutherans such as Chemnitz proposed Protestant models by
which consensus of ordinands could be affirmed. His plan involved a complex
but orderly procedure of nomination, calling by the whole church, consent of
the whole church, sending, presentation, consensus, and confirmation of ministry consensually by clergy and laity.

Ought then the whole multitude (especially where it is very large)
indiscriminately and without order handle the matter of election and
call?

God is not a God of confusion; He rather wants all things to be done
and administered decently and in order in the church. 1 Co 14:40.
Therefore to avoid confusion, at the time of the apostles and also after
their time in the ancient and pure church, the matter of the election
and call of ministers of the Word was always handled according to a

certain order by the chief members of the church in the name and with the consent of the whole church. Thus the apostles first set forth a directive as to what kind of persons are to be chosen for the ministries of the church. Acts 1:15 ff; 6:2 ff. . . . Since the multitude of the church is not always such that it can search out and propose for election those that are fit, the apostles themselves often nominated suitable persons and proposed them to the churches. Titus 1:5; 1 Ti 1:3, 2 Ti 2:2.

Thus Paul sent Titus, Timothy, [and] Silvanus to churches. But the apostles did not thrust those persons on the churches without either invitation or consent, but nominated or presented them to the churches, which then approved and confirmed that nomination or election with their own free election, as Luke describes this custom with the word *cheirotonia*, Acts 14:23.

Finally, after the church had grown into a large multitude, a presbytery was arranged and set up already at the very time of the apostles to handle this matter. 1 Ti 4:14. In this [presbytery], according to the accounts of Tertullian and Ambrose, some were chosen and appointed, from all the orders or members of the church, to take care of and administer these and similar church matters in the name and with the consent of the whole church. And thus the call remained that of the whole complete church, yet with proper and decent order observed. The church immediately following diligently followed these apostolic footsteps. And since the government also began to embrace the doctrine of the Gospel, the whole matter of the election and call of ministers was ordinarily best distributed among the three chief orders of the church, namely clergy, the pious ruler, and the faithful people. Many notable old canons are quoted regarding this rite, Dist. 23, 24, 62, 65, and 67. And the old church histories testify that at times the bishops and clergy proposed persons to be called, at times a pious ruler nominated [them], at times the people requested [them], but they then presented those proposed, nominated, and requested persons to the other orders or members of the church, that the election might be approved and confirmed by their judgment and consent, Cyprian, Book 1, Ep. 4; Augustine, Ep. 100. From this there still remain the words nomination, request, presentation, consensus, confirmation, and conferring; from these words, rightly considered, it can be understood how and with what order the call of ministers of the church both was once regulated and ought to be properly administered in our time. (Chemnitz, *MWS*, Sec. 26, pp. 34–35)

Calvin asked for concurrence in the calling and appointment of a minister:

The order is that ministers first elect such as ought to hold office; afterwards that he be presented to the Council; and if he is found worthy the Council receive and accept him, giving him certification to produce finally to the people when he preaches, in order that he be received by the common consent of the company of the faithful. If he be found unworthy, and show this after due probation, it is necessary to proceed to a new election for the choosing of another. (Calvin, *Draft of Ecclesiastical Ordinances*, 1541, *SW*, pp. 230–231)

The principle of mutual concurrence of ordaining clergy concerning the authenticity of the call was a crucial assumption of ordination. One way of symbolizing this important point was by having more than one authorized person lay hands upon the ordinand, thus providing evidence of concurrence:

We command that a bishop be ordained by three bishops, or at least by two; but it is not lawful that he be set over you by one; for the testimony of two or three witnesses is more firm and secure. But a presbyter and a deacon are to be ordained by one bishop and the rest of the clergy. (*Constitutions of the Holy Apostles*, Bk. III, sec. II, Ch. xx, ANF VII, p. 432)

Luther proposed a hypothetical exception to the rule that the pastor must be consecrated by a bishop:

If a little group of pious christian laymen were taken captive and set down in a wilderness, and had among them no priest concescrated by a bishop, and if there in the wilderness they were to agree in choosing one of themselves, married or unmarried, and were to charge him with the office of baptising, saying mass, absolving and preaching, such a man would be as truly a priest as though all bishops and popes had consecrated him. (Luther, *Babylonian Captivity*, WML II, p. 67)

VII. ❧ THE ACT OF ORDINATION

The laying on of hands is a complex liturgical act that combines and symbolizes these key themes: earnest intercession for divine assistance and spiritual discernment, acknowledgement of divine calling, appointment, entrustment, consecration, public blessing, commissioning, and sending forth to office. All of these themes have deep roots in the prophetic, priestly, and regal traditions of Hebrew scripture. When the Christian pastoral writers sought to account for the meaning of ordinal laying on of hands, there was assumed to be a profound continuity linking Old and New Testament views of calling and sending, wherein Old Testament types were fulfilled and transmuted through Christ's ministry. The patristic synthesis of these themes was continued and further developed by the Reformers. The Lutheran teacher Martin Chemnitz concisely summarized these themes in his description of what occurs in ordination:

The rite of laying on of hands was common in the Old Testament when something was to be put solemnly in the sight of God, as it were, and committed to Him in a special way. Gn 48:14; Lv 1:2,4; Mk 10:16. And since public functions were at times entrusted to certain persons by laying on of hands (Nm 27:18–20; Dt 3:28, 34:9), therefore the apostles, in the ordination of ministers, out of Christian liberty retained and used that common rite as a thing indifferent [and] helpful in teaching many things. Acts 6:5–6; 13:3; 1 Ti 4:14; 5:22; 2 Ti 1:6. And thus also the ancient church observed the act of ordination without anointing and without other superstitions, simply with laying on of hands (Dist. 23 of the Council of Carthage). Therefore we also in our churches observe the same rite. For through laying on of hands the person called is set before God, as it were, so that there might be a public and outward testimony that the call is not only a human matter, but that God Himself calls, sends, and appoints that person for the ministry, though by regular and legitimate means. Moreover, by this solemn act he that is to be ordained is obligated and, as it were, consecrated to Christ for the ministry. Besides, by that rite, as in the sight of God, the church is entrusted to the minister and, on the other hand, the minister to the church, through whose ministry, namely, God wants to teach, exhort, administer the Sacraments, and work effectively in us. But the laying on of hands in ordination is observed chiefly because of the common prayers of the church, that they may be made with greater diligence and warmer desire. For it is, as it were, a public reminder of the difficulty of the ministry, which cannot be made able except by God. 2 Co 3:5–6. Therefore that minister is presented to the Lord of the harvest through laying on of hands, and the church, reminded of the institution of the ministry and of the divine promises attached to it, reminds God of His promises and asks that by their power He would graciously be with the present minister with His Spirit, grace, blessing, efficacy, working, governance, and direction. (Chemnitz, *MWS*, Sec. 30, pp. 36–37)

Public attestation to the authenticity of God's call is made effectual by Holy Spirit amid the earnest prayers of the Church for the presence of the Spirit in empowering this ministry.

Thomas Aquinas stated a medieval consensus that since Order is the cause of one's being made dispenser of other sacraments, ordination must be viewed as a sacrament:

Now just as sanctifying grace is necessary in order that man receive the sacraments worthily, so is it that he may dispense them worthily. Wherefore as in Baptism, whereby a man is adapted to receive the other sacraments, sanctifying grace is given, so is it in the sacrament of Order whereby man is ordained to the dispensation of the other sacraments. (Thomas Aquinas, *Summa Theologica*, Suppl., Q35, Art 1, III, p. 2683)

Although Catholics and Protestants differ as to whether to call this rite a sacrament, there remains substantial similarity in their description of these fundamental elements of ordination. Anglican William Wake provided a mediating view:

The imposition of hands in Holy Orders, being accompanied with a blessing of the Holy Spirit, may perhaps upon that account be called a kind of particular Sacrament. Yet since that grace which is thereby conferred, whatever it be, is not common to all Christians, nor by consequence any part of that federal blessing which Our Blessed Saviour has purchased for us, but only a separation of him who receives it to a special employ, we think it ought not to be esteemed a common Sacrament of the whole Church, as Baptism and the Lord's Supper are. (William Wake, An Exposition of the Doctrine of the Church of England, Article XV, pp. 45f.; *Angl.*, p. 377)

There are five elements of the act of ordination, according to Chemnitz: public testimony, commitment of ministry, solemn vow, authorization to teach, and the church's intercession. Lacking any of these elements, ordination is misconceived:

First . . . [the] rite of ordination is nothing else than the kind of public testimony by which the call of that person who is ordained is declared before God and in His name to be regular, pious, legitimate, and divine.

Second: By that rite, as by a public designation or declaration, the ministry is committed in the name of God and of the church to him who has been called.

Third: By this very thing also, as by a solemn vow, he who has been called becomes obligated to the church in the sight of God to render the faithfulness in the ministry that the Lord requires in His stewards, regarding which He will also judge them. 1 Co 4:2.

Fourth: The church is reminded that it is to recognize that this pastor has divine authority to teach, and to hear him in the name and place of God.

Fifth, and this is most important: That rite is to be observed for this reason, that the whole church might, by common and earnest prayers, commit to God the ministry of him who is called, that He, by his Holy Spirit, divine grace, and blessing, might be with his ministry. (Chemnitz, *MWS*, Sec. 29, p. 136)

The most direct route into an interpretation of ordination is found in the earliest ordination prayers of the patristic church, as in Hippolytus, the Apostolic Constitutions, and early liturgies. Here is an early ordinal prayer that makes clear a fundamental assumption of ordination: that all efficacy in ministry depends upon God. The Church is praying that the "president" (presbyter, elder, priest) be given and receive apostolic authority to remit sin:

O Thou Ruler and Lord of all, Father and God, do Thou guard the shepherd with the flock. Thou art the cause, Thou the power. We are that which is helped; Thou the helper, the physician, the saviour, the wall, the life, the hope, the refuge, the joy, the expectation, the rest, in a word, Thou art all things to us. In order that we may attain eternal salvation, do Thou co-operate, preserve, protect. Thou canst do all things. For Thou art the Ruler of rulers, the Lord of lords, the Governor of kings. Do Thou give power to the president to loose what ought to be loosed, to bind what ought to be bound. Do Thou make him wise. Do Thou, as by his name, protect the Church of Thy Christ as a fair bride. For Thine is eternal glory. Praise to the Father and the Son and the Holy Ghost to all ages. Amen. (Clementina, *Homilies*, Hom. III, Ch. LXXII, ANF VIII, p. 251)

This ordinal prayer was used by Luther:

Lord God, heavenly, merciful Father, Thou hast commanded us to ask, to seek, and to knock and hast promised to hear us if we call upon Thee in the name of Thy Son. On this Thy promise we rely, and we pray Thee to send this servant of Thy Word . . . into Thy harvest, to stand by him, to bless his office and ministry, to open the ears of the believers for the blessed course of Thy Word that Thy name may be praised, Thy kingdom be increased, and Thy church grow. Amen. (Luther, *Table Talk*, W-T, #5376; WLS 3, pp. 1106–1107)

Luther understood himself to be called and duly ordained to ministry and teaching. When desperate challenges arose and hazards faced him, he recalled his ordination to preaching and teaching:

I have often said and still say that I would not take the wealth of the world for my doctorate. For truly I would finally have to lose courage and despair of the great, weighty matter that rests on me if I had begun it as a meddler *(Schleicher)*, without call and command. But now God and all the world must bear me witness that I have begun it publicly in the discharge of my doctorate and the office of the ministry and have brought it thus far with God's grace and help. (Luther, "Infiltrating and Clandestine Preachers, 1532," WLS 3, p. 1176; cf. WA 30 III, p. 522; cf. LW, Vol. 40, pp, 387–388)

Under hazardous conditions of persecution, according to Hippolytus, the church has at times given its special blessing to ministries, not by the formal laying on of hands, but with an assumption of *de facto* conferring of the office of *presbuteros*, to confessors or martyrs who suffer for Christ:

But if a confessor (*omologetes*) has been in chains in prison for the Name, hands are not laid on (*cheirotonein*) him for the diaconate (*diakonia*) or the presbyter's (*presbuteros*) office. For he has the office (*time*) of the presbyterate by his confession (*homologia*). (Hippolytus, *The Apostolic Tradition*, X, sec. i, p. 18)

One of the most intriguing speculations emerging from this passage is that it may have included both men and women, for both were confessors imprisoned for the name of Christ. This has indirect relevance to the ensuing discussion of the ordination of women, since it suggests that women as well as men who were in chains suffering persecution may have been considered *presbuteros* by virtue of their risk-laden confession.

VIII. 🥨 THE OFFICE OF *DIAKONOS*

Having set forth the general understanding of ordination, it is fitting now to review successively the three distinguishable orders of ministry: the diaconate, the presbyterate, and the episcopacy.

Diakonos, from which our word "deacon" comes, means servant or minister. *Diakonia* means service. Each order of ministry is involved in serving, *diakonia*. The overseer (*episkopos*) does not cease to be servant in overseeing. *Diakonia* is the foundation of ministry, serving others as Christ has served us, and thereby participating in Christ's serving ministry. The general ministry of the church is a serving ministry, on whose behalf a representative ministry is set aside, a *diakonia* commissioned to serve on behalf of the whole church.

Of special interest to us in this context is whether or to what degree the *diakonoi* were responsible for pastoral care or counsel. In the Clementine literature we have an early indication, suggesting that *diakonoi* were deeply involved in assisting the leadership in person to person ministries, attentive to emergent needs, social or personal pain, poverty or illness, especially where a church member was on the brink of a misguided action. In such cases, the deacon was to be the "eyes" of the one who has primary oversight and responsibility for the flock:

Let the deacons of the church, going about with intelligence, be as eyes to the bishop, carefully inquiring into the doings of each member of the church, ascertaining who is about to sin, in order that, being arrested with admonition by the president, he may perhaps not accomplish the sin. Let them check the disorderly, encouraging them not to forget to assemble to hear the discourses. . . . Let the deacons keep an eye out for those who are suffering from illness, and let them bring them to the notice of the congregation who do not know of them, that they may visit them, and supply their wants. (Clementina, *The Epistle of Clement to James*, Ch. XII, ANF VIII, p. 220)*

Here are some examples of the kinds of tasks assigned to deacons in the third and fourth centuries:

Let the deacons be in all things unspotted, as the bishop himself is to be, only more active. Let there be deacons in numbers proportional to the size of the congregations, that they may minister to the infirm as workers not ashamed. Let the deaconess be diligent in taking care of the women. Let both deacon and deaconess be ready to carry messages, to travel about, to minister, and to serve. . . . Let them not be ashamed to minister to those that are in want, even as the Son of Man "did not come to be served but to serve, and to give up his life as a ransom for many" (Matt. 20:28). . . . We ought therefore also to serve the brothers and sisters in imitation of Christ. For Christ himself said: "Among you, whoever wants to be great must be your servant, and whoever wants to be first must be the willing slave of all" (Matt. 20:26, 27). For this is what Christ himself did, and he did it not in word only, but rather he fulfilled the prophecy that he would serve many faithfully: For during the farewell supper, Jesus rose from the table "and taking a towel, tied it round him. Then he poured water into a basin, and began to wash his disciples' feet and to wipe them with the towel" (John 13:5). By doing this He demonstrated to us His kindness and brotherly affection, that so we also might serve one another similarly. If, therefore, our Lord and Master so humbled Himself, how can you, the labourers of the truth, and administrators of piety, be ashamed to do the same to such of the brethren as are weak and infirm? . . . Visit all those who stand in need of visitation. (*Constitutions of the Holy Apostles*, Bk. III, Ch. xix, ANF VII, p. 432)*

The diaconate was a responsive, mobile ministry, conveying messages, traveling about, going to the sick, not waiting for them to come to the church. The pattern of *diakonia* was Jesus himself, who washed the feet of his disciples.

Some interpreted the Acts of the Apostles to be saying that deacons were to be limited to seven per city. The Synod of Quinisext felt it necessary to interpret this view:

Since the book of the Acts tells us that seven deacons were appointed by the Apostles, and the synod of Neocaesarea in the canons which it put forth determined that there ought to be canonically only seven deacons, even if the city be very large, in accordance with the book of Acts; we, having fitted the mind of the fathers to the Apostles' words, find that they spoke not of those men who ministered at the Mysteries but in the administration which pertains to the serving of tables. (Quinisext Council, A.D. 692, Canon XVI, The Seven Ecumenical Councils, NPNF 2, XIV, p. 373)

Here is an early account by Hippolytus (c. 170–c. 236) concerning the office of deacon, which shows how it was, at that time, distinguished from the presbyterate:

And a deacon when he is appointed (*kathistanai*) shall be chosen according to what has been said before, the bishop [alone] laying hands on him [in the same manner]. Nevertheless we order that the bishop alone shall lay on hands at the ordaining of a deacon for this reason:

That he is not ordained (*cheirotonein*) for a priesthood, but for the service (*huperesia*) of the bishop that he may do [only] the things commanded by him.

For he is not [appointed to be] the fellow-counsellor (*sumboulos*) of the [whole] clergy (*kleros*) but to take charge [of property] and to report to the bishop whatever is necessary.

He does not receive the Spirit which is common to [all] the presbyterate, in which the presbyters share, but that which is entrusted to him under the bishop's authority.

Nor is he appointed (*kathistanai*) to receive the Spirit of seniority which the presbyters share (*metechein*) but to occupy himself with that which is proper that the bishop may trust him and that he may acquaint the bishop with what is fitting. (Hippolytus, *The Apostolic Tradition*, "Of Deacons," sec. ix, p. 15–16)*

The early forms of ordinal prayers for deacons provide ready access to the early church's understanding the primitive diaconate. In Hippolytus is found this ordinal prayer that the Holy Spirit would bless this ministry of serving, and that the deacon would be found worthy of this entrustment:

O God who has created all things and hast ordered them by the Word, Father of our Lord Jesus Christ whom Thou didst send to minister Thy will and reveal unto us Thy desire; grant the [Holy] Spirit of grace and earnestness and diligence upon this Thy servant whom Thou hast chosen to minister to thy church and to bring up in holiness to Thy holiness that which is offered to Thee by Thine ordained high priests [to the glory of Thy Name;] so that ministering blamelessly and in purity [of heart] he may by Thy goodwill be found worthy of this [high and] exalted office, praising Thee, through Thy Child Jesus Christ [our Lord] through whom to Thee with Him [be] glory, might and praise with the Holy Spirit [in the holy Church] now and ever and world without end. Amen. (Hippolytus, *The Apostolic Tradition*, sec. 9, pp. 17–18)

The ordinal prayer of the Apostolic Constitutions asks for empowerment by the Spirit to minister as deacon after the pattern of the martyr Stephen:

O God Almighty, true and faithful God, who art rich to all that call upon you Thee in truth, fearful in counsels, and wise in understanding, powerful and great, hear our prayer, O Lord, and let Thine ears receive our supplication, and "Let thy face shine upon thy servant" (Ps. 119:135) who is to be ordained for Thee to the office of a deacon.

Replenish him with Thy Holy Spirit and with that same power with which Thou didst replenish Stephen, who was Thy martyr, and follower of the sufferings of Thy Christ. Do Thou render him worthy to discharge acceptably the ministration of a deacon, steadily, unblameably, and without reproof. (*The Constitutions of the Holy Apostles*, Bk. VIII, sec. II, Ch. xviii, ANF VII, pp. 491–492, NEB)*

IX. &. THE ROLE OF THE DEACON IN LITURGY

Since the focus of the diaconate is upon service, one might imagine that liturgical involvement might be diminished, but there is evidence that deacons also maintained an important serving role in liturgy. Justin Martyr gives this primitive account of the deacon's role in the eucharist:

When the president has given thanks and the whole congregation has assented, those whom we call deacons give to each of those present a portion of the consecrated bread and wine and water, and they take it to the absent. (Justin Martyr, *First Apology*, sec. 65, LCC I, p. 286)

Under some circumstances it was understood that the deacon could administer baptism:

Let the deacon, when the presbyter is not present, of necessity baptise. (Hippolytus, *The Apostolic Tradition*, sec. 14, p. 49)

In Hippolytus, an early third century presbyter of Rome, we have a clear canonical rule laid down concerning the exceptional circumstances under which the faithful may receive communion from a deacon:

If the faithful (*pistos*) should be present at a supper (*deipnon*) without the bishop, but with a presbyter or deacon present, let them similarly partake in orderly fashion. But let every one be careful to receive the blessed bread (*eulogion*) from the hand of the presbyter or deacon. Similarly a catechumen shall receive the same bread, but exorcised.

If laymen only are met together without the clergy (*klerikos*) let them act with discipline (*episteme*). For the layman (*laos*) cannot make a blessing [or, make the blessed bread]. (Hippolytus, *The Apostolic Tradition*, Sec. 11–12, p. 48)

Richard Hooker stated the view that the diaconal office combines service to the poor with liturgical service:

Deacons were stewards of the Church to whom at the first was committed the distribution of Church goods, and thereby the care of providing for the poor, and the charge to see that all things of expense might be religiously and faithfully treated. A part also of their office was attendance upon their Presbyters at the time of Divine Service. For this purpose, to set forth the dignity of their calling, Ignatius said that deacons are to the Bishop as if Angelic powers did serve him. (Richard Hooker, *Laws of Ecclesiastical Polity*, Bk. V, Ch. lxxvii; *Angl.*, p. 347)*

X. ❧ DIACONAL CARE FOR THE POOR AND SICK

Some accounts divide the office of deacon into service to the poor and service to the sick. In this way Christian pastoral service is rendered for both social and personal illness. *Diakonia* has to do both with the suffering that emerges from economic limitations in the body politic, and suffering of the individual body. This general distinction appeared in Calvin's reading of the ancient tradition:

There were always two kinds [of deacons] in the ancient Church, the one deputed to receive, dispense and hold goods for the poor, not only daily alms, but also possessions, rents and pensions; the other to tend and care for the sick and administer allowances to the poor. This custom we follow again now for we have procurators and hospitallers. . . . It will be their duty to watch diligently that the public hospital is well maintained, and that this be so both for the sick and the old people unable to work, widowed women, orphaned children and other poor creatures. (Calvin, *Draft Ecclesiastical Ordinances*, 1541, *SW*, pp. 235–236)

Stewardship of property on behalf of mercy to the poor is a key theme of the diaconal office:

Care for the properties of the churches and the collection of income therefrom and of other proceeds designated for the use of the poor of the churches pertain to the office of subdeacons and administrators, so that the deacons may spend themselves completely: first, in the correct distribution of the assets of the churches already collected, namely, to give to each only what he truly needs in order to live to the Lord; secondly, to maintain the discipline of Christ among those who are fed by the churches, so that those who receive food from the churches for this very purpose will strive to live to the Lord. (Bucer, *De Regno Christi*, Poor Relief, Sixth Law, LCC XIX, p. 309)

Calvin similarly stressed the accountability of the deacon for reception and distribution of church income for the poor:

At that time the character of the diaconate was the same as that under the apostles. For they received the daily offerings of believers and the yearly income of the church. These they were to devote to proper uses, that is, to distribute some to feed the ministers, some to feed the poor, but according to the decision of the bishop, to whom they rendered an account annually of their distribution. The fact that the canons everywhere make the bishop the steward of all the possessions of the church is not to be understood as if he personally handled the task. Rather, it was his duty to designate to the deacon the ones to receive public support from the church, and with regard to what was left, to specify to whom it should be given and how much to each. For he had to investigate whether the deacon faithfully executed his responsibility. (Calvin, Inst., Bk. IV, Ch. IV, LCC XXI, p. 1072)

Luther also focused on the diaconal task of assisting in care of the poor:

And the diaconate is not the ministry of reading the Gospel or the Epistle, as is the present practice, but the ministry of distributing the Church's alms to the poor, so that the priests may be relieved of the burden of temporal matters and may give themselves more freely to prayer and the Word. (Luther, *The Babylonian Captivity*, WML II, p. 283)

XI. ❧ THE OFFICE OF *PRESBUTEROS*

The English word priest is a shortening of the Greek *presbuteros*, whose original meaning was elder, or presiding officer, analogous to the *zaqen* of the Jewish congregation. From the first century this office was clearly distinguished from that of deacon:

The presbyter is only to teach, to offer, to baptize, to bless the people, and the deacon is to minister to the bishop, and to the presbyters. (*Constitutions of the Holy Apostles*, Bk. III, sec. XI, ANF VII, p. 432)

Hippolytus provided this early account of a presbyteral ordination:

And when a presbyter is ordained (*cheirotonein*) the bishop shall lay his hand upon his head, the presbyters also touching him. And he shall pray over him according to the previously mentioned form which we gave before over the bishop, praying and saying:
O God and Father of our Lord Jesus Christ. . . . Look upon this Thy servant and impart to him the spirit of grace and counsel, that he may share in the presbyterate and govern Thy people in a pure heart.
As Thou didst look upon the people of Thy choice and didst command Moses to choose presbyters whom Thou didst fill with the spirit which Thou hadst granted to Thy minister, so now, O Lord, grant that there may be preserved among us unceasingly the Spirit of Thy grace, and make us worthy that in faith we may minister to Thee in singleness of heart praising Thee; through Thy child Christ Jesus through Whom

to Thee be glory, might and praise, to the Father and to the Son with the Holy Spirit in the holy Church now and for ever and world without end. Amen. (Hippolytus, *The Apostolic Tradition*, viii, sec. i-ii, p. 13–14)*

This supplication asks that the Spirit may empower this ministry, enlighten this governance, make fruitful this curacy. Similarly the ordinal petition for the *presbuteros* in the Apostolic Constitutions prays for the empowerment of an edifying, healing, teaching, caring ministry.

Look down upon Thy church and increase it. Strengthen those who preside in it, and grant them power, that they may labour both in word and work for the edification of Thy people. Do Thou now also look down upon this Thy servant, who is put into the presbytery by the vote and determination of the whole clergy. Replenish him with the Spirit of grace and counsel to assist and govern Thy people with a pure heart, in the same manner as Thou didst look down upon Thy chosen people, and didst command Moses to choose elders, whom Thou didst fill with Thy Spirit. Do Thou also now, O Lord, grant this, and preserve in us the Spirit of Thy grace, that this person, being filled with the gifts of healing and the word of teaching, may in meekness instruct Thy people, and sincerely serve Thee with a pure mind and a willing soul, and may fully discharge the holy ministrations for Thy people, through Thy Christ, with whom glory, honour, and worship be to Thee, and to the Holy Ghost, for ever. Amen. (*Constitutions of the Holy Apostles*, Bk. VIII, Sec. III, p. 492)*

According to Jerome, the earliest churches were governed by *presbuteroi*, acting consensually:

Hence a presbyter is the same as a bishop, and before ambition came into religion, by the prompting of the devil, and people began to say: "I belong to Paul: I to Apollo; I to Cephas" (I Cor. I. 12), the churches were governed by the direction of presbyters, acting as a body. But when each presbyter began to suppose that those whom he had baptized belonged to him, rather than to Christ, it was decreed in the whole Church that one of the presbyters should be chosen to preside over the others, and that the whole responsibility for the Church should devolve on him, so that the seeds of schism should be removed. (Jerome, LCF, p. 189)

The usual minimal age for presbyteral ordination in the early church was thirty:

Let not a presbyter be ordained before he is thirty years of age, even though he be in all respects a worthy man, but let him be made to wait. For our Lord Jesus Christ was baptized and began to teach in his thirtieth year. (The Council of Neocaesarea, A.D. 315, Canon XI, The Seven Ecumenical Councils, NPNF 2, VIX, p. 84)

XII. ❧ RESPONSIBILITIES OF PRESBYTERS

For almost two millennia Christian lay persons have been served in ministry by persons assigned in the office of *presbuteros* (elder, presbyter, priest). It is at this point that the church's world-wide ministry becomes localized. What do presbuters do? Irenaeus described the *presbuteros* as teacher, steward, expounder of scripture, and moral guide of the congregation:

The church nourishes that kind of presbyter of whom Isaiah spoke: "I will make peace your governor and righteousness your ruler" (Is. 60:17). To such presbyters the Lord referred when he said: "Who then is the faithful and wise servant, whom the master has put in charge of the servants in his household to give them their food at the proper time? It will be good for that servant whose master finds him doing so when he returns" (Matt. 24:45,46). Paul also taught that "in the church God has appointed first of all apostles, second prophets, third teachers" (1 Cor. 11:28). Where, therefore, the gifts of the Lord have been placed, there it behoves us to learn the truth, especially from those who possess that succession of the Church which is from the apostles. Among them we will find what is sound and blameless in conduct, as well as unadulterated and incorrupt in speech. For they preserve this faith of ours in one God who created all things. They increase that love which we have for the Son of God, who accomplished such marvellous dispensations for our sake. They expound the Scriptures to us without danger, neither blaspheming God, nor dishonouring the patriarchs, nor despising the prophets. (Irenaeus, *Against Heresies*, Ch. xxvi, sec. 5, ANF I, p. 498, NIV)*

The presbyter is responsible for the flock:

It is said of the presbyter that he is answerable for all the flock. For God has placed the people under your care, O priests, esteemed leaders in God's house, instructing the people: "Obey your leaders and submit to their authority. They keep watch over you as men who must give an account" (Hebr. 13:17). If you do indeed faithfully watch for the people and pray for them, you shall redeem the souls of those whose offerings support you. But if not, and you become slothful, how and in what way will you give account of them? If you fail to be the intercessor for them in their troubles, then is it not right that you should receive their support? (*Athanasian Canons*, sec. 4, p. 9, NIV)*

Compassionate understanding and love of God and humanity are crucial qualities requisite to presbyteral service:

So now none shall be made a priest but those of understanding, loving God, loving others, such as are able worthily to stand before the altar. (*Athanasian Canons*, sec. 4, p. 8)*

The multifaceted metaphor of the workman was marshalled in the Clementine literature to describe the presbyteral task:

That "the harvest is great, but the workmen are few," this also is well-known and manifest. Let us, therefore, "ask of the Lord of the harvest" that He would send forth workmen into the harvest (Matt. 9:37, 38); such workmen as "shall skilfully dispense the word of truth"; workmen "who shall not be ashamed"; faithful workmen; workmen who shall be "the light of the world"; workmen who "work not for the food that perisheth, but for that food which abideth unto life eternal" (John 6:27); workmen who shall be such as the apostles; workmen who imitate the Father, and the Son, and the Holy Spirit; who are concerned for the salvation of men; not "hireling" workmen; not workmen to whom the fear of God and righteousness appear to be gain; not workmen who "serve their belly"; not workmen who "with fair speeches and pleasant words mislead the hearts of the innocent" (Rom. 16:18). (Clementina, *Two Epistles Concerning Virginity*, ANF VIII, p. 60)

The care of the flock is to be entrusted only to those *presbuteroi* who are accountable to the apostolic tradition, and who have manifested necessary gifts and graces for eldership. Divisiveness, lack of self-constraint, arrogance, and compulsive secrecy are evidences to contrary:

It is incumbent to obey the presbyters who are in the church. For, as I have shown, they possess the succession from the apostles. They, together with the succession of the episcopate, have received the reliable gift of truth, according to the good pleasure of the Father. But it is also incumbent to hold in suspicion others who depart from the primitive succession and assemble themselves together in any place whatsoever . . . . Those, however, who are believed to be presbyters by many but in fact serve their own self-assertive passions and do not place the fear of God supreme in their hearts, who conduct themselves with contempt towards others, and are puffed up with the pride of holding the chief seat, and work evil deeds in secret, pretending that "no one sees us," shall be convicted by the Word. For God does not judge according to outward appearance nor by looking at the face, but into the heart. . . . From all such persons, therefore, it is wise for us to keep aloof, adhering to those who, as I have already observed, hold the doctrine of the apostles, and who, together with the order of priesthood (*presbyterii ordine*), display sound speech and blameless conduct for the confirmation and correction of others. (Irenaeus, *Against Heresies*, Bk. IV, Ch. XXVI, ANF I, p. 497)*

Within their own parishes it is proper to say that presbyters, like bishops, have been given the ministry of administrative oversight:

Peter wrote to presbyters just what we have been saying so that none of them might evasively reply: "I am no bishop, so you cannot charge me with any responsibility." Rather of presbyters he taught that they also are overseers, and that they also shall be held answerable every one of them, for Christ's church and for the district belonging thereabout, just as the bishop also shall be answerable for the town and the districts belonging thereabout which are under his pastorship. (*Athanasian Canons*, sec. 10, pp. 18–19)*

Apart from common consent, it is not advisable that the presbyter go over the heads of episcopal officers and appeal directly to highest government authorities to get one's way:

If any bishop, or presbyter, or any one whatever of the canon shall presume to betake himself to the Emperor without the consent and letters of the bishop of the province, and particularly of the bishop of the metropolis, such a one shall be publicly deposed and cast out, not only from communion, but also from the rank which he happens to have; inasmuch as he dares to trouble the ears of our Emperor beloved of God, contrary to the law of the Church. But, if necessary business shall require any one to go to the Emperor, let him do it with the advice and consent of the metropolitan and other bishops in the province, and let him undertake his journey with letters from them. (Council of Antioch in Encaeniis, A.D. 341, Canon XI, The Seven Ecumenical Councils, NPNF 2, XIV, p. 114)

The presbyter is not a free agent, and is not given liberty or legitimate authorization to separate from the apostolic tradition and promulgate idiosyncratic opinions as Christian teaching:

If any presbyter despises his own bishop and assembles separately, and fixes another altar, when he has nothing to condemn in his bishop either as to piety or righteousness, let him be deprived as an ambitious person . . . . But let these things be done after one and a second, or even a third admonition from the bishop. (*Constitutions of the Holy Apostles*, Ecclesiastical Canons, 32, ANF VII, p. 502)

XIII. ☙ THE BISHOP'S PASTORAL CARE OF THE CHURCH

If the *presbuteros* (elder, priest) is the *poimen* (pastor-shepherd) of the local congregation or parish, the *episkopos* (overseer, bishop) is the *poimen* of the church in a wider area, a jurisdiction or diocese. Many congregations are therefore entrusted to the pastoral care of the bishop, while only one is entrusted to the presbuter. The bishop does not cease being pastor, and does not cease to give pastoral counsel.

Consequently, much of the literature of the pastoral tradition has focused on the pastoral care offered by the bishop. Gregory the Great's *Pastoral Care*, for example, was written primarily to instruct bishops in the care of souls, although its counsel is also applicable to anyone serving in the pastoral office. Gregory began his influential treatise with this admonition on the paradoxical willingness to take on the task of episcopal oversight. Approval and constraint (positive and negative reinforcements) are the assumed tools of the art of pastoral governance. The episcopal office is best received when it is not sought. One who directly pursues it has probably misunderstood it:

> "If anyone sets his heart on being an overseer, he desires a noble task" (1 Tim. 3:1). But while praising the desire, he immediately turns what he has praised to an awesome challenge when he immediately adds: "Now the overseer must be above reproach" (1 Tim. 3:2). . . . The great masters of the art of guiding do both of these simultaneously: they impel by approval and check by alarms. By describing the height of blamelessness, the Apostle sought to restrain his hearers from pride, and, by praising the task which needs doing, dispose them to the life required. It must be noted, however, that this was said at a time when whoever was set over people was usually the first to be led to the tortures of martyrdom. At that time, therefore, it was laudable to seek the office of a bishop, even though through it there was little doubt that one would thereby come in the end to heavier pains. Hence even the office of a bishop itself is defined as a good work, when it is said, "If anyone sets his heart on being an overseer, he desires a noble task" (1 Tim. 3:1). But if anyone should seek, not this ministry of a good work, but the glory of distinction, he becomes himself a witness against himself that he does not desire the office of a bishop. (Gregory the Great, *BPR*, NPNF 2, X, p. 6, NIV)*

The solicitous caring of a parent for the whole family is a penetrating metaphor of the pastoral care of the bishop for the church:

> For it seems that the particular characteristic of the married state is that it gives the man who desires a perfect marriage an opportunity to take responsibility for everything in the home which he shares with his wife. The apostle says that one should appoint bishops who by their oversight over their own house have learned to be in charge of the whole church. (Clement of Alexandria, *On Marriage*, Ch. XII, sec. 79, LCC II, p. 76)

The family analogy extends particularly to the vulnerable and needy— just as parents take special care for children and elderly who are weak or incapacitated, so the episcopal care of the church attends especially to the guardianship of the defenseless. In urging that the bishop call persons "by name," Ignatius revealed a warmly personalizing mode of episcopal leadership in the late first century:

Take care that widows are not neglected; next to the Lord, be yourself their guardian. See that nothing is ever done without consulting you, and do nothing yourself without consulting God—as I am sure you never do. Take a firm stand. Hold services more frequently, and hunt up everyone by name. (Ignatius of Antioch, *Letter to Polycarp*, sec. 4, ECW, p. 128)

The Athanasian Canons urged that the contact between bishop and presbyters be both frequent and candid. The serving role (*diakonia*) remained central to the overseer:

The bishop shall eat often with the *presbuteroi* of the church, that he may learn of their responses, and see for himself the quality of their tranquillity in the fear of God. And he shall stand there and serve them. If they are weak, he shall wash their feet with his own hands. (*Athanasian Canons*, sec. 66, p. 43)*

Just as presbyters visit persons in their flock, so do bishops visit congregations in their diocese. The excitement and importance of episcopal visitation to the congregation is reflected in this passage from the seventeenth century Anglican tradition:

Let every minister be diligent in exhorting all parents and masters to send their children and servants to the bishop at the visitation, or other solemn times of his coming to them, that they may be confirmed. And let him also take care that all young persons may, by understanding the principles of religion, their vow of baptism, the excellence of Christian religion, the necessity and advantages of it, and of living according to it, be fitted and disposed, and accordingly by them presented to the Bishop, that he may pray over them, and invoke the Holy Spirit, and minister the holy rite of confirmation. (Jeremy Taylor, *RAC*, sec. 70; *CS*, p. 22)

In the early phases of the development of episcopacy, it was customary to ask the consent of the people to the election of the bishop. Such a procedure is found in the Apostolic Constitutions:

A bishop to be ordained is to be, as we have already, all of us, appointed, unblameable in all things, a select person, chosen by the whole people, who, when he is named and approved, let the people assemble, with the presbytery and bishops that are present, on the Lord's day, and let them give their consent. And let the principal of the bishops ask the presbytery and people whether this be the person whom they desire for their ruler. And if they give their consent, let him ask further whether he has a good testimony from all men as to his worthiness for so great and glorious an authority; whether all things relating to his piety towards God be right; whether justice towards men has been observed by him; whether the affairs of his family have been well ordered by him; whether he has been unblameable in the course of his life. And if all the assembly together do according to truth, and not according to prejudice, witness that he is such a one, let them the third time, as before God the Judge, and Christ, the Holy Ghost being also present, as well as all the holy and ministering spirits, ask again whether he be truly worthy of this ministry, that so "in the mouth of two or three witnesses every word may be established." And if they agree the third time that he is worthy, let them all be demanded their vote; and when they all give it willingly, let them be heard. And silence being made, let one of the principal bishops, together with two others, stand near to the altar, the rest of the bishops and presbyters praying silently, and the deacons holding the divine Gospels open upon the head of him that is to be ordained, and say to God thus. (*Constitutions of the Holy Apostles*, Bk. VIII, sec. II, Ch. iv, ANF VII, pp. 481–482)

XIV. 🙠   Tasks of Episcopal Care

What kinds of pastoral care does the bishop undertake? The pastoral writers sought to define the office and tasks of episcopacy so as to show how the bishop is both alike and distinguished from other pastors. As a pastor, the bishop has a curacy—a diocese or see. As a minister the bishop has a particular service—that of oversight:

A Bishop is a minister of God, unto whom with permanent continuance there is given not only power of administering the Word and Sacraments, which power other Presbyters have, but also a further power to ordain ecclesiastical persons, and a power of chiefty in government over Presbyters as well as Laymen, a power to be by way of jurisdiction a Pastor even to Pastors themselves. So that this office, as he is a Presbyter or Pastor, consisteth in those things which are common unto him with other pastors, as in ministering the Word and Sacraments: but those things incident unto his office, which do properly make him a Bishop, cannot be common unto him with other Pastors. (Hooker, *Laws of Ecclesiastical Polity*, Bk. VII, Chs. 1–6, Works pp. 143–166; *Angl.* p. 351)

The bishop remains a presbyter, but for the good order of the church is given the unique power to commission other presbyters. This distinction was delineated in medieval times by Jean de Paris:

It is necessary that among these ministers some will be superior and complete in their powers and will confer this priesthood on others in ordination and consecration. These are bishops who though not in any way superior to ordinary priests as far as consecrating the true body of Christ is concerned are, in their supervisory role, superior in what touches the faithful. For bishops are important and complete in their power because they can make other priests which lower clergy cannot do. Whatever concerning the faithful people is of a difficult nature is reserved for the bishop's decision and it is by their authority that priests carry out the charge committed to them. (Jean de Paris, *On Royal and Papal Power*, Ch. 3, p. 83)

The foremost task of pastoral care for the bishop is that of guaranteeing to laity that the apostolic witness will be truly made available to them without distortion or deficit. It is for this purpose that the succession of faithful witnesses to the apostles has been a part of episcopal self-understanding from earliest times, according to Hooker:

In some things every Presbyter, in some things only Bishops, in some things neither the one nor the other, are the Apostles' successors. The Apostles were sent as special chosen eyewitnesses of Jesus Christ, from Whom immediately they received their whole embassage and their commission to be the principal first founders of a House of God, consisting as well of Gentiles as of Jews. In this there are not after them any other like unto them; and yet the Apostles have now their successors upon earth, their true successors, if not in the largeness, surely in the kind of that episcopal function. . . .

We find that throughout all those cities where the Apostles did plant Christianity, so that histories of the times have noted succession of pastors in the seat of one, not of many (there being in every such Church far more pastors), and the first one in every rank of succession we find to have been, if not some Apostle, yet some Apostle's disciple. By Epiphanius the Bishops of Jerusalem are reckoned down from James to Hilarion then Bishop. Of those who claimed that they held the same things which they received from those who had lived with the Apostles themselves, Tertullian spoke in this way: "Let them therefore show the beginnings of their Churches, let them recite their Bishops one by one, each in this way succeeding other so that the first Bishop of them hath had for his author and predecessor some Apostle, or at least some Apostolical person who persevered with the Apostles. For in this way Apostolical Churches are able to bring forth the evidence of their estates. This is what the Church of Smyrna did, having Polycarp whom John did consecrate." Catalogues of Bishops in a number of other Churches,

Bishops, and succeeding one another from the very Apostles' times, are by Eusebius and Socrates collected. (Hooker, *Laws of Ecclesiastical Polity*, Bk. VII, Ch. 1–6, Works, III, pp. 143–151, 151–157; *Angl.*, pp. 353–354)*

Since it is charged with guardianship of apostolic teaching, the episcopal office is by definition a teaching office. The Quinisext Synod set forth the manner in which episcopal leaders must be teachers, prepared to settle disputes about Christian teaching:

It behoves those who preside over the churches, every day but especially on Lord's days, to teach all the clergy and people words of piety and of right religion, gathering out of holy Scripture meditations and determinations of the truth, and not going beyond the limits now fixed, nor varying from the tradition of the God-bearing fathers. And if any controversy in regard to scripture shall have been raised, let them not interpret it otherwise than as the lights and doctors of the church in their writings have expounded it, and in these let them glory rather than in composing things out of their own heads, lest through their lack of skill they may have departed from what was fitting. (Quinisext Synod, A.D. 692, Canon XIX, The Seven Ecumenical Councils, NPNF 2, XIV, p. 374)

During the English parliamentary crisis of 1648, a succinct statement of the nature of episcopacy was presented to the Parliamentary Divines by King Charles I, setting forth reasons why he could not consent to abolish episopal governance in the Church of England:

For the name *Episcopus* or Bishop, His Majesty hath long since learnt from those that are skilful in the greek tongue that it imports properly no more than an "overseer," one that hath the charge or inspection of something committed unto him, as he that is set to watch a beacon or to keep sheep. Whence in the New Testament and in the ecclesiastical use, it is applied to such persons as have the care and inspection of the Churches of Christ committed unto them *in spiritualibus*; as both Bishops and Presbyters have in some sort, but with this difference,—that mere Presbyters are *Episcopi gregis* only, they have the oversight of the flock in the duties of preaching, Administration of the Sacraments, Public Prayer, exhorting, rebuking, etc.; but Bishops are *Episcopi gregis et pastorum* within their several precincts in the acts of external government. So that the common work of both functions is the Ministry of the Gospel. But that which is peculiar to the function of Bishops as distinguished from Presbyters is Church Government. It is not therefore to be wondered if it should happen in the New Testament the word *Episcopus* to be usually applied unto Presbyters, who were indeed overseers of the flock, rather than unto Church Government, who had then a title of greater eminency whereby to distinguish them from ordinary Presbyters,—to wit, that of "Apostles." But when the government of Churches came into the hands of their successors, the names were by common usage (which is the best master of words) very soon appropriated, that of *Episcopus* to the Ecclesiastical Government or Bishop of a Diocese, and that of Presbyter to the ordinary Minister or Priests. (King Charles I, The King's Answer to the Paper Delivered in by the Reverend Divines Attending the Honorable Commissioners Concerning Church Government, pp. 3f.; *Angl.*, p. 368)

The episcopal care of the church is, accordingly, understood in terms of vigilant oversight of the flock, watchfulness, inspection, and spiritual direction within duly authorized precincts. Presbyters also are *episcopari gregis* (overseers of the flock) in the sense of oversight of a local congregation through preaching, sacrament and pastoral care.

The concluding selection gathers up most of these themes on tasks of episcopacy, but in the mode of prayer. Hippolytus provided the clearest Pre-Nicene picture of the office of pastoral oversight of the churches in the ordinal prayer for the consecration of bishops in early third century Rome:

Election
Let the bishop be ordained, being in all things without fault chosen by all the people.

Confirmation
And when he has been proposed and found acceptable to all, the people shall assemble on the Lord's day together with the presbytery and such bishops as may attend. . . .

Consecration
With the agreement of all let the bishops lay hands on him and the presbytery stand by in silence. And all shall keep silence praying in their heart for the descent of the Spirit. After this one of the bishops present at the request of all, laying his hand on him who is ordained bishop, shall pray thus, saying:

Prayer for the Consecration of a Bishop
"O God and Father of our Lord Jesus Christ, Father of mercies and God of all comfort," "Who dwellest on high yet hast respect unto the lowly," "who knowest all things before they come to pass";

Who didst give ordinances unto Thy church "by the Word of Thy grace"; Who "didst foreordain from the beginning" the race of the righteous from Abraham, instituting princes and priests and leaving not Thy sanctuary without ministers; Who from the foundation of the world hast been pleased to be glorified in them whom Thou has chosen;

And now pour forth that Power which is from Thee, of "the princely Spirit" which Thou didst deliver to Thy Beloved Child Jesus Christ, which He bestowed on Thy holy Apostles who established the Church which hallows Thee in every place to the endless glory and praise of Thy Name.

Father "who knowest the hearts of all," grant upon this Thy servant whom Thou hast chosen for the episcopate to feed Thy holy flock and serve as Thine high priest, that he may minister blamelessly by night and day, that he may unceasingly behold and propitiate Thy countenance and offer to Thee the gifts of Thy holy Church. (Hippolytus, *The Apostolic Tradition*, III. i-iv, pp. 4–5)*

The church's prayer is that the power of the Holy Spirit may "pour forth" its effective empowerment upon the bishop's care of the flock. It is addressed to the holy One who meets humanity in lowly places, who knows and comforts, who has not left himself without witnesses to his insurmountable goodness.

The selections of Part Five have clarified the meaning of ordination, its biblical grounding, and the reasoning that has accompanied orders. The classical pastoral writers set forth explicit principles to guide the calling, examining, and selection of candidates for ordination. The ordinal examination assesses not only doctrinal adequacy, but sufficiency of development of personal, interpersonal, and behavioral qualities requisite for soul care. Each of three tasks or "orders" has distinguishable responsibilities: insuring that right doctrine is taught in a given region (*episkopos*), that the people of a local congregation are properly counseled and provided with Word and Sacrament (*presbuteros*), and that through service the discipline of the community is maintained (*diakonos*). Without ordination the care of souls would be lacking in an ordering principle, apostolic grounding, and means for quality control in the selection of clergy.

6 Women in Ministry

THERE IS EVIDENCE from Luke 8:1–3, Romans 16:1–16, and Philippians 4:2–3, that women were deeply involved in the ministries of the earliest Christian communities. Paul referred to Euodia and Syntyche as "these women who shared my struggles in the cause of the gospel" (Phil. 4:2). He spoke of Phoebe as "a fellow Christian who holds office in the congregation at Cenchreae" (Rom. 16:1), and especially to "Prisca and Aquila, my fellow-workers in Christ Jesus. They risked their necks to save my life, and not I alone but all the gentile congregations are grateful to them. Greet also the congregation at their house" (Rom. 16:3–5). Luke spoke of Mary of Magdala, Joanna and Susanna who had journeyed with Jesus "from town to town and village to village, proclaiming the good news of the kingdom of God" (Luke 8:1 NEB).

There can be no doubt that women have carried significant responsibilities and played crucial roles in the general ministry of the church, in care for the sick, care for the poor, and care for the dying. The question we wish to explore here is the extent to which it is proper to speak of women in the classical pastoral tradition as being involved in the care of souls, that is, a sacred representative ministry, as distinguished from a more general understanding of the ministry of the *laos*. The following passages will at least reveal that there are a variety of views to be considered. We will first cite some passages that show evidence of various types of ministries in which women have been engaged, and then selections that show evidence that the pastoral tradition had genuine concern for fairness in the use of language. For although the patriarchalism has been present, it has not been the only voice.

I. ✱ Ministries in Which Women Have Been Engaged

One indisputable way in which women have ministered is through the order of deaconess. The recollection of the role of women in salvation history is celebrated in this moving pre-Nicene prayer for the blessing of the ordination of a deaconess:

O Eternal God, the Father of our Lord Jesus Christ, the Creator of man and of woman, who didst replenish with the Spirit Miriam, and Deborah, and Anna, and Huldah; who did not think it unfit that Thy only begotten Son should be born of a woman; who also in the taber-

137

nacle of the testimony, and in the temple, didst ordain women to be keepers of Thy holy gates,—do Thou now also look down upon this Thy servant, who is to be ordained to the office of a deaconess, and grant her Thy Holy Spirit, and cleanse her "from all that can defile flesh or spirit" (2 Cor. 7:1), that she may worthily discharge the work which is committed to her to Thy glory, and the praise of Thy Christ, with whom glory and adoration be to Thee and the Holy Spirit for ever. Amen. (*The Constitutions of the Holy Apostles*, Bk. VIII, sec. III, Ch. xx, ANF VII, p. 492, NEB)*

This is a prayer to God to enliven a ministry undertaken by women. The key phrase, also found in the ordinal prayers for the diaconate and presbyterate, is: "Grant thy Holy Spirit." It is the prayer of the whole church for the blessing and empowerment of this ministry. It assumes a long memory of the ways in which God has chosen and ordained women and replenished them by the Spirit. A series of names was recollected: Miriam, Deborah, Anna, and others. Deaconess was a Christian office to which women were ordained, following the earlier Jewish tradition of ordaining women as gatekeepers of the tabernacle. The view that women have never been ordained to anything ignores an important part of the Christian pastoral tradition.

All parties can also agree that one indisputable way in which women have participated in Christian ministry is "through their resources," or through ministries of temporal support. The key text from Luke 8:3 is: "The women provided for them [Jesus and the disciples] out of their own resources." This text has recurred in the tradition where women's ministries have been discussed. Here is one such text from the Clementine literature:

Many holy women, again, ministered to holy men of their substance, as the Shunammite woman ministered to Elisha. . . . To Jesus Christ our Lord women ministered of their substance; but they did not live with him; but chastely, and holily, and unblameably they behaved before the Lord. (Clementina, *Two Epistles Concerning Virginity*, Ch. XV, ANF VIII, p. 65)

It was early acknowledged that there are some things men cannot do in ministry as well as women, for example, care for women:

Ordain also a deaconess who is faithful and holy, for the ministrations towards women. For sometimes he cannot send a deacon, who is a man, to the women, on account of unbelievers. Thou shalt therefore send a woman, a deaconess, on account of the imaginations of the bad. For we stand in need of a woman, a deaconess, for many necessities; and first in the baptism of women, the deacon shall anoint only their forehead with the holy oil, and after him the deaconess shall anoint them. (*Constitutions of the Holy Apostles*, Bk. III, sec. II, ANF VII, p. 431)

Under the circumstances of a highly constricted sexual ethic, men minister to women in certain ways, but stand in need of women where their own ministries are limited. Part of this is explained by taboos against male priests touching women, but the general principle is that some aspects of sacred ministry are better performed by women. To avert scandal in the baptism of women, the deacon had one role, the deaconess another. Hence in this very early period, women had a kind of liturgical role, and were not blocked out of representative liturgical leadership altogether, even during the strongest periods of the alleged hegemony of patriarchalism.

The tradition of women being given prophetic gifts is very old indeed. Here is a recollection in the Apostolic Constitutions of the calling and authorization of women to prophesy:

> Now women prophesied also. Of old, Miriam the sister of Moses and Aaron, and after her Deborah, and after these Huldah and Judith— the former under Josiah, the latter under Darius. The mother of the Lord did also prophesy, and her kinswoman Elisabeth, and Anna; and in our time the daughters of Philip: yet were not these elated against their husbands, but preserved their own measures. Wherefore if among you also there be a man or a woman, and such a one obtains any gift, let him be humble, that God may be pleased with him. For says He: "Upon whom will I look, but upon him that is humble and quiet, and trembles at my words?" (Is. 66:2). (*Constitutions of the Holy Apostles*, Book VIII, Sec. I, ANF VII, p. 481)

Accordingly, it was not considered a novel or unusual thing in the early church if women received prophetic inspiration. For the Jewish tradition had known numerous prophetic women. And the memory of the women in the holy family—Mary, Elizabeth and Anna—were thought of as prototypes of prophetic Christian women. Models of prophetic women who have at the same time maintained their domestic covenants and responsibilties, can be seen in both Old and New Testaments. These models did not have merely the character of private inspiration, but of publicly declared prophetic witness. Next we ask whether women were viewed as learned teachers whose gifts were, on the basis of their piety and education, acknowledged by bishops of the early tradition? It seems so, according to one of the earliest pastoral writers, Ignatius, the bishop of Antioch around the turn of the first century:

> Salute thou also Mary my daughter, distinguished both for gravity and erudition, as also "the Church which is in her house." (Col. 4:15). May my soul be in place of hers: she is the very pattern of pious women. (Ignatius of Antioch, *Epistle to Hero*, sec. 9, ANF I, p. 115)

The bishop, Ignatius, was indicating to his readers that his official affirmation was being given to the church in Mary's house. By saying, "May my soul be in the place of hers," he was apparently blessing and approving her ministry in her house as if it were his own ministry, and as if hers were an extension of his. If that passage is ruled out as a reference to the early ministry of women, it must be asked what could qualify as such.

The example of Miriam, the sister of Moses, leading the women of the redeemed community in praise of God, became an early Christian prototype for thinking of women leading in songs of praise:

> "When the children of Israel had crossed over the Sea of Suth, Moses and the children of Israel sang the praises of the Lord, and said: We will praise the Lord, because He is exceedingly to be praised" (Exod. 15:1). And, after that Moses had finished singing praises, then Miriam, the sister of Moses and Aaron, took a timbrel in her hands, and all the women went out after her, and sang praises with her, women with women apart, and men with men apart. (Clementina, *Two Epistles Concerning Virginity*, Ch. XIV, ANF VIII, p. 65)

It remains a significant question today as to whether women shall be "with women apart." Shall women do things on their own, without predisposing definitions from the male-oriented tradition? The pastoral tradition at times clearly affirmed the separable identity of women, viewed in relation to the purpose of God in the creation of women and men.

According to the Council of Chalcedon, deaconesses were ordained, as were men, by laying on of hands with specific age limitations and only after rigorous ordinal examination:

> A woman shall not receive the laying on of hands as a deaconess under forty years of age, and then only after searching examination. (Chalcedon, A.D. 451, Canon XV, The Seven Ecumenical Councils, NPNF 2, XIV, p. 279)

The age at which nuns and deaconesses may enter orders was debated repeatedly. Here is a canon of the late seventh century:

> For although the great Basil in his holy canons decreed that she who willingly offers to God and embraces virginity, if she has completed her seventeenth year, is to be entered into the order of virgins: nevertheless, having followed the example respecting widows and deaconesses, analogy and proportion being considered, we have admitted at the said time those who have chosen the monastic life. For it is written in the divine Apostle that a widow is to be elected in the church at sixty years old: but the sacred canons have decreed that a deaconess shall be ordained at forty, since they saw that the Church by divine grace had gone forth more powerful and robust and was advancing still further, and they saw the firmness and stability of the faithful in observing the

divine commandments. (Quinisext Synod, A.D. 692, Canon XL, The Seven Ecumenical Councils, NPNF 2, XIX, p. 384)

May women preach under some circumstances and still remain responsible to Paul's injunction against usurpation of authority? Luther offered this observation:

You must pay no attention to distinctions when you want to look at Christians. You must not say: "This is a man or a woman; this is a servant or a master; this person is old or young." They are all alike and only a spiritual people. Therefore they are all priests. All may proclaim God's Word, except that, as St. Paul teaches in 1 Cor. 14:34, women should not speak in the congregation. . . . If, however, only women were present and no men, as in nunneries, then one of the women might be authorized to preach. (Luther, "Sermons on the First Epistle of St. Peter, 1523," LW, Vol. 30, p. 55; cf. WA 12, p. 308)

This is a remarkable conclusion about the priesthood of the whole church, as a priesthood that includes women as well as men. Luther was willing to affirm Paul's rabbinic assumptions about the ordering of men and women in worship, but only on the Pauline basis that the gospel transcends the law. God permits that external ordering to remain in this world under the conditions of sin, but there is no distinction between men and women as to intrinsic dignity or authority. Externally there is super- and sub-ordination, but inwardly and spiritually there is no distinction of worth. Women may preach the word authoritatively under some circumstances, in Luther's view.

II. ❧ FAIRNESS IN LANGUAGE

Did early Christian writers recognize and attempt to correct the problem of generic pronouns, that language addressed to one sex is applicable to the other? Apparently this is an issue that Tertullian had reflected upon deliberately:

Though my words may seem to be addressed to one sex only, what I say is applicable to persons of both sexes, for there is one law which governs all. (Tertullian, *On Monogamy*, sec. 10, ACW 13, p. 93)

Clement of Alexandria explicitly sought to clarify that the Greek term *anthropos* (often translated mankind or humankind) intends to make reference both to men and women:

The very name "mankind" is a name common to both men and women. Similarly, the Attic Greeks called, I believe, not only the boy

but also the girl by the one name of "child." . . . Notice, too, that "sheep"
is the general name used for the male and female. (Clement of Alexandria, *Christ the Educator*, Bk. I, Ch. 4.11, FC 23, p. 12)

This may hardly seem a concession or an act of progress, until one recalls the
context in which many considered women less adequately representative of humanity than men. Some crucial ideas were understood in the feminine gender.
Origen did not hesitate to speak of the soul in the feminine:

> For the soul, therefore, these things will include a certain self-per-
> ception, by which she ought to know how she is constituted in herself.
> (Origen, *Song of Songs*, Bk. 2, ACW 26, p. 134)

Catherine of Siena, along with many other writers, spoke of the soul as feminine:

> The soul cannot persevere except by the union of her three powers
> [intellect, memory, will]. (Catherine of Siena, *A Treatise of Discretion*, p.
> 133)

III. ❧ EQUALITY OF SOULS BEYOND SEXUAL DIFFERENCES

The consuming interest of pastoral care is the nurture and growth of the soul.
The soul is the inner, energizing, vital center of personal existence, given by
God. The soul is the life of the body, that without which the body is a corpse,
without which personality is lifeless.

It is pertinent to ask whether, despite historical differences, souls are considered equal in the pastoral tradition. Further, despite the fact that feminine,
neuter, or masculine language has in various periods been applied to the soul,
can the soul be said to be masculine or feminine?

> Souls, themselves by themselves, are equal. Souls are neither male
> nor female. (Clement of Alexandria, *The Stromata, or Miscellanies*, Bk.
> VI, Ch. XII, ANF II, p. 503)

Soul does not have sexual identity. Soul enlivens a body which has sexual identity. Soul is not sexually differentiated. Although soul care is attentive to sexual
differences, because the body-soul unity is inseparable, the soul itself transcends sexual difference. The concern of soul care is the nurture of excellent
habitual behavior patterns (*arete*, or virtues) in the soul. Clement of Alexandria
argued that the virtue practiced by women is not fundamentally different from
the virtue practiced by men.

> Let us recognize, too, that both men and women practise the same
> sort of virtue. Surely, if there is but one God for both, then there is
> but one Educator for both.

One Church, one virtue, one modesty, a common food, wedlock in common, breath, sight, hearing, knowledge, hope, obedience, love, all are alike [in man and woman]. They who possess life in common, grace in common, and salvation in common have also virtue in common and, therefore education too. The Scripture says: "For in this world, they marry and are given in marriage," for this world is the only place in which the female is distinguished from the male, "but in that other world, no longer" (Matt. 22:30). There, the rewards of this life, lived in the holy union of wedlock, await not man or woman as such, but the human person. (Clement of Alexandria, *Christ the Educator*, Bk. I, Ch. 4.10, FC 23, pp. 11–12)

Remarkably, the implication is, even in the third century, that the education of men and women should be the same. So also echoes John Chrysostom of the equality of the souls men and women:

Has she not the same kind of soul as thou? Has she not been vouchsafed the same privileges by God? Does she not partake of the same table? (Chrysostom, *Homilies on Ephesians*, Hom. XV, NPNF 1, XIII, p. 124)

That there are not two tables in Christianity for the eucharist, nor two baptisms, for women as distinguishable from men, is no incidental or minor point. Many pastoral writers argued for the perfect complementarity of the sexuality of men and women. Complementarity implies that male sexuality requires female sexuality, and female requires male. One cannot have one without the other. Since both are absolutely required to accomplish the divinely given purpose of sexuality, neither sex, it is argued, can be superior:

The male differs from the female only in that part of his body in which is the power of injecting seed and propagating mankind. And in this there is a great proof of providence, from the necessary difference of members; but more in this, where under a likeness of form there is found to be diversity of use and variety of office. For males and females equally have teats, but only those of the female are filled with milk; that, as soon as they have brought forth, the infant may find nourishment suited to him. But if we see the members in man arranged with such method, that in all the rest there is seen to be similarity of form, and a difference only in those in which their use requires a difference, and we neither see anything superfluous nor anything wanting in man, nor in woman anything deficient or in excess, who will not, from all these things, acknowledge the operation of reason, and the wisdom of the Creator? (Clementina, *Recognitions of Clement*, Bk. VIII, Ch. xxxii, ANF VIII, p. 174)

In the original divine creation of sexuality, there are no excesses or deficiencies, only radical complementarity. Yet absolute equality is hardly possible in a tragically self-assertive world:

This article wants to make all men equal and to turn the spiritual kingdom of Christ into a worldly, external kingdom. This is impossible, for a state in which there is no inequality of persons—so that some are free, others captive; some are masters, others subjects—cannot exist in this world. (Luther, "Admonition to Peace: A Reply to the Twelve Articles of the Peasants in Swabia, 1525," WLS I, p. 438; cf. WML IV, p. 240, and WA 18, p. 327)

Ignatius pleaded that women not be mistreated:

Do not hold women in abomination, for they have given you birth, and brought you up. It is fitting, therefore, to love those that were the authors of our birth. (Ignatius of Antioch, *Epistle to Hero*, sec. 4, ANF I, p. 114)*

IV. 🙿 GIFTS OF WOMEN

The Christian community is blessed with many gifts, which in their complementarity are sufficient for the well-being and growth of the community. However, as Paul pointed out, gifts differ—for it would not enhance the strength of the community if every one had the same gift. In this context, some writers have argued that women are more prone to receive some spiritual gifts than men. Luther, for example, spoke of the special capacity of women for faith:

When the female sex begins to embrace Christian doctrine, it is more fervent in faith than the male sex, as may be seen in the case of Anastasia. Magdalene was more courageous than Peter (John 20;1ff). (Luther, *Table Talk*, W-T 2, #1858; WLS 3, p. 1460)

John Chrysostom commended as a model for both men and women the compassionate life-style of certain gifted women:

Their only meal is in the evening, a meal not even of herbs nor of bread, but of flour and beans and pulse and olives and figs. They spin without intermission, and labor far harder than their handmaids at home. What more? they will take upon them to wait upon women who are sick, carrying their beds, and washing their feet. Nay, many of them even cook. So great is the power of the flame of Christ; so far does their zeal surpass their very nature. . . . Hearken about the women of old; they were great characters, great women and admirable; such were Sarah, Rebekah, Rachel, Deborah, and Hannah; and such there were also in the days of Christ. (John Chrysostom, *Homilies on Ephesians*, Hom. XIII, NPNF 1, XIII, p. 116)

Clement of Alexandria commended the virtues of self-reliance and educational discipline as concerns that are just as relevant to women as men:

It is not then possible that man or woman can be conversant with anything whatever, without the advantage of education, and application, and training; and virtue, we have said, depends not on others, but on ourselves above all. (Clement of Alexandria, *The Stromata, or Miscellanies*, Bk. IV, Ch. XIX, ANF II, p. 432)

Palladius provided examples among the martyrs and ascetics of women who carried on extraordinary ministries of witness and hospitality, founding monasteries and helping travellers, as in the case of Melania:

Melania the thrice blessed was Spanish by birth and later a Roman. She was the daughter of Marcellinus, one of the consuls, and wife of some man of high rank, I forget which. She was widowed at twenty-two and was counted worthy of divine love, and she told no one, for she would have been stopped at that time, when Valens held rule. She had a trustee named for her son, and taking every movable piece of her property she put it on board ship and set off for Alexandria at full speed with illustrious women and children.

And there she sold her possessions and changed her holdings into gold. She went to Mount Nitria and met Pambo, Arsisius, Sarapion the Great, Paphnutius of Scete, Isidore the Confessor, and Dioscorus, bishop of Hermopolis. And she spent up to half a year with them, making the rounds of the desert and seeking out all the holy men . . . . After they were recalled from exile, she built a monastery in Jerusalem and lived there twenty-seven years heading a company of fifty virgins. Close by dwelt also the very noble Rufinus from the Italian city of Aquileia; his way of life was like hers, and he was a most staunch man, later deemed worthy of the priesthood—a more learned and reasonable man was never found.

So for twenty-seven years they both entertained with their own private funds the bishops, solitaries, and virgins who visited them, coming to Jerusalem to fulfil a vow. They edified all their visitors and united the four hundred monks of the Pauline schism by persuading every heretic who denied the Holy Spirit and so brought them back to the Church. They bestowed gifts and food on the local clergy. . . .

No one failed to benefit by her good works, neither in the east nor in the west, neither in the north nor in the south. For thirty-seven years she practiced hospitality; from her own treasury she made donations to churches, monasteries, guests, and prisons. (Palladius, *The Lausiac History*, No. 47–54; ACW 34, pp. 123–134)

Melania was also cited for scholarly competencies in theology:

Melania . . . was most erudite and fond of literature, and she turned night into day going through every writing of the ancient commentators—three million lines of Origen and two and a half million lines of Gregory, Stephen, Pierius, Basil, and other worthy men. And she did not read them once only and in an offhand way, but she worked on them, dredging through each work seven or eight times. Thus it was possible for her to be liberated from "knowledge falsely so called" (I Tim. 6:20) and to mount on wings, thanks to those books—by good hopes she transformed herself into a spiritual bird and so made the journey to Christ. (Palladius, *The Lausiac History*, No. 55, sec. 3, ACW 34, pp. 136–137)

From the beginning of primal human history women have played decisive roles in the history of salvation:

"When the term was completed, God sent his own Son, born of a woman" (Gal. 4:4). The enemy would not have been justly conquered unless it had been a man [made] of woman who conquered him. . . . Because of this the Lord also declares himself to be the Son of Man, so renewing in himself that primal man from whom the formation /of man/ by woman began. (Irenaeus, *Against Heresies*, sec. 21, LCC, p. 391, NEB)*

Women were thought by Palladius to be as courageous as men in the witness to faith. In his Lausaic History, he recounts some of the women who had played significant and inspired roles in Christian mission:

I must also commemorate in this book the courageous women to whom God granted struggles equal to those of men, so that no one could plead as a excuse that women are too weak to practice virtue successfully. . . . Among these was the Roman matron Paula, who was mother of Toxotius, a woman highly distinguished in the spiritual life. . . . I knew Basianillia, too, the wife of Candidianus the general; she practiced virtue zealously and carefully and still is vigorously fighting the good fight. And I knew Photeina, too, a maiden of the highest renown, a daughter of Theoctistus, the priest of Laodicea. And in Antioch I came across a woman also of great reknown who held converse intimately with God, the deaconess Sabiniana, aunt of John, bishop of Constantinople. (Palladius, *The Lausiac History*, No. 41, sec. 1–2, 4, ACW 34, pp. 117–118)

In African Christianity of the fourth century it was assumed that women may have the calling and competencies to teach women catechumens:

Widows and dedicated women (*sanctimoniales*) who are chosen to assist at the baptism of women, should be so well instructed in their office as to be able aptly and properly to teach unskilled and rustic women how to answer at the time of their baptism to the questions put to them, and also how to live godly after they have been baptized. (Fourth Council of Carthage, A.D. 398, Canon XII, The Seven Ecumenical Councils, NPNF 2, VIX, p. 41)

These selections cannot form a fully adequate Christian teaching about women in ministry. The deposit of faith given in Jesus Christ was a fully adequate revelation as it was grasped by the apostolic writers, but certain dimensions of that revelation have taken an exceptionally long time to fully recognize and develop amid the tragic conflicts of history. Why did such achievements as those of the Protestant Reformation take so long? Why was political toleration so slow in coming? Why did it take so long to recognize the will of Christ concerning human slavery? We remain slow learners also with respect to the equality of women and men. The Christian community is still trying to understand fully what was essentially given in the Christian gospel.

7 Preparation for Care of Souls

For a task so consequential as caring for souls, an appropriate regimen of preparation has always been thought important. Key pastoral writers for almost two millenia have been thinking and writing about what we today call theological curriculum—that course of study and intellectual, moral, and spiritual preparation requisite for the practice of pastoral care.

Many issues are explored by the pastoral writers under this heading: Is intellectual formation less important than moral and spiritual aspects of pastoral formation? What personality characteristics or behavioral patterns are thought to be crucial to ministry, so much so that care of souls can hardly function without them? How important are pastoral role models in developing competencies for ministry? What subjects are considered non-omissible in a curriculum of theological studies? In addition to scripture study, how heavily are historical, philosophical, literary, scientific, and psychological inquiries to be weighed?

I. ❧ What Makes a Good Care-Giver?

Classic pastoral writers have largely affirmed that preparation for soul care requires a well-proportioned regimen which involves seasonable, practical knowledge of scripture and tradition, keen moral awareness, practiced spiritual discipline, the development of intellectual rigor and logical reflection, accurate observation, prudential judgment, and common sense grounded in eschatological awareness. But how are these to be balanced porportionally? In what sequence are they to be pursued? Does one depend upon another?

First, gaining an appropriate confidence in oneself, learning to trust one's own ability to make reasonable judgments, is an important step toward readiness for ministry. No one is going to prepare you for ministry, wrote Lactantius, if you do not ready yourself. For a vocation that speaks so much of relying upon God, this vocation, ironically, requires a high degree of self-reliance:

It is therefore right, especially in a matter on which the whole plan of life turns, that everyone should place confidence in himself, and use his own judgment and individual capacity for the investigation and weighing of the truth, rather than through confidence in others to be deceived by their errors, as though he himself were without understanding. God has given wisdom to all alike, that they might be able

148

both to investigate things which they have not heard, and to weigh things which they have heard. . . . Since wisdom—that is, the inquiry after truth—is natural to all, they deprive themselves of wisdom, who without any judgment approve of the discoveries of their ancestors, and like sheep are led by others. (Lactantius, *The Divine Institutes*, Ch. VIII, ANF VII, p. 51)

Pastoral inquirers are encouraged to learn to rely upon their own perception, reasoning, and judgment, to weigh evidence fairly, and not blindly follow spurious authoritarianisms. One who presumes to guide another's conscience needs a conscience well-guided. Luther warned care-givers:

Therefore I admonish you, especially those of you who are to become instructors of consciences, as well as each of you individually, that you exercise yourselves by study, by reading, by meditation, and by prayer, so that in temptation you will be able to instruct consciences, both your own and others, console them, and take them from the Law to grace, from active righteousness to passive righteousness, in short, from Moses to Christ. (Luther, *Lectures on Galatians*, 1535, LW 26, p. 10)

For Luther, it was not merely knowing conceptually the difference between law and gospel that was the center of care of souls, but the existential application of that distinction to the counselor's own existence. In this same spirit, John Chrysostom compared preparation for care of souls to an athletic contest in which many types of rigorous preparation come to focus upon one single moment—the race (by analogy the moment of being required to provide good counsel to another in trouble):

People who are keen for athletic fitness need doctors and trainers and a careful diet and continual exercise and any amount of precautions. For the neglect of a small detail in these matters upsets and spoils the whole scheme. Then what about those whose vocation is to look after this Body which has to contend, not against flesh and blood, but against the unseen powers? (John Chrysostom, *On the Priesthood*, Ch. IV, sec. 2, p. 114)

The kind of reasoning most pertinent to care of souls is practical, prudential reasoning that rightly envisions fitting means to good ends. Anything knowable, however, is capable of being sinfully distorted. The misuse of knowledge has been the primordial human problem in the history of the family of Adam. Good knowing emerges out of good living:

Scripture clearly says, "In the beginning God planted in the midst of the garden the tree of knowledge and the tree of life" (Gen. 2:9); thereby showing that the way of life lies through knowledge. It is only because the first-created couple used it improperly that, through the wiles of the serpent, they were stripped of all they had. Without knowledge there can be no life, and without life there can be no trustworthy knowledge; which is why the two trees were planted side by side. The Apostle saw the force of this when he told us, "knowledge makes a windbag, but love is a builder" (1 Cor. 8:1); that was his rebuke to the knowledge which is exercised without regard to the lifegiving precepts of the truth. For a man who claims to know, but is without the knowledge which is real and attested by life, knows nothing. (*Epistle to Diognetus*, ECW, sec. 12, p. 183)

Ministry cannot proceed effectively without the acquisition of hardwon skills which cannot be substituted by the pretense of piety. Preparation for ministry is crucial because so many souls hang in the balance of its effectiveness. Richard Baxter reflected on the curious irony that God would allow so much to depend upon ministry:

It is a lamentable case, that in a message from the God of heaven, of everlasting moment to the souls of men, we should behave ourselves so weakly, so unhandsomely, so imprudently, or so slightly, that the whole business should miscarry in our hands, and God should be dishonoured, and his work disgraced, and sinners rather hardened than converted; and all this through our weakness or neglect! How often have carnal hearings gone home jeering at the palpable and dishonourable failings of the preacher! . . . What skill is necessary to deal in private with one poor ignorant soul for his conversion! . . . I know that laziness hath learned to allege the vanity of all our studies, and how entirely the Spirit must qualify us for, and assist us in our work; as if God comanded us the use of means, and then warranted us to neglect them. (Baxter, *RP*, 70–71)

In reviewing numerous reasons why pastors may tend to feel internal resistances to acting pastorally, Baxter mused on the intrinsic difficulty and subtlety of this task:

Here sloth will tie the hands of many. . . . Many of us have also a foolish bashfulness which makes us backward to begin relationships, and to speak plainly to others. We are so modest, it seems, that we blush to speak for Christ, or contradict the devil, or save a soul, while, at the same time, we are less ashamed of shameful works. . . . We have commonly a great deal of unskilfulness and unfitness for this work. Alas! How few know how to deal with an ignorant, worldly man, for his conversion! To get within him and win upon him; to suit our speech to his condition and temper; to choose the meetest subjects, and follow them with a holy mixture of seriousness, and terror, and love, and meekness, and evangelical allurements—oh! who is fit for such a thing? (Baxter, *RP*, pp. 192–93)*

Three closely intertwined spiritual disciplines (prayer, temptation, and meditation) are required to practice pastoral guidance with understanding:

There is none like to Luther's three masters: Prayer, Temptation, Meditation. Temptation stirs up holy meditation; meditation prepares to prayer; and prayer makes profit of temptation and fetcheth all Divine knowledge from Heaven. Of others I may learn the theory of Divinity, of these only, the practice. Other masters teach me, by rote, to speak, parrot-like of Heavenly things; these alone, with feeling and understanding. (Joseph Hall, *Meditations and Vows*, I, lxxxv, Works, VIII, p. 24; *Angl.*, p. 615).

The complex relation of study to the practice of ministry has long fascinated pastoral writers. The Anglican pastor, John Earle, offered this penetrating analysis in 1628 of the need for a well-timed melding of knowing and doing, of preparation and action, of mind and spirit:

The good pastor is one that knows the burden of his calling and has studied to make his shoulders sufficient. He has not been hasty to launch forth from his port, the University, but awaited the ballast of learning and the wind of opportunity. Divinity is not the beginning but the end of his studies, to which he takes the ordinary stair and makes the Arts his way. He counts it not profaneness to be polished with human reading, or to smooth his way by Aristotle to scholastic theology. He has sounded both religions, and anchored in the best, and is a Protestant out of judgement, not faction; not because his country, but his reason, is on this side. The Ministry is his choice, not refuge; and yet the pulpit not his itch, but fear. His discourse there is substance, not all rhetoric. He utters more things than words. His speech is not helped with enforced action, but the matter acts itself. . . . In Simoniacal purchases he thinks his soul goes in the bargain, and is loath to come by promotion so dear. Yet his worth at the length advances him, and the price of his own merit buys him a living. He is no base scraper of his tithes and will not wrangle for the odd egg. The lawyer is the only man he hinders, by whom he is spited for taking up quarrels. He is a main pillar of our Church, though not yet Dean or Canon, and his life our religion's best apology. His death is his last sermon, where in the pulpit of his bed he instructs men to die by his example. (John Earle, *Microcosmography*, sec. 3, pp. 5–7; *Angl.*, p. 728–729)*

II. ❧ ROLE MODELS OF PASTORAL INTEGRATION

The effectiveness of pastoral practice is improved by carefully studying the best practitioners of pastoral care. One may learn good counsel by observing the best counselors at close range. Most pastoral writers have strongly commended the study of the example of excellent ministers. The best preparation for pastoral service, therefore, may be more like an apprenticeship to an excellent sculptor, or a medical internship, than academic study in a university:

It is the example of such men as these, my brothers, that we must make our own. It is written, "Seek ye the company of the holy, for they who seek their company shall themselves be made holy." And it says somewhere else, "With the innocent you shall be innocent, with the chosen you shall be chosen, with the wayward you shall be wayward" (Ps. 18:26,27). (Clement of Rome, *To the Corinthians*, sec. 46, ECW, p. 47)

St. Frances de Sales commented upon the importance of role models for ministry. He especially noted that several models in combination may be best:

Look at St. Anthony, honoured by God and by men on account of his great sanctity. Tell me, how did he reach such heights of holiness and perfection? Was it by much reading, or by conferences and frequent Communions, or by the multitudes of sermons which he heard? Not at all; he became so great a Saint by making use of the example of the holy hermits, taking the abstinence of one, the prayer of another, like a diligent bee, going hither and thither, pilfering and storing up the virtues of the servants of God, to make the honey of sanctity by these holy examples. (Francis de Sales, Conference VII, *SC*, p. 114)

In his biography of St. Anthony, Athanasius had earlier described the period during which Anthony was preparing for his vocation. This is the passage from which Frances de Sales got his "diligent bee" image:

Now there was then in the next village an old man who had lived the life of a hermit from his youth up. Antony, after he had seen this man, imitated him in piety. And at first he began to abide in places outside the village: then if he heard of a good man anywhere, like the prudent bee, he went forth and sought him, nor turned back to his own place until he had seen him; and he returned, having got from the good man as it were supplies for his journey in the way of virtue. So dwelling there at first, he confirmed his purpose not to return to the abode of his fathers nor to the remembrance of his kinsfolk; but to keep all his desire and energy for perfecting his discipline. He worked, however, with his hands, having heard, "he who is idle let him not eat," (2 Thes. 3:10) and part he spent on bread and part he gave to the needy. And he was constant in prayer, knowing that a man ought to pray in secret unceasingly. For he had given such heed to what was read that none of the things that were written fell from him to the ground, but he remembered all, and afterwards his memory served him for books.

Thus conducting himself, Antony was beloved by all. He subjected himself in sincerity to the good men whom he visited, and learned thoroughly where each surpassed him in zeal and discipline. He observed the graciousness of one; the unceasing prayer of another; he took knowledge of another's freedom from anger and another's loving-kindness; he gave heed to one as he watched, to another as he studied; one he admired for his endurance, another for his fasting and sleeping on the ground; the meekness of one and the long-suffering of another he watched with care, while he took note of the piety towards Christ and the mutual love which animated all. Thus filled, he returned to his own place of discipline, and henceforth would strive to unite the qualities of each, and was eager to show in himself the virtues of all. With others of the same age he had no rivalry; save this only, that he should not be second to them in higher things. And this he did so as to hurt the feelings of nobody, but made them rejoice over him. So all they of that village and the good men in whose intimacy he was, when they saw that he was a man of this sort, used to call him God-beloved. And some welcomed him as a son, others as a brother. (Athanasius, *Life of Anthony*, sec. 3–4, NPNF 2, IV, p. 196)

According to Athanasius' account of the most dominant figure among the desert fathers, Anthony the Great, academic learning cannot of itself suffice in preparation for counsel. Native intelligence mixed with rigorous spiritual discipline count for more:

Antony also was exceeding prudent, and the wonder was that although he had not learned letters, he was a ready-witted and sagacious man. At all events two Greek philosophers once came, thinking they could try their skill on Antony; and he was in the outer mountain, and having recognised who they were from their appearance, he came to them and said to them by means of an interpreter, "Why, philosophers, did ye trouble yourselves so much to come to a foolish man?" And when they said that he was not a foolish man, but exceedingly prudent, he said to them, "If you came to a foolish man, your labour is superfluous; but if you think me prudent become as I am, for we ought to imitate what is good. And if I had come to you I should have imitated you; but if you to me, become as I am, for I am a Christian." But they departed with wonder, for they saw that even demons feared Antony.

And again others such as these met him in the outer mountain and thought to mock him because he had not learned letters. And Antony said to them, "What say ye? which is first, mind or letters? And which is the cause of which—mind of letters or letters of mind? (Athanasius, *Life of Anthony*, sec. 72–73, NPNF 2, IV, p. 215)

Taking Paul as role model, Richard Baxter commended a single biblical text, Acts 20:19–35, as a worthy basis upon which a young pastor might well organize an entire year of preparatory study, because it so aptly summarized the pastoral task:

I think this one speech deserves a twelvemonth's study, more than most things young students spend their time upon. O brethren! Write it on your study doors. Set it in capital letters as your copy, that it may be ever before your eyes. If we could well learn only two or three lines of it, what preachers should we be!

(a) Our general business—SERVING THE LORD IN ALL HUMILITY AMID SORROWS AND TRIALS.

(b) Our special work—KEEP WATCH OVER YOURSELVES AND OVER ALL THE FLOCK.

(c) Our doctrine—REPENTANCE BEFORE GOD AND TRUST IN OUR LORD JESUS CHRIST.

(d) The place and manner of teaching—I TAUGHT YOU IN PUBLIC AND IN YOUR HOMES.

(e) His diligence, earnestness, and affection—I NEVER CEASED TO COUNSEL EACH OF YOU, AND HOW I WEPT OVER YOU.

(f) His faithfulness—I HAVE KEPT BACK NOTHING; I HAVE DISCLOSED TO YOU THE WHOLE PURPOSE OF GOD.

(g) His disinteredness and self-denial for the sake of the gospel—I HAVE NOT WANTED ANYONE'S MONEY OR CLOTHES FOR MYSELF; YOU ALL KNOW THAT THESE HANDS OF MINE EARNED ENOUGH FOR THE NEEDS OF MYSELF AND MY CONPANIONS. I SHOWED YOU THAT IT IS OUR DUTY TO HELP THE WEAK IN THIS WAY, BY HARD WORK, AND THAT WE SHOULD KEEP IN MIND THE WORDS OF THE LORD JESUS, WHO HIMSELF SAID, "HAPPINESS LIES MORE IN GIVING THAN IN RECEIVING."

(h) His patience and perseverance—FOR MYSELF, I SET NO STORE BY LIFE; I ONLY WANT TO FINISH THE RACE, AND COMPLETE THE TASK WHICH THE LORD JESUS ASSIGNED TO ME.

(i) His prayerfulness—I COMMEND YOU TO GOD AND TO HIS GRACIOUS WORD, WHICH HAS POWER TO BUILD YOU UP AND GIVE YOU YOUR HERITAGE AMONG ALL WHO ARE DEDICATED HIM.

(j) His purity of conscience—THAT BEING SO, I HERE AND NOW DECLARE THAT NO MAN'S FATE CAN BE LAID AT MY DOOR.

Write all this upon your hearts, and it will do yourselves and the Church more good than twenty years' study of those lower things. (Baxter, *RP*, pp. 229–230, NEB)*

III. ❧ JOYS AND BENEFITS OF PASTORAL STUDY AND MEDITATION

Pastors often regard study time as the most fruitful and rewarding aspect of ministry. Others become so distracted by pastoral tasks that little time seems left for study or meditation. The early pastoral writers placed a high premium upon an intentional effort to maintain regular study time. Origen thought that tranquillity in study was necessary to ready one for the storms of pastoral service. His metaphor was that of building a house in good weather prior to a storm:

When a house is being built which is to be made as strong as possible, the building takes place in fine weather and in calm, so that nothing may hinder the structure from acquiring the needed solidity. And thus it turns out so strong and stable that it is able to withstand the rush of the flood, and the dashing of the river, and all the agencies accompanying a storm which are apt to find out what is rotten in a building and to show what parts of it have been properly put together. And more particularly should that house . . . be built at a time when God can add His free co-operation to the projector of so noble a work, when the soul is quiet and in the enjoyment of that peace which passes all understanding, when she is turned away from all disturbance and not buffeted by any billows. . . . All this is said by way of apology to you, reverend Ambrosius. It is at your sacred encouragement that I have made up my mind to build up in writing the tower of the Gospel; and I have therefore sat down to count the cost to see whether I can finish it, lest I should be mocked by the beholders because I laid the foundation but was not able to finish the work. The result of my counting, it is true, has been that I do not possess what is required to finish it; yet I have put my trust in God, who enriches us with all wisdom and all knowledge. If we strive to keep His spiritual laws we believe that He does enrich us; He will supply what is necessary so that we shall get on with our building, and shall even come to the parapet of the structure. (Origen, *Commentary on John*, Bk. VI, Ch. 1, ANF X, p. 349)*

While engaged in study, one does not cease doing the work of the pastor. For study is an activity without which soul care cannot wisely proceed. Study is therefore not something that can be considered a luxury of ministry, or an ancillary option, but essential to the task of ministry. But like slow-growing seeds, this sort of investment of time does not always have an immediate return:

My concern should be that others receive from me [what God has taught me in Scripture] and that I strive to present this in the most attractive form, to teach the ignorant, to admonish and encourage those who have knowledge, to comfort troubled consciences properly, to awaken and strengthen negligent and sleepy hearts, and so on, as St. Paul did (1 Timothy 4; 2 Timothy 4; Titus 3), and as he also commanded his pupils Timothy and Titus to do. This should be my concern: how others get it [Christian truth] from me. I should, however, study and beseech God. Studying is my work. This work God wants me to do, and if it pleases Him, He will bless it. It may well happen that I study for a long time, and yet He does not grant me success. Then in a year or two, and when it pleases Him, He grants it plentifully and superabundantly in an hour. (Luther, "Sermon on Matthew 6:24–34," WA 10 I, 2, p. 378; WLS 2, pp. 927–928)

The pastoral writers have often urged that morning be intentionally set aside regularly for study. Henry Isaacson spoke with affectionate amusement of the fixed habit of Anglican Bishop Lancelot Andrewes:

From the hour he arose, his private devotions finished, to the time he was called to dinner, which, by his own order, was not till twelve at noon at the soonest, he kept close at his book, and would not be interrupted by any that came to speak with him, or upon any occasion, public prayer excepted. Insomuch that he would be so displeased with scholars that attempted to speak with him in a morning, that he would say "He doubted they were no true scholars that came to speak with him before noon." (Henry Isaacson, On Lancelot Andrewes, 1650, Andrewes' Miscellaneous Works, LACT, xxv; *Angl.*, p. 729)

However crucial study time may be, it is not so absolutely important that it can legitimately crowd out all time for direct openness to God in mediation and prayer. St. Teresa of Avila highly commended seasons of quiet when objective and academic learning would be put aside in favor of the simplicity of prayer.

What the soul has to do at these seasons of quiet is merely to go softly and make no noise. By noise, I mean going about with the understanding in search of many words and reflections with which to give thanks for this benefit. . . . In these periods of quiet, then, let the soul repose in its rest; let them put their learning aside; the time will come when they will use it in the Lord's service and will esteem it so much that they would not have failed to acquire it for all the treasures imaginable, simply because they can serve His Majesty with it and for this purpose find it a great help. But in the sight of Infinite Wisdom, believe me, there is more value in a little study of humility and in a single act of it than in all the knowledge in the world. So in this state there is no room for argument but only for a plain recognition of what we are, a presenting of ourselves in our simplicity before God, whose will is that the soul should become a fool. (Teresa of Avila, Life, Ch. XV, Works, I, pp. 157–159)

Anthony, the preeminent desert father, after a period of engagement in the world, strongly felt a compelling need to leave the busy-ness of the world in order to discover himself anew in the presence of God. Athanasius reported this transition:

When the duke, as he is called, entreated him [Anthony] to stay, he replied that he could not linger among them, and persuaded him by a pretty simile, saying, "Fishes, if they remain long on dry land, die. And so monks lose their strength if they loiter among you and spend their time with you. Wherefore as fish must hurry to the sea, so must we hasten to the mountain." (Athanasius, *Life of Anthony*, NPNF 2, IV, p. 218)

According to Baxter, one of the reasons that ministry is freely supported by lay benevolence is that ministers remain free to make a full-time and unimpeded inquiry on behalf of the supportive community of faith into scripture and Christian wisdom:

It is something that you are maintained by other men's labours. This is for your work, that you may not be taken off from it, but, as Paul requireth, may "give yourselves wholly to these things," (1 Tim. 4:15) and not be forced to neglect men's souls, whilst you are providing for your own bodies. . . . But you have far greater privileges than this. . . . To be daily employed in the consideration of the blessed nature, works, and ways of God! Others are glad of the leisure of the Lord's day, and now and then of an hour besides, when they can lay hold upon it. But we may keep a continual Sabbath. We may do almost nothing else, but study and talk of God and glory, and engage in acts of prayer and praise, and drink in his sacred, saving truths. . . . To live among such excellent helps as our libraries afford, to have so many silent wise companions whenever we please. . . . You are the stewards of his mysteries, and rulers of his household; and he that entrusted you, will maintain you in his work. . . . If you will put forth your hand to relieve the distressed, he will wither the hand that is stretched out against you. (Baxter, *RP*, pp. 128–129)

Bishop Joseph Hall wrote rhapsodically of the special joys and benefits of pastoral study, amid the ever-changing rhythms of pastoral practice:

Other artisans do but practise; we, still learn. Others run still in the same gyre, to weariness, to satiety; our choice is infinite. Other labours require recreations; our very labour recreates our sports. We can never want either somewhat to do, or somewhat that we would do.

How numberless are those volumes which men have written of arts, of tongues! How endless is that volume, which God hath written of the world, where every creature is a letter, every day a new page! Who can be weary of either of these? To find wit in poetry; in philosophy, profoundness; in mathematics, acuteness; in history, wonder of events; in oratory, sweet eloquence; in Divinity, supernatural light and holy devotion; as so many rich metals in their proper mines, whom would it not ravish with delight?

After all these, let us but open our eyes. We cannot look anywhere in this in this universal Book of our Maker, without seeing a lesson worth our study, worth taking out. What creature has not its miracle? What event fails to challenge observation? And if, weary of foreign employment, we are inclined to look home into ourselves, there we find a more private world of thoughts, which set us on work anew, more busily, not less profitably. Now our silence is vocal, our solitariness popular, and we are shut up to do good unto many.

And, if once we be cloyed with our own company, the door of conference is open. Here interchange of discourse, besides pleasure, benefits us; and he is a weak companion from whom we return not wiser.

I could envy, if I could believe, that Anchorite who, secluded from the world and pent up in his voluntary prison-walls, denied that he thought the day long, while yet he hungered for learning to vary his thoughts. Not to be flooded with the same conceit is difficult exceeding human strength; but, to a man so furnished with all sorts of knowledge that, according to his dispositions, he can change his studies, I should wonder that ever the sun should seem to pace slowly. How many busy tongues chase away good hours, in pleasant chat, and complain of the haste of night! What ingenuous mind can be soon weary of talking with learned authors, the most harmless and sweetest of companions? What a heaven lives a scholar in, that at once, in one close room, can daily converse with all the glorious Martyrs and Fathers, that can single out, at pleasure, either sententious Tertullian, or grave Cyprian, or resolute Jerome, or flowing Chrysostom, or divine Ambose, or devout Bernard, or, who alone is all these, heavenly Augustine; and talk with them and hear their wise and holy counsels, verdicts, resolutions: yea, to rise higher, with courtly Isaiah, with Learned Paul, with all their fellow-Prophets, Apostles: yet more, like another Moses, with God Himself, in them both! Let the world despise us. While we have these delights, we cannot envy those in the world. We cannot wish ourselves other than we are.

Besides, the way to all other contentments is troublesome: the only recompence is in the end. To delve in the mines, to scorch in the fire, for the getting, for the finding of gold, is a slavish toil. The comfort is in the wedge, to the owner, not the labourers. But our very search of knowledge is delightsome. Study itself is our life, from which we would not be barred from a world. How much sweeter then is the fruit of study, the conscience of knowledge! In comparison, the soul that has once tasted it, easily contemns all human comforts. (Joseph Hall, Epistles, Fourth Decade, No. iii.; *Angl.*, p. 760)*

Anglican Thomas Traherne felt that the time spent in study was so valuable that he was willing to give up other temporal benefits for it. He deliberately chose a reduced income in order to gain time for study:

When I came into the country, and being seated among silent trees and meads and hills had all my time in mine own hands, I resolved to spend it all, whatever it cost me, in search of happiness and to satiate that burning thirst which Nature had enkindled in me from my youth. In which I was so resolute, that I chose rather to live upon ten pounds a year, and to go in leather clothes, and feed upon bread and water, so that I might have all my time clearly to myself, than to keep many thousands per annum in an estate of life where my time would be devoured in care and labour. And God was so pleased to accept of that desire, that from that time to this I have had all things plentifully provided for me, without any care at all, my very study of Felicity making me more to prosper than all the care in the whole world. So that through His blessing I live a free and a kingly life as if the world were turned again into Eden, or much more, as it is at this day. (Thomas Traherne, Centuries of Meditations, p. 186; *Angl.*, p. 776)

IV. ❧ THE PASTOR'S BOOKS

The pastor's work and the pastor's books are inseparable. Since dialogue with scripture and tradition is so central to pastoral care, it is to be expected that the life of the pastor will be deeply enmeshed in the meditative reading, thoughtful study, and care of good books. Since the pastor's time is limited, selection of excellent books is a consequential pastoral decision.

Luther counseled that fewer books should be better read than many poorly. The classical pastoral writers should be read to lead to scripture. Even the best of the classical writers, as they themselves testified, can never adequately substitute for scripture:

The number of theological books must also be lessened, and a selection made of the best of them. For it is not many books or much reading that makes men learned; but it is good things, however little of them, often read, that make men learned in the Scriptures, and make them godly, too. Indeed the writings of all the holy fathers should be read only for a time, in order that through them we may be led to the Holy Scriptures. As it is, however, we read them only to be absorbed in them and never come to the Scriptures. We are like men who study the sign-posts and never travel the road. The dear fathers wished, by their writings, to lead us to the Scriptures, but we so use them as to be led away from the Scriptures, though the Scriptures alone are our vineyard in which we ought all to work and toil. (Luther, "An Open Letter to Christian Nobility," WML II, p. 151)

Anglican Gilbert Burnet provided a brief summary of curriculum for clergy. His list of books commended to clergy gives us the gist of the priorities prevailing in one period (late seventeenth century), emphasizing biblical, patristic, historical, and medical writers.

With the Study of the Scriptures, or rather as a part of it comes in the Study of the Fathers, as far as one can go. In these their Apologies and Epistles are chiefly to be read, for they give us the best view of those Times. Basil's and Chrysostom's Sermons are by far the best. To these Studies, History comes in as a noble and pleasant Addition. It gives one broad perspectives on the Providence of God, the nature of Man, and the Conduct of the World. This is above no Man's Capacity. Admittedly some Histories are better than others, yet almost any Histories one can get one's hands on is better read than none at all. If one can find one's way through it, he ought to begin with the History of the Church, starting with Josephus, and go on with Eusebius, Socrates, and the other Historians. They are commonly bound together. Then go to other later Collectors of Ancient History, followed by the History of our own Church and Country; then the Ancient Greek and Roman History, and after that, as much History, Geography, and Books of Travels as can be had, will give an easy and useful Entertainment, and will furnish one with great variety of good Thoughts, and of pleasant as well as edifying Discourse. As for all other Studies, everyone must follow his Inclinations, his Capacities and that which he can procure to himself. . . . The Study and Practice of Physick, especially that which is safe and simple, puts the Clergy in a capacity of doing great acts of Charity, and of rendering both their Persons and Labours very acceptable to their People. It will procure their being soon sent for by them in Sickness, and it will give them great advantages in speaking to them of their Spiritual Concerns when they are being especially careful of their health, but in this nothing that is sordid must mix.

 These ought to be the chief Studies of the Clergy. But to give all these their full effect, a Priest that is much in his Study ought to Employ a great part of his Time in secret and fervent Prayer, for the

Direction and Blessing of God in his Labours, for the constant assistance of his Holy Spirit, and for a lively Sense of Divine Matters, that so he may feel the Impressions of them grow deep and strong upon his Thoughts. (Burnet, *Of the Pastoral Care*, Ch. VIII; *CS*, p. 85)*

Jeremy Taylor's brief account of a good library of pastoral care placed a strong emphasis upon pastoral guidance for penitents (derived largely from ancient canon law and penititential advisories), solid ethical case studies of pastoral care (cases of conscience), wise scriptural exposition, and books that store a "treasure of comforts and advices":

Every minister ought to be well skilled and studied in saying his office, in the rubrics, the canons, the articles, and the homilies of the Church, that he may do his duty readily, discreetly, gravely, and by the public measures of the laws. To which also it is very lawful that it be added, that every minister study the ancient canons of the Church, especially the pententials of the Eastern and Western churches. Let him read good books, such as are approved by public authority; such which are useful, wise, and holy; not the scribblings of unlearned parties, but of men learned, pious, obedient, and disinterested; and among these, such especially which describe duty and good life, which minister to faith and charity, to piety and devotion; cases of conscience, and solid expositions of Scripture. Concerning which, learned and wise persons are to be consulted. . . . Let every minister be sure to lay up a treasure of comforts and advices, to bring forth for every man's need in the day of his trouble; let him study and heap together instruments and advices for the promoting of every virtue, and remedies and arguments against every vice; let him teach his people to make acts of virtue, not only by external exercise, but also in the way of prayer and internal meditation. (Jeremy Taylor, *RAC*, Ch. VII., sec. 80–83; *CS*, pp. 24–26)

Luther's recommended reading list strongly favored the classical and most reliable (not new and trendy) biblical commentaries, as well as poetry, law, medicine, and history, with a stress upon quality, not quantity:

My advice is not to heap together all manner of books indiscriminately and think only of the number and size of the collection. I would make a judicious selection, for it is not necessary to have all the comentaries of the jurists, all the sentences of the theologians, all the *quaestiones* of the philosophers, and all the sermons of the monks. Indeed, I would discard all such dung, and furnish my library with the right sort of books, consulting with scholars as to my choice.

First of all, there would be the Holy Scriptures, in Latin, Greek, Hebrew, and German, and any other language in which they might be found. Next the best commentaries, and, if I could find them, the most

ancient, in Greek, Hebrew, and Latin. Then, books that would be helpful in learning the languages, such as the poets and orators, regardless
of whether they were pagan or Christian, Greek or Latin, for it is from
such books that one must learn grammar. After that would come books
on the liberal arts, and all the other arts. Finally, there would be books
of law and medicine; here too there should be careful choice among
commentaries.

Among the foremost would be the chronicles and histories, in whatever languages they are to be had. For they are a wonderful help in
understanding and guiding the course of events, and especially for observing the marvelous works of God. (Luther, "To the Councilman of
All Cities in Germany That They Establish and Maintain Christian
Schools," LW 45, pp. 375–376)

In what follows, we have a rare account from the third century that reveals
how important the proper care of a library was considered to be by one early
Christian writer. Written by Theonas, bishop of Alexandria (282–300 A.D.) to
the chief chamberlain of the Emperor (possibly Diocletian), it provided a rec-
ommendation on the sort of person to whom one should entrust a highly val-
ued collection of books and manuscripts:

The most responsible person, however, among you, and also the most
careful, will be he who may be entrusted by the emperor with the cus-
tody of his library. He will himself select for this office a person of
proven knowledge, a serious person adapted to understanding weighty
affairs, and ready to reply to all applications for information, such a
one as Philadelphus chose for this charge, and appointed to the super-
intendence of his most noble library—I mean Aristeus, his confidential
chamberlain, whom he sent also as his legate to Eleazar, with most magnificent gifts, in recognition of the translation of the sacred Scriptures;
and this person also wrote the full history of the Seventy Interpreters.
If, therefore, it should happen that a believer in Christ is called to this
same office, he should not despise that secular literature and those
Gentile intellects which please the emperor. To be praised are the poets
for the greatness of their genius, the acuteness of their inventions, the
aptness and lofty eloquence of their style. To be praised are the orators; to be praised also are the philosophers in their own class. To be
praised, too, are the historians, who unfold to us the order of exploits,
and the manners and institutions of our ancestors, and show us the
rule of life from the proceedings of the ancients. On occasion also he
will endeavour to laud the divine Scriptures, which, with marvellous
care and most liberal expenditure, Ptolemy Philadelphus caused to be
translated into our language. . . . He ought, therefore, to know all the
books which the emperor possesses. He should often turn them over,

and arrange them neatly in their proper order by catalogue. If, however, he has to get new books, or old ones transcribed, he should be careful to obtain the most accurate copyists. If that cannot be done, he should appoint learned men to the work of correction, and recompense them justly for their labours. He should also cause all manuscripts to be restored according to their need, and should embellish them, not so much with mere superstitious extravagance, as with useful adornment. . . . As he is able, he should, with all modesty, suggest to the emperor that he should read, or hear read, those books which suit his rank and honour, and minister to good use rather than to mere pleasure. He should himself first be thoroughly familiar with those books. (Theonas of Alexandria, *Epistle to Lucianus*, sec. 7, ANF VI, p. 160)

This selection, primarily about the appointment and qualifications for royal librarian, provides telling evidence that (1) at a very early date, long before the more comfortable Constantinian era, Christian pastors had serious interests in the care, ordering and maintenance of books and libraries; (2) in this primitive time Christian leaders were critically reading philosophers, poets, and historians; and (3) careful attention was being given to technical matters like ancient manuscript restoration, proper cataloguing, and accurate transcription.

The daily necessities of pastoral work will strongly influence the pastor's choice of books. Baxter summarized the point:

I confess I think NECESSITY should be the great disposer of a minister's course of study and labour. If we were sufficient for everything, we might attempt everything and take in order the whole Encyclopaedia: but life is short, and we are dull, and eternal things are necessary, and the souls that depend on our teaching are precious. I confess, necessity hath been the conductor of my studies and life. It chooseth what book I shall read, and tells me when, and how long. It chooseth my text, and makes my sermon. (Baxter, *RP*, p. 113)

George Herbert strongly commended the patristic commentaries as healthy grist for the preacher's mill:

Commenters and Fathers, who have handled the places controverted, the Parson will by no means turn aside. He does not study others in such a way as to neglect the grace of God in himself or what the Holy Spirit would teach him personally. In this way he assures himself that God in all ages has had his Servants to whom he has revealed his Truth, as well as to him. One Country does not produce all things, that there may be commerce; so neither has God opened, or will open all to one, that there may be a traffic in knowledge between the servants of God, for the planting both of love, and humility. So the parson will have at least one Commentary upon every Book of Scripture, and ploughing with this, and his own meditations, he enters into the secrets of God treasured in the holy Scripture. . . . The Country Parson reads both the Fathers and the Schoolmen, and to these he adds the later Writers, or a good proportion of them. Out of all of these he comes to compile a Book, and Body of Divinity, which is the storehouse of his Sermons, and which he preaches all his Life, yet each time diversely clothed, illustrated, and enlarged. (Geo. Herbert, *CP*, Ch. III, IV, CWS, p. 59)*

The lives of early Christian saints and martyrs provide a powerful source of inspiration for the parson:

He often reads the lives of the primitive monks, hermits and virgins; and wonders not so much at their patient suffering, and cheerful dying under persecuting emperors (though that indeed be very admirable), as at their daily temperance, abstinence, watchings and constant prayer and mortifications, in the times of peace and prosperity. (Geo. Herbert, *CP*, Ch. IX, CWS, p. 66)*

Trithemius, the influential Abbot of Sponheim (1462–1516), thought that the excellence of learned theological scholars should not so intimidate the pastor that he would be unable to do insightful primary scholarship of his own:

If our own studies cannot approach [others], should we not then refrain completely from studying theology? Should the excellence of what others have said prevent us from getting absorbed in reading Scripture? Quite to the contrary. Though we may never attain the level of Augustine or Gregory, we should at least emulate those whose erudition admittedly depended on the scholarship of others. (Johannes Trithemius, *In Praise of Scribes*, Preface, p. 31)

V. 🙠 Pastoral Study of Scripture

Of the many books of the pastor's library, one book stands as that which transforms one's understanding of all other books. The Word the Bible speaks is not a passing flurry of human ideas, but an eternal Word.

The highest importance has been placed upon the study of scripture to ground pastoral teaching, preaching, and counsel. Although this is often viewed as a distinctive Protestant emphasis, it is surprising how widely patristic, medieval, and Reformation pastoral writers have substantially agreed that rigorous scripture study is required for the Christian care of souls. Hugh of St. Victor wrote:

There are books and books. For some are books written by God, and others are those that men write. The books that men write are made of the skins of dead animals or some other corruptible material, and, as these last for only a short time, the books themselves grow old and in their own way are reduced to nothing, leaving no vestige of themselves behind. And all who read these books will die some day, and there is no one to be found who lives for ever. These, therefore, being made of dead things by mortal beings who are going to die, cannot bestow enduring life on those who read and love them. They are certainly not worthy to be called books of life, . . . if I can find a book the eternal origin, the deathless being, and the knowledge whereof is life, the writing whereof is indelible, the sight desirable, the teaching easy, the wisdom sweet, the depth unfathomable, a book whereof the words are countless and yet all one Word, this book will be a book of life. (Hugh of St. Victor, *SSW*, p. 88)

Luther argued his priorities with disarming hyperbolic zeal:

You cannot read too much in Scripture; and what you read you cannot read too carefully, and what you read carefully you cannot understand too well, and what you understand well you cannot teach too well, and what you teach well you cannot live too well. (Luther, Introduction to J. Spangenberg's *Postil*, 1542, WA 53, p. 218; WLS 3, p. 1110)

Since scripture offers God's own address to the heart by means of the Spirit, it is to be read and re-read and ever-again reappropriated in ever-new ways. For a given passage of scripture is not meant to be read only once, as if it spoke only to that one occasion:

Concerning the letters of princes it is stated in a proverb that they should be read three times; but surely the letters of God—for this is what Gregory calls Scripture—should be read seven times three, yes, seventy times seven or, to say even more, countless times. For they are divine wisdom, which cannot be grasped immediately at the first glance. (Luther, "Lectures on Genesis Chapters Fifteen to Seventeen, 1536," LW 3, p. 114)

The pastor who does not know Hebrew and Greek is left at a considerable disadvantage:

St. Augustine, too, is compelled to confess, when he writes in *De doctrina Christiana*, that a Christian teacher who is to expound Scripture has need also of the Greek and the Hebrew languages in addition to the Latin; otherwise it is impossible for him not to run into obstacles everywhere. In fact, difficulty and labor are incurred even when a person does know languages well. (Luther, "To the Councilmen of All Cities in Germany That They May Establish Christian Schools," 1524, WLS 1, p. 95; cf. WML IV, pp. 116f.; WA 15, p. 40)

All forms of knowing may be brought to good use in teaching, with the knowledge of scripture at the center:

> It is an ill Mason that refuseth any stone: and there is no knowledge, but, in a skilful hand, serves either positively as it is, or else to illustrate some other knowledge. He condescends even to the knowledge of tillage, and pasturage, and makes great use of them in teaching, because people, by what they understand, are best led to what they understand not. But the chief and top of his knowledge consists in the book of books, the storehouse, and magazine of life and comfort, the Holy Scriptures. There he sucks, and lives. In the Scriptures he finds four things; Precepts for life, Doctrines for knowledge, Examples for illustration, and Promises for comfort: these he hath digested severally. (George Herbert, *CP*, Ch. 1, CWS, p. 55)

The scripture does not need our criticism as much as our lives need the criticism of scripture. When we think of ourselves as critics of scripture, as if we stood above scripture and making imperious judgments from on high about it, then we may easily miss the force of what scripture has to say to us:

> We are to search, says He, not to sit in judgment; not to be masters, but pupils; not to inject our notions into Scripture, but get Christ's testimony out of it; and as long as Christ is not found aright in it, it is also not being searched aright. (Luther, Inscription, WA 48, p. 143; WLS 1, p. 80)

The Bible's counsel cannot be fully grasped by objective historical study without prayer and attentiveness. We may do harm to others if we rush into the Bible unprepared, "with pig's feet," only grabbing what we want to use immediately, without listening carefully to its inner address:

> Since Holy writ wants to be dealt with in fear and humility and penetrated more by studying (*studio*) with pious prayer than with keenness of intellect, therefore it is impossible for those who rely only on their intellect (*nudo ingenio*) and rush into Scripture with dirty feet, like pigs, as though Scripture were merely a sort of human knowledge not to harm themselves and others whom they instruct. So utterly do they fail to differentiate; and they move about in Scripture without any reverence. That is why so many dare to be teachers. As soon as they have learned grammar, they profess, without any further study, to know theology and say: Oh, well, the Bible is an easy matter! Particularly those do this whose bellies have been distended by the husks of those swine, the philosophers. (Luther, "Sermon on the Eighth Commandment, 1517," WA 1, p. 507; WLS 1, p. 78)

What the pastor seeks most in the study of scripture is not objective, historical knowledge, but the inner meaning of the divine address, personally appropriated:

It is the sight of you, Lord, that I have sought; and all the while in my meditation the fire of longing, the desire to know you more fully, has increased. When you break for me the bread of sacred Scripture, you have shown yourself to me in that breaking of bread, and the more I see you, the more I long to see you, no more from without, in the rind of the letter, but within, in the letter's hidden meaning. (Guido, The Ladder of Monks, Vol. 2, Sec. VI, CFS, p. 73)

The benefits of scripture study were summarized by Trithemius:

Scripture purifies the heart of man, enlightens the mind of its lovers and gently intoxicates the senses. . . . There is no bitterness in its company, no pain in sharing its life, only gladness and joy. Its words are words of surprising and pleasant order. The yearning of those who love Scripture keeps on growing, satiety never leads to disgust, the hunger of the just causes joy, excess is never resented, and the frequent difficulties which must be overcome are praised. Its promise of eternal life to all the faithful teaches the knowledge of things and events which lead to salvation.

Scripture records the past truthfully, interprets the present more intelligibly than we can conceive it, and proclaims the future with certainty, as if it were already real. It is permeated with truth, radiates divine virtue and announces to the reader all things necessary for salvation.

If Scripture is read with a sincere mind, it offers nothing but profit and pleasure, meat for the strong and nourishing food for the weak. Its sense of history proclaims the truths of the past, its allegories strengthen faith, its imagery teaches morals, and its mystical interpretation raises the mind to our heavenly home. (Johannes Trithemius, *In Praise of Scribes*, Ch. 2, pp. 39–41)

Scriptures may also be employed to support false teaching:

The followers of every heresy gather the occasions of their error from the God-inspired Scriptures, corrupting in their evil minds the things rightly said through the Holy Spirit. (Chalcedon, A.D. 451, The Letter of Cyril to John of Antioch, The Seven Ecumenical Councils, NPNF 2, XIV, p. 253)

VI. ❧ THE PASTORAL STUDY OF SCIENCE, PHILOSOPHY, PSYCHOLOGY, AND LITERATURE

From previous selections it is clear that preparation for pastoral care cannot be limited strictly to acts of piety, prayer, and scripture study, however important these may be. For the theological curriculum requires a broader base of human learning. The debate about the fundamental elements of a theological curriculum goes back many centuries, antedating the emergence of the modern university. One question repeatedly discussed is the extent to which the curriculum of theological students should include scientific studies. In his eulogy to Origen, a model of Christian teaching and learning, Gregory Thaumaturgus (c. 213–c. 270), bishop of Neocaesarea, spoke of the breadth of Origen's interest in understanding the natural world, and its profound effect upon his own theological education:

Nor did he confine his efforts merely to that form of the mind which it is the lot of dialectics to regulate. He also took seriously that humble capacity of mind which shows itself in our amazement at the magnitude, wondrousness, magnificent and absolutely wise construction of the world. . . . That, too, he aroused and corrected by other studies in natural science, illustrating and distinguishing the various divisions of created objects, and with admirable clearness reducing them to their pristine elements, taking them all up perspicuously in his discourse, and going over the nature of the whole, and of each several section, and discussing the multiform revolution and mutation of things in the world, until he carried us fully along with him under his clear teaching. By those reasonings which he had partly learned from others, and partly found out for himself, he filled our minds with a rational instead of an irrational wonder at the sacred economy of the universe, and irreproveable constitution of all things. This is that sublime and heavenly study which is taught by natural philosophy—a science most attractive to all. And what need is there now to speak of the sacred mathematics, viz., geometry, so precious to all and above all controversy, and astronomy, whose course is on high? These different studies he imprinted on our understandings, training us in them, or calling them into our mind, or doing with us something else which I know not how to designate rightly. And the one he presented lucidly as the immutable groundwork and secure foundation of all, namely geometry; and by the other, namely astronomy, he lifted us up to the things that are highest above us, while he made heaven passable to us by the help of each of these sciences, as though they were ladders reaching the skies. (Gregory Thaumaturgus, "Oration and Panegyric," Argument VIII, ANF VI, p. 30)*

Gregory was speaking of his own theological education, his primary theological mentor, the one who converted him to Christianity, Origen. Gregory's theological education apparently embraced speculative mathematics, cosmology, geometry, astronomy, and what was then known of natural evolutionary history ("the multiform mutation of things in the world"). All of these subjects were viewed as being intrinsically related to theology, not optional addenda.

The same Origen wrote to Gregory on the manner and extent to which Christian teachers should make use of philosophy and psychology. It is in this letter that Origen's memorable adaptation of the metaphor of "spoiling the Egyptians" occurred, as an analogy of the legitimate use of philosophy by Christian theology:

Your natural good parts might make of you a finished Roman lawyer or a Greek philosopher, so to speak, of one of the schools in high reputation. But I am anxious that you should devote all the strength of your natural good parts to Christianity for your end; and in order to this, I wish to ask you to extract from the philosophy of the Greeks what may serve as a course of study or a preparation for Christianity, and from geometry and astronomy what will serve to explain the sacred Scriptures, in order that all that the sons of the philosophers are wont to say about geometry and music, grammar, rhetoric, and astronomy, as fellow helpers to philosophy, we may say about philosophy itself, in relation to Christianity.

Perhaps something of this kind is shadowed forth in what is written in Exodus from the mouth of God, that the children of Israel were commanded to ask from their neighbours, and those who dwelt with them, vessels of silver and gold, and rainment, in order that, by spoiling the Egyptians, they might have material for the preparation of the things which pertained to the service of God. . . . How useful to the children of Israel were the things brought from Egypt, which the Egyptians had not put to a proper use, but which the Hebrews, guided by the wisdom of God, used for God's service? (Origen, Letter to Gregory, sec. 1, ANF IV, p. 393)

Tertullian commented on the cognitive habits of mind required by Christian apologetics. He lived in a hostile political environment characterized by massive state persecutions of Christians. His subject was psychology, the study of the *psyche*, the soul, and its own testimony of itself:

A great love for research and an even greater memory are required of a student who would gather, from the most accepted works of the philosophers, poets, and any other teachers of secular learning and wisdom, reasonable arguments for the truth of Christianity, in order to convict its rivals and persecutors by their own learned apparatus of error in themselves, and, thus, of their injustice toward us. (Tertullian, Testimony of the Soul, Ch. 1, FC 10, p. 131)*

Tertullian argued that Christian psychology and counsel must guard against excessive dependency upon autonomous philosophies or unsubstantiated psychological opinions. He warned about a too-easy alliance between the academy and the church, between "Athens and Jerusalem":

Indeed heresies are themselves instigated by philosophy. From this source came the Aeons, and I known not what infinite forms, and the trinity of man in the system of Valentinus, who was of Plato's school. From the same source came Marcion's better god, with all his supposed tranquility—he came out of the Stoics. Then, again, the opinion that the soul dies is held by the Epicureans; while the denial of the restoration of the body is taken from the aggregate school of all the philosophers. When matter is made equal to God, then you have the teaching of Zeno. When any doctrine is alleged touching a god of fire, then Heraclitus comes in. The same subject-matter is discussed over and over again by the heretics and the philosophers; the same arguments are repeatedly involved. . . . Unhappy Aristotle! who invented for these men dialectics, the art of building up and pulling down; an art so evasive in its propositions, so farfetched in its conjectures, so harsh, in its arguments, so productive of contentions—embarrassing even to itself, retracting everything, and really treating of nothing! From whence do thes "interminable myths and geneologies" (1 Tim. 1:4) spring, and "foolish speculations" that are "unprofitable and pointless" (Tit. 3:9) and teaching that "will spread like gangrene" (2 Tim 2:17). From all these, when the apostle would restrain us, he expressly names philosophy as that which he would have us be on our guard against. Writing to the Colossians, he says, "Be on your guard; do not let your minds be captured by hollow and delusive speculations, based on traditions of man-made teaching and centered on the elemental spirits of the universe and not on Christ" (Col. 2:8). He had been at Athens, and had in his interviews with its philosophers become acquainted with that human wisdom which pretends to know the truth while it only corrupts it, and is itself divided into its own manifold heresies, by the variety of its mutually repugnant sects. What indeed has Athens to do with Jerusalem? What concord is there between the Academy and the Church? What between heretics and Christians? Our instruction comes from "the porch of Solomon" who had himself wrote: "Set your mind upon the Lord, as is your duty,and seek him in simplicity of heart" (Wisdom of Solomon 1:1). Away with all attempts to produce a mottled Christianity of Stoic, Platonic, and dialectic composition! (Tertullian, *On Prescription Against Heretics*, Ch. VII, ANF III, p. 246, NEB)*

Luther similarly argued that philosophical and psychological speculations on the soul are not to be uncritically taken to be normative for pastoral care:

In this regard my advice would be that Aristotle's Physics, Metaphysics, On the Soul, Ethics, which have hitherto been thought his best books, should be altogether discarded, together with all the rest of his books which boast of treating the things of nature, although nothing can be learned from them either of the things of nature or the things of the Spirit. Moreover no one has so far understood his meaning, and many souls have been burdened with profitless labor and study, at the cost of much precious time. I venture to say that any potter has more knowledge of nature than is written in these books. It grieves me to the heart that this damned, conceited, rascally heathen has with his false words deluded and made fools of so many of the best Christians. God has sent him as a plague upon us for our sins. . . . My friends the theologians have spared themselves pains and labor; they leave the Bible in peace and read the Sentences. I should think that the Sentences ought to be the first study of young students in theology and the Bible ought to be the study for the doctors. But now it is turned around; the Bible comes first, and is put aside when the bachelor's degree is reached, and the Sentences come last. . . . What, then, are we to do? I know of no other way than humbly to pray God to give us Doctors of Theology. Pope, emperor and universities may make Doctors of Arts, of Medicine, of Laws, of the Sentences; but be assured that no one will make a Doctor of Holy Scripture, save only the Holy Ghost from heaven, as Christ says in John 6:45, "They must all be taught of God Himself." Now the Holy Ghost does not concern Himself about red or brown birettas or other decorations, nor does He ask whether one is old or young, layman or priest, monk or secular, virgin or married; nay He spake of old by an ass, against the prophet who rode upon it. (Luther, "An Open Letter to the Christian Nobility," sec. 25, WML II, p. 146–151)

It was a central dilemma of pastoral care in Luther's day as our own that scripture's address could not be heard above the clamor of philosophers, speculators, and naturalistic reductionists.

In one of Christianity's earliest post-New Testament writings, Justin Martyr sought to define philosophy:

"What, then, is philosophy?", he says, "and what is happiness? Pray tell me, unless something hinders you from saying." "Philosophy, then," said I, "is the knowledge of that which really exists, and a clear perception of the truth; and happiness is the reward of such knowledge and wisdom." (Justin Martyr, *Dialogue with Trypho*, ANF I, p. 196)

This apparently innocuous quote shows clearly that one of the earliest writings of the Christian tradition was thinking of philosophy as a companion discipline of theology, intrinsically relevant to the Christian pastoral interest in authentic human happiness.

Tertullian spoke to the question of the extent to which the ancient pagan poets need be read for the soul's good. Characteristically Tertullian held a paradoxical view of such literary study. The crucial distinction is that between learning and teaching. Clergy and laity were open to read the pagan poets, but clergy were forbidden to teach them as if they were true Christian doctrines:

We know it may be said, "If teaching literature is not lawful to God's servants, neither will learning be likewise"; and, "How could one be trained unto ordinary human intelligence, or unto any sense or action whatever, since literature is the means of training for all life? How do we repudiate secular studies, without which divine studies cannot be pursued?" Let us see, then, the necessity of literary erudition; let us reflect that partly it cannot be admitted, partly cannot be avoided. Learning literature is allowable for believers, rather than teaching, for the principle of learning and of teaching is different. If a believer teach literature, while he is teaching doubtless he commends, while he delivers he affirms, while he recalls he bears testimony to, the praises of idols interspersed therein. (Tertullian, *On Idolatry*, Ch. X, ANF III, p. 66)

In Gregory Thaumaturgus' panegyric on Origen, he reveals that his theological teacher had a very independent, critical mind, not prone simply to take as final the theories of rhetoricians on the proper style of communication. Origen taught and conveyed those independent habits of mind to his theological students:

That capacity of our mind which deals critically with words and reasonings, was educated in a rational manner; not according to the judgments of illustrious rhetoricians—whatever Greek or foreign honour appertains to that title—for theirs is a discipline of little value and no necessity: but in accordance with that which is most needful for all. (Gregory Thaumaturgus, "Oration and Panegyric," ANF VI, p. 30)

Baxter objected to psychological and philosophical studies which prematurely ruled out faith's response to revelation:

O that all our students in our universities would well consider this! What a poor business is it to themselves, to spend their time in acquiring some little knowledge of the works of God, and of some of those names which the divided tongues of the nations have imposed on them, and not to know God himself. . . . Nothing can be rightly known, if God be not known; nor is any study well managed, nor to any great purpose, if God is not studied. . . . No man that hath not the vitals of theology, is capable of going beyond a fool in philosophy. . . .They read divinity like philosophers, as if it were a thing of no more moment than a lesson of music, or arithematic, and not the doctrine of everlasting life; this is that blasteth so many in the bud, and pestereth the

Church with unsanctified teachers! Hence it is, that we have so many worldlings to preach of the invisible felicity, and so many carnal men to declare the mysteries of the Spirit; and I would I might not say, so many infidels to preach Christ, or so many athiests to preach the living God: and when they are taught philosophy before or without religion, what wonder if their philosophy be all or most of their religion! (Baxter, *RP*, pp. 56–60)

Hugh of St. Victor had earlier made a similar point that knowledge that would systematically restrict itself to empirical objects would be extremely limited knowledge:

Sight is restricted in its scope, and it is therefore quite unable to take in very large things; because it is dim, it does not discern those that are very small; and, because it is slow, when it is directed towards distant objects, even though it spans the intervening space, it is impeded by the very distance itself. For it is not sharp-sighted, it does not penetrate inwards, but roves about only over those things that outwardly appear. Moreover it can neither look back to events past, nor forward to those that are to come.

I have said this to show you under what imitations this bodily vision labours, since it cannot see a thing that is not planted straight in front of it. And even then, very large objects are beyond it because of their size, the very small elude it by their minuteness, the far-off ones escape it by their distance, and the inward ones are hidden from it by their obscurity. So when you hear yourself invited to "see," it is not the sight of this eye that I would have you think about. You have another eye within, much clearer than that one, an eye that looks at the past, the present, and the future all at once, which sheds the light and keenness of its vision over all things, which penetrates things hidden and searches into complexities, needing no other light by which to see all this, but seeing by the light that it possesses of itself. (Hugh of St. Victor, *SSW*, p. 158)

Jean Gerson was astounded at how deeply faddism had corrupted pastoral care in his time (1363–1429). He urged pastors to avoid the temptations of what he called a harmful type of "curiosity":

Curiosity is that corruption by which man, having rejected the more useful things, devotes himself to those things which are less beneficial, things which he cannot attain and which are harmful to him. Of course, when one considers the end to which such an activity leads according to time, place, person, generation, station in life, profession and state, then this judgment of what is more and less beneficial changes in accordance with the different circumstances. Indeed, what is found to be harmful and improper for one is fitting and even commanded for another.

Singularity is that corruption by which man, having rejected the more useful things, devotes himself to foreign and unusual teachings. Here, as with curiosity, it is necessary to take the end of the activity into account before a final value judgment is made.

You see, then, that, although by reason of their different subjects their faces are distinguished by various individual features, curiosity and singularity, as is the custom with sisters, are alike in many ways. Each is guilty of forsaking the more useful things. And each forsakes these things out of a desire to establish its own pre-eminence. Curiosity does it in order to know what is improper; singularity in order to excel over others. (Jean Gerson, "Against the Curiosity of Scholars," p. 29)

VII. ❧ Pastoral Formation and Moral Development

Intrinsic to preparation for pastoral care is the spiritual and moral formation of the pastor. Most leading pastoral writers have commented extensively on these themes, and few have neglected them. One gains the cumulative impression that this concern was generally regarded as exceedingly important in most periods of the pastoral tradition.

Central to the following selections is a crucial assumption: The soul-guide's own behavior must correspond with the spirit of moral guidance given to others. Otherwise the care-receiver loses confidence in the integrity and congruity of the care-giver. The pivotal issue: Can one correct something in another that remains in oneself uncorrected?

You cannot put straight in others what is warped in yourself. (Athanasius, On the Incarnation, Sec. 14, p. 24)

Similarly, can one rightly teach what one does not practice?

He also said, "If a man understands something and does not practise it, how can he teach it to his neighbour? (Poemen, Sayings of the Desert Fathers, sec. 197, p. 163)

In writing on patience, Tertullian, with disarming candor, confessed his own personal lack of it. He then poignantly asked himself about the plausibility of his teaching patience to others:

I fully confess unto the Lord God that it has been rash enough, if not even impudent, in me to have dared compose a treatise on Patience, for practising which I am all unfit, being a man of no goodness; whereas it were becoming that such as have addressed themselves to the demonstration and commendation of some particular thing, should themselves first be conspicuous in the practice of that thing, and should regulate the constancy of their admonishing by the authority of their personal conduct, for fear their words blush at the deficiency of their deeds. And would that this "blushing" would bring a remedy, so that shame for not exhibiting that which we go to suggest to others should prove a tutorship into exhibiting it. . . . So I, most miserable, ever sick with the heats of impatience, must of necessity sigh after, and invoke, and persistently plead for, that health of patience which I possess not. (Tertullian, *Of Patience*, Part VI, Ch. 1, ANF III, p. 707)

The principle is that the teacher must embody the behavior he teaches. Insofar as one fails to do so, it is best to acknowledge that candidly, as did Tertullian, rather than pretend. The pastoral writers worked diligently to maintaing a plausible balance between teaching and example:

Example alone is not sufficient instruction. . . . By distinguishing the two he shows that example is one thing and instruction another, and that each requires the other for perfection edification. (John Chrysostom, *On the Priesthood*, Ch. IV, sec. 8, p. 125)

Black Moses, a third century African ascetic, was among the most warmly remembered of the desert fathers. He subtly taught that more decisive than the correspondence between teaching and behavior is the correspondence between prayer and behavior:

If a man's deeds are not in harmony with his prayer, he labours in vain. The brother said, "What is this harmony between practice and prayer?" The old man said, "We should no longer do those things against which we pray." (Black Moses, Sayings of the Desert Fathers, p. 120)

This is a simple teaching, profound in its implication. For one who no longer does those things against which one prays will either have an exemplary life or very short prayers.

In praising Origen's method of teaching, Gregory Thaumaturgus recalled how closely integrated were Origen's teaching of the virtues and his own actual embodiment of them. Origen's profoundest teaching was Origen's life:

For it is in this way, Origen used to say, that heavenly virtues will gradually ripen in the soul: first, *prudence*, which is able to distinguish those things that are moving in the mind from that which exists objectively, and from knowledge that accrues from external sources, whether good or evil. Similarly *temperance* is the power that makes the right selection among these things in their beginnings; and *righteousness*, which assigns what is just to each; and that virtue which is the conserver of them all—*fortitude*. And therefore he did not accustom us to a mere profession in words, as if to say that prudence, for instance, is merely the knowledge of good and evil, or of what ought to be done, and what ought not: for that would be indeed a vain and profitless study, if there was simply the doctrine without the deed. Worthless would be that prudence which fails to do the things that ought to be done, or turn us away from those things that ought not to be done. . . . Nor, again, did he content himself with the mere assertion that temperance is simply the knowledge of what ought to be chosen and what ought not; though the other schools of philosophers do not teach even so much as that, and especially the more recent, who are so forcible and vigorous in words. . . . and yet they are incapable of delivering the truth as to prudence, so that one shall do the things which are dictated by prudence. . . . So not in mere words did this teacher go over the truths concerning the virtues with us. Rather he incited us much more to the practice of virtue, and stimulated us by the deeds he did more than by the doctrines he taught. (Gregory Thaumaturgus, "Oration and Panegyric," IX, ANF VI, p. 31)*

If the pastor has not experienced what he teaches at a deep level of integration into one's feelings, the teaching will ring emotively hollow:

These things are never well known till they are felt, nor well felt till they are possessed; and he that feeleth them not himself, is not likely to speak feelingly of them to others, nor to help others to the feeling of them. (Baxter, *RP*, p. 81)

If the pastor's behavior does not correspond with the pastor's ideas, the ideas are rightly suspect. Baxter cajoled his fellow pastors:

If God's threatenings be true, why do not you yourselves fear them? If they be false, why do you needlessly trouble men with them, and put them into such frights without a cause?. . . . You who teach others, shall you not be taught yourselves? You who say that others should not commit adultery, or be drunk, or covetous, are you such yourselves? You who make your boast of the law, do you through breaking the law dishonor God? What! Shall the same tongue speak evil that speaks against evil? (Baxter, *RP*, p. 68)

The depth of the pastor's moral awareness depends significantly upon the extent to which the pastor has learned to distinguish means and ends. Pastoral counsel often focusses upon the complex relation of ends and means in making fundamental life choices. Ignatius Loyola thought that this was the pivotal issue around which other issues of counseling would finally turn:

In every good choice, in so far as it depends upon us, the direction of our intention should be simple. I must look only to the end for which I am created, that is, for the praise of God our Lord and for the salvation of my soul. Therefore, whatever I choose must have as its purpose to help me to this end. I must not shape or draw the end to the means, but the means to the end. Many, for example, first choose marriage, which is a means, and secondarily to serve God our Lord in the married state, which service of God is the end. Likewise there are others who first desire to have benefices, and afterward to serve, God in them. These individuals do not go straight to God, but want God to come straight to their inordinate attachments. Acting thus, they make a means of the end, and an end of the means, so that what they ought to seek first, they seek last. My first aim, then, should be my desire to serve God, which is the end, and after this, to seek a benefice or to marry, if it is more fitting for me, for these things are but means to the end. Thus, nothing should move me to use such means or to deprive myself of them except it be only the service and praise of God our Lord and the eternal salvation of my soul. (Ignatius Loyola, *Spiritual Exercises*, pp. 82–83)

Nothing, therefore, befits good counsel more than examining the differences between means and ends.

Suppose a pastor has a duty to speak, yet his life is not consistent with what his speech would wish to say. Should he keep silent? The pastor knows he must speak out, yet he also is aware that in speaking out he will by his behavior undermine what he has a duty to say—an issue profoundly felt in many actual situations of ministry. Guerric of Igny provided a subtle self-analysis and a biblical response:

Although I look askance at this consolation if I say without doing, if while my tongue makes its contribution my life lacks merit I have perhaps to be afraid rather lest God should say to me in my sins: "Why do you tell of my justice and discourse of my covenant with your mouth." (Ps. 49:16). But what am I to do? If I do not speak my pain will not be appeased, and if I keep silent it will not depart from me. Fear harasses me in either case and I am hemmed in on both sides. My position and my duty demand that I should speak, my life contradicts what I say. But I remember the words which I found on the Wise Man's lips: "Let the soul of him who toils toil for himself, since his mouth has compelled him." (Prov. 16:26). I will speak then, not as my position requires but as my understanding allows, or rather as the Lord grants, in whose hand are we and our utterances. (Guerric of Igny, CFS 32, *Liturgical Sermons*, Vol. 2, Sermon 39, sec. 4, CFS 32, pp. 119–120)

When confronted by a situation where a clear confession of faith is called for, the pastor must not delay and temporize, but speak with seasonable promptness. Timing is the essence of communication. A delayed witness may speak more through its delay than its intended witness.

He who when asked concerning the right faith, puts off his answer for a long while, does nothing else but deny the right faith. For in questioning and answering on things which are of faith, it is not he who is found first or second, but he who is the more ready with a right confession, that is acceptable to God. (Second Council of Constantinople, A.D. 553, Extracts from the Acts, Session I, The Seven Ecumenical Councils, NPNF 2, XIV, p. 303)

Quality care-giving is situationally aware of intricate complexities that arise out of a given interpersonal situation. Any such situation is sufficiently complex to make and keep the pastor humble. In praying for divine guidance to guide others, Aelred of Rievaulx was keenly aware of his limits:

O Good Shepherd Jesus, good, gentle, tender Shepherd, behold a shepherd, poor and pitiful, a shepherd of your sheep indeed, but weak and clumsy and of little use, cries out to you. To you, I say, Good Shepherd, this shepherd, who is not good, makes his prayer. He cries to you, troubled upon his own account, and troubled for your sheep. For when in bitterness of soul I view my former life, it scares and frightens me that I should be called shepherd, for I am surely crazy if I do not know myself unworthy of the name. (Aelred of Rievaulx, *The Pastoral Prayer*, sec. 1–2, CFS 2, pp. 105–106)

Moral gravity, personal humility, and honesty with oneself characterize this ironic medieval prayer.

Not only is it positively the case that good moral practice confirms good pastoral teaching, but also negatively that bad practice may invalidate whatever may be otherwise good in one's preaching or counsel. The deeds of the pastor can undo his preaching, in Baxter's view:

Take heed to yourselves, lest your example contradict your doctrine, . . . lest you unsay with your lives, what you say with your tongues. . . . He that means as he speaks, will surely do as he speaks. One proud, surly, lordly word, one needless contention, one covetous action, may cut the throat of many a sermon, and blast the fruit of all that you have been doing. (Baxter, *RP*, p. 63)

Nothing is more likely to turn persons away from a pastor's guidance than that pastor's own behaviors that clearly reveal that he does not take his own precepts seriously:

When they observe that our actions are unworthy of the words we utter, they turn to blasphemy, saying that it is a myth and a deception. (II Clement, Sec. V, par. 13, AF, p. 66)

It is a primary responsibility of the care-giver to attend carefully to whether his life corresponds with his words, according to Gregory:

While he is obliged to speak what is good to those under his charge, he must first observe the matters of which he speaks. He is, therefore, ensnared with the words of his mouth, in that he is constrained by the exigency of right reason not to allow his way of life to be relaxed in a way that does not accord with his teaching. In other words, in the presence of the strict Judge he is constrained to accomplish in his own conduct what he clearly prescribes in words to others. (Gregory the Great, *Pastoral Care*, Part III, Ch. 4, ACW 11, p. 98)

Menno Simons understood the moral inconsistency and vulnerability in which the counselor places himself if he does not listen to his own counsel:

It is not enough that in appearance a man speaks much of the Word of the Lord. It must also be verified by devout and unblamable conduct, as the Scriptures teach. . . . Behold, dear reader, so should every preacher and teacher be minded who would rightly govern and rule in the church of God. For if anyone were to reproach and teach others and he himself be reproachable and untaught, he will have to hear, Why do you teach others and do not teach yourself first? (Menno Simons, *Foundation of Christian Doctrine*, 1539, CWMS, pp. 169–170)

Few come under harsher judgment of the pastoral tradition than those who play easy with words:

For these are they "who by good words and fair speeches lead astray the hearts of the simple, and, while offering them blessings, lead them astray" (Rom. 16:18). Let us, therefore, fear the judgment which awaits teachers. For a severe judgment will those teachers receive "who teach, but do not," (Matt. 23:3). . . . These, moreover, are like "the blind man who leads the blind man, and they both fall into the ditch." (Matt. 15:14). And they will receive judgment, because in their talkativeness and their frivolous teaching they teach natural wisdom, and the "frivolous error of the plausible words of the wisdom of men" (cf. Col. 2:8). (Clementina, *Two Epistles Concerning Virginity*, Ch. XI, ANF VIII, p. 59)

Good teaching and good actions mutually confirm one another:

These are the two causes of offense to hearers; doctrine and life. If a man leads a good life but preaches bad doctrine, this is a great offense, because he should not be believed. If, on the other hand, he teaches good doctrine but leads a bad life, people say: If what he teaches were true, he himself would live it. (Luther, "Sermon on John 8:46–50, 1528," WA 27, p. 78; WLS 3, p. 1123)

VIII. ❧ PUBLIC DEMEANOR AND THE DOUBLE STANDARD DILEMMA

It is precisely due to the highly public character and moral expectations of the office of pastor that public scrutiny tends to fasten more intently on clerical than lay scandal or misbehavior. Chrysostom commented on how difficult it is to keep pastoral misdeeds out of public view, using an athletic analogy:

The priest's shortcomings simply cannot be concealed. On the contrary, even the most trivial soon get known. The weakest athlete can keep his weakness secret as long as he remains at home and pits himself against nobody; but when he strips for the contest, he is soon shown up. (John Chrysostom, *On the Priesthood*, Ch. III, sec. 14, p. 85)

Among the remains of the second and third century were found fragments of a treatise of one Apollonius "Concerning Montanism." This document reveals how the church of that period was testing prophetic claims by public fruits:

It is proper, too, that all the fruits of a prophet should be examined. Tell me: Does a prophet dye his hair? Does a prophet use stibium [dark, cosmetic eyeshadow] on his eyes? Is a prophet fond of dice? Does a prophet lend money on interest? (Apollonius, *Concerning Montanism*, sec. 5, ANF VIII, p. 776)*

John Chrysotom argued that the misdeeds of a well-known person may harm others proportional to the breadth of the reputation:

The sins of ordinary men are committed in the dark, so to speak, and ruin only those who commit them. But when a man becomes famous and is known to many, his misdeeds inflict a common injury on all. (John Chrysostom, *On the Priesthood*, Ch. III, sec. 14, p. 85)

In the light of the public character of the office and the extent of expectation attached to it, it should not surprise pastors that their actions are subjected to extraordinary public surveillance. There are investigative press reporters (or their equivalents) "sitting at the gate" just waiting for someone to stumble, according to Augustine:

Why do they sit at the gate, and what do they watch for, if it be not for this, that so soon as any bishop or clergyman or monk or nun has fallen, they may have ground for believing, and boasting, and maintaining that all are the same as the one that has fallen, but that all cannot be convicted and unmasked. . . . The moment that any crime is either falsely alleged or actually proved against any one who makes a profession of piety, these men are incessant and unwearied in their efforts to make this charge be believed against all religious men. (Augustine, *Letters*, Letter LXXVIII to Church of Hippo, NPNF 1, I, p. 347)

There can be no doubt that pastors are subjected to special public scrutiny. Those who argue absolutely against any form of "double standard" for clergy and laity sometimes oversimplify the case by thinking flatly that both should be judged on a stringently equal basis with precisely the same criteria applied, and with no reference to the any special claims of the pastoral office. John Chrysostom accurately described the problem:

As long as the priest's life is well regulated in every particular point, their intrigues cannot hurt him. But if he should overlook some small detail, as is likely for a human being on his journey across the devious ocean of this life, all the rest of his good deeds are of no avail to enable him to escape the words of his accusers. That small offence casts a shadow over all the rest of his life. Everyone wants to judge the priest, not as one clothed in flesh, not as one possessing a human nature, but as an angel, exempt from the frailty of others. (John Chrysostom, *On the Priesthood*, Ch. III, sec. 14, p. 86)

Many classic writers held clergy to a more rigorous moral performance than laity, but the underlying reasoning does not thereby dissolve into a double standard. For if one holds that both clergy and laity ought to practice what they profess, and that clergy must show the way to doing this, then the dissonance of a double standard is reduced. If clergy only were held to be under this claim of moral congruence of word and deed, then the laity would be encouraged to moral laxity. Ambrose's maxim: *the preceptor must keep the precept*. Where clergy live better lives than laity it is by grace:

The life of a priest ought to surpass others as its grace surpasses, and he who binds others by his precepts ought himself to keep the precepts of the law in himself. (Ambrose, *Letters*, Letters to Priests, FC 26, p. 345)

Baxter argued that there was a quietly providential purpose in the high visibility of the pastor's sins:

There are many eyes upon you, and there will be many to observe your falls. . . . If other men may sin without observation, so cannot you. And you should thankfully consider how great a mercy this is, that you have so many eyes to watch over you, and so many ready to tell you of your faults; and thus have greater helps than others, at least for restraining you from sin. . . While you are as lights set upon a hill, think not to lie hid. . . . Do your work as those that remember that the world looks on them, and that with the quick-sighted eye of malice, ready to make the worst of all, to find the smallest fault where it is, to aggravate it where they find it, to divulge it and to take advantage of it to their own designs and to make faults where they cannot find them. (Baxter, *RP*, pp. 75–76)

As an expression of the set-apartness of ministry, canonical rules were developed during the patristic period on the clothing of clergy:

> None of those who are in the catalogue of the clergy shall wear clothes unsuited to them, either while still living in town or when on a journey; but they shall wear such clothes as are assigned to those who belong to the clergy. (Synod of Quinisext, A.D. 692, Canon XXVII, The Seven Ecumenical Councils, NPNF 2, XIV, p. 377)

Whether clergy may drink wine, sometimes viewed as a test case of public demeanor, was answered in this way by one of the Athanasian canons:

> No deacon nor anyone that is counted of priesthood shall drink wine to drunkenness. They shall not drink in the holy places nor shall any priest drink wine during the day, except a cup or two. And when they have drunk, they shall not go forth from the town, lest any have the likeness of Christ in contempt. In the Paschal days may none of the priests drink wine at all, nor shall they eat meat. What wine remains over from the altar at the *Pascha* shall be given unto the sick poor. (*Athanasian Canons*, sec. 29–30, p. 31)*

Shall clerics enter taverns? The African Council provided:

> That the clergy are not to enter taverns for eating or drinking, nor unless compelled to do so by the necessity of their journey. (African Code, A.D. 419, Canon XL, The Seven Ecumenical Councils, NPNF 2, XIV, p. 461)

Shall clerics operate taverns?

> Let no cleric be permitted to keep a "public house." For if it be not permitted to enter a tavern, much more is it forbidden to serve others in it and to carry on a trade which is unlawful for him. (Synod of Quinisext, A.D. 692, Canon IX, The Seven Ecumenical Councils, NPNF 2, XIV, p. 369)

Shall clerics sue others clerics in court?

> If any Clergyman have a matter against another clergyman, he shall not forsake his bishop and run to secular courts; . . . Litigious clerics shall be punished according to canon, if they despise the episcopal and resort to the secular tribunal. (Chalcedon, A.D. 451, Canon IX; Ancient Epitome of Canon IX, The Seven Ecumenical Councils, NPNF 2, XIV, p. 274)

IX. ❧ CLERGY HOMOSEXUALITY AND SEXUAL NORMS

Although the sexual ethic of clergy has undergone various changes and remains subject to continuing debate, there has been no period of Christian pastoral history that has concluded that the sexual behavior of the clergy can be completely ignored. Here is an example of a seventh century directive on clerical sexual values:

He who has been joined in two marriages after his baptism, or has had a concubine, cannot be bishop, or presbyter, or deacon, or at all on the sacerdotal list; in like manner, that he who has taken a widow, or a divorced person, or a harlot, or a servant, or an actress, cannot be bishop, or presyter, or deacon, or at all on the sacerdotal list. (Council of Quinisext, A.D. 692, Canon III, The Seven Ecumenical Councils, NPNF 2, XIV, p. 363)

Individual masturbation was regarded as less culpable in priests than mutual mastubation, fornication or homosexuality, which involve the joint consent of two persons:

Some sin with themselves alone; some commit mutual masturbation; some commit femoral fornication; and finally, others commit the complete act against nature. The ascending gradation among these is such that the last mentioned are judged to be more serious than the preceding. Indeed, a greater penance is imposed on those who fall with others than on those who defile only themselves. (Pietro Damiani, *Book of Gomorrah*, sec. 1, p. 29)

Habitual homosexuals were not ordained:

It seems utterly preposterous to us that those who are habitually defiled with this festering contagion would dare either to be promoted to orders or to remain in their rank if already promoted since it is proved to be contrary to reason and against the canonical decrees of the fathers. . . . Scripture attests that he struck down Onan, the son of Judah, with premature death for this nefarious crime, "Onan knew that the descendants would not be counted as his, so whenever he had relations with his brother's wife, he wasted his seed on the ground in order that children not be born in the name of his brother" (Gen. 38:9) . . . . So from this we clearly gather that any male who falls into sin with a male—into that crime, as we showed above, which is surely to be punished by death in the judgment of the Old Law—even if he burns with the zeal of psalm-singing, and is distinguished in his love of prayer, and leads a full religious life under a witness of approved reputation, can indeed receive full pardon for his offence, but he is never permitted to aspire to ecclesiastical orders. (Pietro Damiani, *Book of Gomorrah*, sec. 3, pp. 32–33)

The question arose as to whether the urgent need for priests in short supply might make it relatively more acceptable to ordain homosexuals:

But perhaps someone will say, "There is an imminent necessity and there is no one to perform a sacred function in the church. The judgment which was first based on the pronouncement of divine justice is reasonably modified by the proposed necessity of the situation." . . . Will a judgment be owed in favour of one man which, if upheld, will result in the destitution of a whole people? Will what is not relaxed for the benefit of an immense multitude be violated for the benefit of a single person? But now let the great preacher himself also come forward and let what he thinks of this vice be more expressly known. He says in the Epistle to the Ephesians, "Make no mistake about this: no fornicator, no unclean or covetous person has any inheritance in the kingdom of Christ and of God." (Eph. 5:5). Consequently, if an unclean man has no inheritance at all in heaven, by what presumption, by what rash pride should he continue to possess a dignity in the Church which is no less the Kingdom of God? (Pietro Damiani, *Book of Gomorrah*, sec. 4, p. 35)

It was argued that the corruption of one homosexual priest may effect others, especially subordinates. Those who understood themselves to be homosexual were counseled away from sacred ministry:

Therefore, the person who is still bound by earthly desires should beware lest, by more gravely igniting the anger of the strict Judge, he become the author of the ruin of his subordinates while he takes pleasure in his exalted position. So, if culpable vice still rules over him, a person should prudently take stock of himself before he dares to assume the position of the sacerdotal office, lest one who is perverted by his own crime should desire to become the intercessor for the faults of others. Be careful, be careful, and be afraid of igniting inextinguishably God's fury towards you; fear lest you provoke more sharply by your very prayers the one you offend openly by acting evilly. Intent on your own ruin, beware of becoming responsible for the ruin of another. The more moderately you now fall into sin, the more easily will you rise by means of the outstretched hand of penance through the mercy of God. (Pietro Damiani, *Book of Gomorrah*, pp. 72–73)

Whenever the issue of clergy homosexuality was argued, it was usually argued more on biblical than sociological or psychological grounds. The fundamental concern was for the integrity of the community, which each member had a fiduciary duty to protect:

For who would turn a deaf ear; yes, who would not tremble to the core when he hears the Apostle, as a thundering trumpet, say of such men, "For this reason God has given them up to the vileness of their own desires, and the consequent degradation of their bodies." (Rom.

1:24). . . . "In consequence, I say, God has given them up to shameful passions. Their women have exchanged natural intercourse for unnatural, and their men in turn, giving up natural relations with women, burn with lust for one another; males behave indecently with males, and are paid in their own persons the fitting wage of such perversion. Thus, because they have not seen fit to acknowledge God, he has given them up to their own depraved reason." (Rom. 1:26–28). . . . What else is it for one who is unworthy of an ecclesiastical order to try to break into the office of the sacred altar but to abandon the threshold and to endeavour to enter through the impenetrable barrier of the wall? Because a free passage does not appear for their feet, such men are deceived by their own presumption and are compelled rather to remain in the outer vestibule, while they promise themselves they can reach the sanctuary. . . . Let the indolent superiors of clerics and of priests hear; let them hear and let them greatly fear being participants in the guilt of others, even though they feel safe as far as they themselves are concerned. I refer to those who close their eyes to the correction of their subordinates' sins and offer them the freedom of sinning through an ill-advised silence. (Pietro Damiani, *Book of Gomorrah*, sec. 5, pp. 37, 39–40)

Should pastors with impugnity keep silent when homosexual practice increases?

But if the doctor shrinks in horror from infected wounds, who will take the trouble to apply the cauter? If the one who is to heal becomes nauseated, who will lead sick hearts back to health? Vice against nature creeps in like a cancer and even touches the order of consecrated men. (Pietro Damiani, *Book of Gomorrah*, Preface, p. 27)

X. ❧ THE PASTOR AS MORAL ROLE MODEL

The pastor as teacher of the good life cannot avoid being in some sense a model for others in the search for the good life. Since the pastor speaks of the truth, hearers look preeminently to the pastor for truth-telling. Since the pastor is often heard speaking of love and justice, it will not miss the notice of hearers whether the pastor's behavior is unloving and unjust. Jeremy Taylor recognized that even the best deeds can become distorted:

Be not satisfied, when you have done a good work, unless you have also done it well: and when you have, then be careful that vainglory, partiality, self-conceit, or any other folly or indiscretion, snatch it not out of your hand, and cheat you of the reward. (Jeremy Taylor, *RAC*, Ch. II, sec. 23; *CS*, p. 10)

Taylor's point is subtle. Even when the pastor does a good deed, it may be subject to being distorted by a meanly inclined will, which then takes away whatever good the deed itself might have accomplished. Yet this need not imply that the pastor is morally spotless:

No one is free from sin, excepting Him that became flesh for us. For it is written "No man is pure from filthiness; no, not though he be but one day old" (Job 16:4 LXX). It is for this purpose that the lives and conduct of the ancient holy men and patriarchs were described; not that we may reproach them from our reading, but that we ourselves may repent, and have hope that we also shall obtain forgiveness. For their blemishes are to us both security and admonition, because thenceforth we learn that when we have offended if we repent we shall have pardon. For it is written: "Who can boast that he has a clean heart? and who dare affirm that he is pure from sin?" (Prov. 20:9). No one therefore is without sin. But you must therefore labor to the utmost of your power to be blameless. (*Constitutions of the Holy Apostles*, Bk. II, sec. III.xviii, ANF VII, p. 403) *

When ideal visions of the pastoral role-model are presented, they may seem impossible to actualize. But these ideal pictures are treated realistically and humanely by the greatest of the pastoral writers. It is not as if these ideal paradigms were subject to complete, simple, immediate, or absolute fulfillment, but that they remain significant ideals even if not often or absolutely realized. The sociological principle is that the congregation's moral awareness is not likely to rise above the level of its leadership. The Apostolic Constitutions drew this picture of the pastoral leader:

Let him be prudent, humble, apt to admonish with the instructions of the Lord, well-disposed, one who has renounced all the evil projects of this world and all heathen lusts; let him be orderly, sharp in observing the deceitful, and taking heed of them, but yet a friend to all; just, discerning. Whatever qualities are commendable to all, let the bishop possess them in himself. For if the pastor be unblameable as to any wickedness, he will compel his own disciples, and by his very mode of life press them to become worthy imitators of his own actions. As the prophet somewhere says, "And it will be, as is the priest, so is the people" (Is. 24:2). (*Constitutions of the Holy Apostles*, Bk. II, sec. II, ANF VII, p. 398)

How far toward perfectionistic absolutism do these claims go? A good case in point concerns whether bastards, who had no control over their parentage, may be ordained as pastors:

Very many men who have been born out of wedlock are, notwithstanding, not only thought worthy of being counted among the flock of our brethren; they often are even chosen for positions of authority over them. (Methodius, *The Symposium*, Logos 2, Theophila, sec. 3, ACW 27, p. 51)

One can do nothing about the circumstances of one's birth, but one is responsible for one s behavior. Since lechery is willed, it is a far different case:

> Chambering and wantonness are regarded as crimes so great, that anyone stained with these sins is deemed unworthy not merely of holding office in the church, but also of participation in the sacraments. (Augustine, *Letters*, Letter XXII to Bishop Aurelius, A.D. 392, Ch. 3, NPNF 1, I, p. 239)

According to the Visitation Articles of Archbishop Laud (1635), many aspects of the minister's outward behavior remain of legitimate interest to the church. Even though questions such as the following are in many ways culturally determined, or shaped by changing social mores, and to modern readers privacy-invasive, nonetheless in their historical context it was thought fair and appropriate to ask:

> Does your minister use such decency and comeliness in his apparel, as is enjoined by the 47th Canon? Is he of sober behaviour, and one who does not engage in such bodily labor as is not seemly for his function and calling? Is your minister noted or any other way defamed for having obtained his benefice or his orders by simony, or in any other way reputed to be a simoniacal person, or any way noted to be a schismaic, or schismatically affected, or reputed to be an incontinent person? Do any such persons table or lodge in his house? Or is he a frequenter of taverns, inns, or alehouses, or any place suspected for ill rule? Or is he a common drunkard, a common gamester, or player at dice, a swearer or one who does not apply himself at his study, or is otherwise offensive or scandalous to his function or ministry? (William Laud, Visitation Articles, 1635, sec. 21–22, pp. 77–78; *Angl.*, pp. 707–708)*

One might object that these are private matters, incidental to the quality of ministry, and the rights of privacy should apply to ministers as well as any other citizen. But that objection assumes that we are dealing essentially with a civil right. The privilege and calling of ministry is not a civil right, since states grant civil rights, but no state can ordain canonically to ministry. The minister who voluntarily affirms the call to ministry and takes up the task of teaching Christian faith and practice, cannot appeal to the right of privacy when his behavior fails to correspond with his teaching.

Every emergent situation brings potential learning and opportunity for ministry. Although the pastor is called to a rhythm of labor and rest, there is never a moment or occasion in which one ceases being a pastor:

Had you but one ignorant old man or woman to teach, what a hard task it would be, even though they should be willing to learn! But if they be as unwilling as they are ignorant, how much more difficult will it prove! But to have such a multitude of ignorant persons, as most of us have, what work will it find us! . . . O brethren, what a field of work is there before us! Not a person that you see but may find you work. . . . Let us, then, be up and doing, with all our might; difficulties must quicken, not discourage us in so necessary a work. If we cannot do all, let us do what we can. . . . Consider that it is by your own voluntary undertaking and engagement that all this work is laid upon you. No man forced you to be overseers of the Church. (Baxter, *RP*, pp. 125– 127)

The selections in Part Seven have focussed upon the preparation of the care- giver, a task so consequential that it deserves a well-proportioned regimen of preparation that involves seasonable, practical knowledge of scripture and tra- dition, keen moral awareness, spiritual discipline, intellectual rigor, and wise prudential judgment. The effectiveness of pastoral practice is improved by carefully studying the best practitioners of pastoral care. While engaged in study, one does not cease doing the work of a pastor. The selection of pastoral books is a consequential pastoral decision, aiming toward classic depth rather than trendy opinion. Spiritual and moral formation is intrinsic to the preparation of the pastor. The preceptor must embody the precept if one's guidance is to be taken seriously. Sexual accountability is a major cornerstone of the pastor's moral formation. The pastor as a teacher of the good life cannot avoid becom- ing a model for others who search for the good life.

Conclusion

SEVEN MAJOR CONCLUSIONS may be drawn from these varied selections from classical pastoral wisdom:

(1) The self-understanding of the care-giver precedes and shapes all pastoral acts; for caregiving does not occur without a care-giver.

(2) The chief formative metaphor for soul care is the good shepherd caring for the vulnerable flock amid a perilous world— a metaphor that combines consoling, healing, guiding, nurturing, leading, and guarding images of caring for persons.

(3) The authority of the care-giver is to serve the health of souls, the authorization for service being grounded in the apostolic witness to God's care for the world.

(4) Ordination to soul care means that one is set apart representatively on behalf of the general ministry of the whole church, assuming that sacred and public ministry through Word, sacrament, and order is not affirmed so as to deny, but enhance, the general ministry of the laity.

(5) Ordination to soul care occurs inwardly by divine calling, outwardly by due confirmation of the church, in the orders of *diakonos, presbuteros, and episkopos*, through rigorous examination of competences requisite to care of persons.

(6) The calling to soul care is not limited to one gender, either in scripture or tradition.

(7) Care of souls requires rigorous preparation in scripture and tradition, aptness to teach, intellectual gifts, spiritual discipline, historical perspective, moral awareness, and the prevailing correspondence of words and deeds to make one's counsel credible.

Abbreviations

ACW   Ancient Christian Writers. Edited by J. Quasten, J. C. Plumpe, and W. Burghardt. 44 vols. New York: Paulist Press, 1946ff.

AF   *The Apostolic Fathers.* Edited by J. N. Sparks. New York: Thomas Nelson, 1978.

ANF   Ante-Nicene Fathers. Edited by A. Roberts and J. Donaldson. 10 vols. 1866–1896. Reprint ed., Grand Rapids: Eerdmans, 1979.

Angl.   *Anglicanism: The Thought and Practice of the Church of England, Illustrated from the Religious Literature of the Seventeenth Century.* Edited by P. E. More and F. L. Cross. London: SPCK, 1935.

BCP   *Book of Common Prayer* (1662 unless otherwise noted). Royal Breviar's edition. London: SPCK, n.d.

BPR   *Book of Pastoral Rule.* Gregory the Great, NPNF 2, X, 1-94.

CC   *Creeds of the Churches.* Edited by John Leith. Richmond, VA: John Knox Press, 1979.

CFS   Cistercian Fathers Series. 44 vols. Kalamazoo, MI: Cistercian Publications, 1968ff.

COCL   Classics of the Contemplative Life. Edited by J. M. Hussey, 8 vols. London: Faber and Faber, 1960ff.

CS   *The Curate of Souls.* Edited by John R. H. Moorman, London: SPCK, 1958.

CSS   Cistercian Studies Series. 68 vols. Kalamazoo, MI: Cistercian Publications, 1968ff.

CWMS   *Complete Writings of Menno Simons* (c. 1496–1561). Edited by John C. Wenger, Scottdale, PA: Herald Press, 1956.

CWS   Classics of Western Spirituality. 30 vols. to date. Edited by Richard J. Payne et. al. New York: Paulist Press, 1978ff.

ECF   *Early Christian Fathers.* Edited by H. Bettenson. London: Oxford University Press.

ECW   Early Christian Writers: The Apostolic Fathers. Translated by Maxwell Staniforth. London: Penguin Books, 1968.

FC   Fathers of the Church. Edited by R. J. Deferrari. 74 vols. to date. Washington, DC: Catholic University Press, 1947ff.

FER   The Fathers for English Readers. 15 vols. London: SPCK, 1878–90.

Inst.   Institutes of the Christian Religion, by John Calvin. LCC, vols. 21 and 22. Philadelphia: Westminster Press, 1960.

KVJ   King James Version, 1611 (also called the Authorized Version)

LACT   Library of Anglo-Catholic Theology. 99 vols. Oxford University Press, 1841–63.

LCC   Library of Christian Classics. 26 vols. Edited by J. Baillie, J. T. McNiell, and H. P. Van Dusen. Philadelphia: Westminster Press, 1953–61.

LCF   *Later Christian Fathers.* Edited by H. Bettenson. London: Oxford University Press, 1970.

LF   A Library of Fathers of the Holy Catholic Church. Edited by E. B. Pusey, J. Kebel, J. H. Newman, and C. Marriott. 50 vols. Oxford: J. H. Parker, 1838–88.

Loeb   Loeb Classical Library. Edited by Page, Capps, Rouse. Cambridge, MA: Harvard University Press, 1912ff.

LPT   Library of Protestant Thought. Edited by John Dillenberger. 13 vols. New York: Oxford University Press. 1964–72.

LW   Luther's Works. Edited by J. Pelikan and H. T. Lehmann. 54 vols. St. Louis: Concordia, 1953ff.

MPG   J. B. Migne, ed., Patrologia Graeca. 162 vols. Paris: Migne, 1857–76.

MPL   J. B. Migne, ed., Patrologia Latina. 221 vols. Paris: Migne, 1841–1865. General Index, Paris, 1912.

MPLS   J. B. Migne, ed., Patrologia Latina: Supplementum. 4 vols. Edited by A. Hamman, Turnhout, Belgium: Editions Brepols.

MWS   *Ministry of Word and Sacrament: An Enchiridion,* by Martin Chemnitz (1595). St. Louis: Concordia, 1981.

NE   *A New Eusebius: Documents Illustrative of the History of the Church to A.D. 337.* Edited by J. Stevenson (based on B. J. Kidd). London: S.P.C.K., 1957.

NEB   New English Bible

NIV   New International Version

NPNF   A Select Library of the Nicene and Post-Nicene Fathers of the Christian Church. 1st Series, 14 vols.: 2nd series, 14 vols. Edited by H. Wace and P. Schaff. New York: Christian, 1887–1900.

OCC   Our Christian Classics, ed. James Hamilton. London: Nisbet, 1858.

PW   Practical Works, Richard Baxter. 23 vols. London: James Duncan, 1830.

RAC   *Rules and Advices to the Clergy of the Diocese of Nown and Connor,* 1661, Jeremy Taylor, Works, ed. R. Heber, 1839, vol. xiv.

RSV   Revised Standard Version

SC   *Spiritual Conferences* (1628), St. Francis de Sales. Westminster, MD: Newman, 1943.

SCG   Summa contra Gentiles, On the Truth of the Catholic Faith, Thomas Aquinas. 4 vols. New York: Doubleday, 1955–57.

SSW   *Selected Sacred Writings*, Hugh of St. Victor. London: Faber and Faber, 1962.

ST   Summa Theologica, Thomas Aquinas. Edited by English Dominican Fathers. 3 vols. New York: Benziger, 1947–48.

SW   *John Calvin, Selections from His Writings.* Edited by John Dillenberger. Missoula, MT.: Scholars' Press, 1975.

TCL   Translations of Christian Literature. Edited by Sparrow Simpson and Lowther Clarke. London: SPCK, 1917ff.

WA   "Weimarer Ausgabe," D. Martin Luthers Werke. Kritische Gesamtausgabe, Weimar, 1883ff.

W-Br.   Weimarer Ausgabe, D. Martin Luther, Briefwechsel, Kritische Gesamtausgabe, Weimar, 1930ff., Letters.

WLS   What Luther Says. Edited by E. Plass. 3 vols. St. Louis: Concordia, 1959.

WML   Works of Martin Luther. Philadelphia Edition. 6 vols. Philadelphia: Muhlenberg Press, 1943.

WA-T   Weimarer Ausgabe. D. Martin Luther, Tischreden, Kritische Gesamtausgabe, Table Talk, 1912ff.

WSD   *Writings on Spiritual Direction,* ed. J. M. Neufelder and Mary C. Coelho. New York: Seabury Press, 1982.